MADE IN HUDDERSFIELD

Made in Huddersfield

the post-industrial Pennine landscape

Jack Ramsay

for the old adventure playground

NORTH OF WATFORD PUBLISHING
PO Box A56, Huddersfield, West Yorkshire, England HD1 1TU

Made in Huddersfield
special Huddersfield Edition of 2000 copies hardback only

first published . . . July 1989

British Library Cataloguing in Publication Data

Ramsay, Jack
Made in Huddersfield: the post industrial
Pennine landscape.
1. Yorkshire. Pennines. Social Life.
I. Title
942.8085'8

ISBN 1 – 871939 – 00 – 3

SPECIAL ACKNOWLEDGEMENTS

to **Mr Ivan Lee,** editor of the *Huddersfield Daily Examiner* for permission to reproduce quotations from various editions of his newspaper

to **Gordon Peate** and **Martine Brown** of Gordon Peate Photography, Manchester, for full access to such superb darkroom facilities, talk, food, and comments on the manuscript

to **Carol Stanley** for comments on the finished manuscript

and to **Diana Henderson**, the abstract painter, for reading the completed manuscript, and whose company and suggestions and astonishing wisdom on all matters have been a source of unending inspiration for at least six years past

book and jacket designed by Jack Ramsay
typeset in 12pt Baskerville by Lloyd-Williams, Southport, Merseyside
author's photographs laser-scanned by Spectrum Photo-Litho, Stanningley, Leeds
printed in duo-tone and bound by Netherwood Dalton and Co, Huddersfield

made in Milnsbridge, Huddersfield between 1987 and 1989

prologue

Other than old photographs I have no visual memory of my Father whatsoever. I was four years old when he died in 1965, and the only recollection I have of even being in his presence is a blurred vision of us both driving in an Austin A35 van, down by the cattle market at Fartown, off Bradford Road, at the bottom end of Huddersfield town centre. Although I can remember this one incident reasonably clearly, I can only see the car's crude dashboard and a black railway viaduct and some gable ends of terraced houses passing outside the window. I know I am with my Father, but the person at the wheel of the vehicle is an indistinct figure with no features and no voice.

For several months after his death, until everything had been sorted out, both my Mother and me stayed with an Aunt and Uncle and their two children in their terraced house up Quarmby Road, near the Co-Op at Paddock Head. Despite my always knowing them as Auntie and Uncle, they were not relatives as such but the couple who my Mother and Father had gone about with when all four of them were courting. My only recollections of staying in the house with them at the time are a Jack and Jill storybook, bare varnished floorboards, and getting a marble stuck in my throat and being shaken upside down by the ankles to dislodge it. Apparently, after my Father died, my Mother had to keep telling me he had gone away on business and would be off for a long time, whenever I enquired as to where he was. Then one day somebody discourteously and abruptly informed me that he was dead—which caused an almighty great bust up—and I am told I 'screamed blue murder'.

Like my Father before her, my Mother died suddenly, in 1981. I had gone away to art college in Manchester and was in the second week of adjusting to new lodgings and a new routine, whilst at the same time sweating profusely about the relationship I was involved in with a girl I was engaged to marry, which was in the awkward process of disintegrating. Pressurized by the bereavement more than ever before, a couple of weeks after the funeral the engagement crumbled and we parted (although we were to be reunited for a time later, thank God). Shortly after this I took our two dogs away to a home for unwanted animals near Leeds. I had gone back to live at home and was commuting daily to college in Manchester, but being out of the house for over twelve hours a day and leaving the dogs couped up was too much for them to bear, and the overpowering smell on returning home in the evening was becoming unbearable for me. Their screams from behind the door of an old barn as I left them for the last time sometimes haunt me now. By that time, such a rush of change in the space of mere days meant that any more grief I might have felt at the loss of the two dogs had been replaced by a sort of bitterly expectant cynicism that things could only get worse. I wallowed in the mire of self pity, indulging in quantities of drink and one night stands I have experienced neither before nor since.

The winter of 1981 up to Christmas was the coldest I had ever known. The very air itself felt to be freezing at the back of your throat as you inhaled outside. People passing you in the street let off sudden but regular bursts of dense vapour that shot out from the top of their hunched figures like gasps of steam from little human valves. It lingered in clouds about their heads as they walked along for longer than I could remember having noticed before, and always showed up most under the streetlamps at night. During the same week the engagement finished, I arrived home one such cold evening to find a note pushed through my letterbox by a neighbour from further up the terrace. He'd found my cat dead outside his back door earlier in the day and had placed it in a bag for me in my yard. I'm sure I smiled when I read this. The cat was curled inside a plastic supermarket carrier bag. It was frozen stiff. I looked inside the container and saw it had a dreadful twisted expression to its mouth which I had no wish to linger over. I lifted the bag up by the handles and was very aware of how heavy the animal suddenly felt, how alien to me was its cold fur. I had lifted the cat up many times, but always with both hands. Only when they are suspended by one hand in a polythene bag like so much dead meat do you realize that cats are quite heavy objects. I was both appalled and unnerved by the fact that as it was lifted vertically in the bag, its curled up posture did not change. I also felt alarmingly indifferent to it, it was like it was somebody else's and had never belonged to me. There was a thick, hardened layer of rock-hard snow and ice on the ground. I dug my heel into it, to no avail. I winced and swore under my breath and shivered from the cold and looked up then down the overgrown back yards behind our terrace, contemplating what I might do with the corpse of the animal. Only those who have experienced the godforsaken intolerable misery and the debilitating after effects of sudden death in the family, the terrifying, methodical manner by which you have to dispose of familiar clothes and the most intimate and personal of the deceased's possessions, will understand what I mean when I refer to how the numbing, deadening sensations that grip the emotions and the brain, the bitterness and anger and fists smashing into the unbreakable wall of inner frustrations, can make you do the strangest of things. Such grief is almost invariably a reaction as much to the horrifying helplessness of your own vile predicament as it is sorrow for the person who has died. How will *you* carry on? How will *you* adjust to the reality of somebody who has always been there suddenly not being there any more? You are frightened at how *you* must face the future, which is why death is such a hideous thing which is why, in turn, you grieve: there is nothing *you* can do about it. Death is absolute and final and cannot be manipulated by the land of the living through a bit of suffering but we'll make do until we get to the all's-well-in-the-end conclusion. *You* have to accept death or go under.

So, senses numbed as they were, my body pierced by the sub-zero cold, that damnable self pity swimming that even the strongest of minds ought not to be able to deter, I concluded what I would do with the body of the cat. I had quickly established the ground was too hard to seriously contemplate digging a hole. I returned to the house, brought out some newspapers and some cellotape, wrapped the animal up and put it in the dustbin. It was the final horrifying indignity after more than a dozen years together, but I couldn't be bothered, under the circumstances, to do anything else. It was too cold and it was too much mental effort, and in the awful, lifeless existence you go through following death, the sombre train journeys you fester throughout, the appetite for anything and everything that is constantly placated by the sickening empty void that tries forever to enlarge in the pit of the stomach, what would ordinarily necessitate the most minimal of efforts to muster under normal circumstances becomes excrutiatingly difficult to bear even thinking about.

As I put the lid back down onto the dustbin I distinctly remember looking up to the massive six storied textile mill towering at the bottom of the yard with the rest of its associated buildings, not ten feet from where I was standing. This house, this yard, the whole surrounding environment, had been my playground during adolescence. The mills held an odd, elegiac kind of solid security for me. They made the neighbourhood. Then I had cursed at myself when I recollected how I'd thought of that security once, coming home on the last bus about a year previously, from the home of the girl to whom I had been engaged to marry. It was about 11.00pm, the street lamps—always so comely in the dark—were glowing orange as they passed outside the condensation on the bus window, and I'd thought of this house, this environment, this cindered back yard by these mills, the warm base of home, and had felt a sudden mental stab of utter contentment that overcame me with a rush, like an inner warming of hands in front of the fire of happiness. Things were going really well. I was beaming with the self-centered smarmy confidence of the typical 18 or 19 year old student who takes himself very seriously, who is full of himself and his increasing self awareness and heightening thinking abilities, but who is as yet completely naïve to the reality of the world that exists beyond the school gates. At such an age you are so blasé and inexperienced with life, but more importantly so inexperienced with people, you can do anything: you can change that world. After my 'design education' was complete, London beckoned, marriage to a lovely young lady, and the modest routine of an average family life would no doubt follow. The old Northern milltown would be stored in a siding in the goods yard of childhood memories, the station of the mainstream was calling. I was on the right track, and the express train was heading straight for it at full speed.

But trains can be diverted or take a different route or stop at all the wrong stations from those listed on the timetable. Life deals its sudden cruel blows and knocks us from our pedestals; reminds us, in fact, just who and what we really are. We may be lucky enough to start with a fan of aces and turn up trumps throughout it, or we may start with a real bad hand. Not only we people, but towns and environments too. Places change. Places receive their sudden cruel blows. As I looked up at those big mills when I put the dead cat in the dustbin—the animal had been the final tenuous living vestige from the environment of my upbringing and my adolescence, now being wrapped up in the *Huddersfield Daily Examiner* to be left behind forever—I felt a sudden, crazy, sentimental affiliation to the old buildings in front of me and the security they represented. Daft as it sounds, the mills made me feel a little better inside. At least they were still there, breathing their precious life-giving properties into the neighbourhood, into that grubby back yard, in a way I had been so conscious of for so long, looking out at them from my bedroom window above. But little did I know that the mills were on their last legs. Changes were afoot. Those mills were about to be dealt their bad hand.

A redundant miner being interviewed on a local magazine programme on TV a few years later commented on the closure of his village pit in South Yorkshire. He described the mine as being the heart from which the rest of the town had fed. I knew exactly what he meant. He was not making a strictly sentimental observation, for if I remember correctly, the village had grown in a circle around the pit-head with the mine being right in the middle. The village grew to serve the pit and the pit served the village. The place was instantly recognizable and drew its nourishment from the revolving pit-head gear. Watch any TV documentary about the effects of a large factory's closure on such a community, notice how the people being interviewed, like this miner, consistently refer to the industry that has gone as giving the place its purpose, its buzz. Its life.

Places that held such strengths for the people who have lived in them, places that gave off an indescribable sensation to most of their dependents of being buoyant, holding them safely up by a thick rubber life-ring on the surface of the ocean of the living could, it seemed, never change. But they did change. They sprung a slow leak. Moreover, in some such places, it was as though somebody had come along and shattered their confidence in this ocean of the living as surely as if they had punctured it with a spike. Before you knew where you were, both you and your familiar environment were sinking. You floundered together, your whole suburb or village floundered as it struggled and splashed to come up for air.

Death is a hideous thing. Whether it is the death of a loved one, of a village, or when in the news it was always that of an old industrial suburb, a mine, a steelworks, a shipyard, or a textile mill, for a great many people it constitutes the biggest and hardest change they must face and its after effects were, and for that matter still are, intolerable. Lives can be devastated and are never quite the same again.

It is a hideous thing, this shutting down of the living, whatever form it takes.

Near Millgate, Paddock Foot

Pre-industrial Revolution Weavers Cottage, Longwood

PART ONE

1

I remember the demolition men came to the mills during early April 1983.

At first the roof slates went, then the roof timbers and joists, neatly stacked ready for sorting before being bundled onto the backs of heavy, rumbling lorries that threaded their way tortuously up Church Street in a constant puther of dust; up past the handful of pre-industrial revolution weavers' cottages and the cobbled charm of Church Lane adjoining on the left; up past the few scrawny allotments and the cobblers with its faded 1960's advertisements pasted to its original tongued-and-grooved Victorian counter at the corner of Ballroyd Lane on the right; and away with their forlorn cargoes to some anonymous building regurgitation plant, goodness knows where.

The lorries were noisy, cumbersome, and absurdly out of place. They were driven by engines not designed for the steep gradients or the narrow winding backstreets of the Colne Valley millscapes. They seemed, like the big men sat behind their steering wheels, to be possessed of that determinedly stoic sense of purpose tinged with scheming menace which hangs over any demolition site like the staid glare of the galley-hand over his slaves as the ship heads into battle. The arrival on Grove Street below of their steel caterpillar-tracked brethren, the bulldozers, diggers, and cranes, was like a procession of low-loaders returning from a trip to the lost Amazonian jungle where prehistoric creatures still roam. The machines were the captive dinosaurs, drugged and chained down, being brought back to civilization in a state of slumber, but liable to stir and awaken at any moment. Their powerful hydraulic limbs were folded and clamped ominously; the big shovels were the focal points, the jaws of the beasts bearing the battle scars of demolition: buckled teeth: scratched paint: the dried mud caked on the stale matter around their jowls, hardened from relentless tearing at a building's flesh. The machines came poised, ready to feed mercilessly and without remorse on the valley's decaying carcass of industry—*Look, we're very sorry to be destroying yet another chunk of this region's once great textile muscle, but you see it is no longer needed, and therefore these buildings simply have to come down, so down they will come and there's not a bloody thing you can do about it.* The few local people bothering to stand and watch the convoy of lorries grinding this way and that reminded me of a mournful congregation gathering to watch the smouldering remnants of their church the morning after the arson attack the night before: stunned, empty expressions, gaping morosely at a fixed point in space, welded inextricably to the dawning realization that a great gobbet of their lives has been bitten away phlegmatically, abruptly, and without warning. Whether or not that handful of people standing with me had actually been part of Sunnybank Mills I did not know and did not bother to ask (although the sorrowful shaking of heads suggested they might have been) but one thing was for sure: we were all of us experiencing the same overwhelming sense of loss: we were all of us feeling the same sense of bitter, helpless regret that most people surely feel as they assemble to witness some large building, or quarter of their environment, that has been such an integral part of the established fabric of the layout of the townscape that they have known so well for so long, once it is being razed to the ground.

In the built-up industrial areas of the big milltowns and steeltowns of the North, the removal of such a segment was usually a large one covering many acres. When it had gone, it left an enormous blank space that interrupted—and continues to interrupt in a great many places—the flow of everything else around it like a front tooth ripped out of the huge, rambling mouth of industry. As you approached the South Yorkshire steel city of Sheffield from Barnsley on the train, perched atop a long embankment and clattering over a succession of viaducts plunging through the wastelands of *emptiness* and scrapyards, piled high with rusty wreckage exploiting the death of steel, the simile was compounded to the full as you realized that Sheffield had lost most of its big industrial teeth leaving only a huge toothless grimace. The mighty jaws of Northern industry that once gobbled up coal and ore and raw human fodder from miles around to spit out immortal phrases such as "STEEL MAKING CAPITAL OF THE WORLD" were now ravaged by the disease of manufacturing decline; kicked in the mouth by the demon of recession as it stomped across the industrial North wearing steel toe-capped boots that showed no affiliation but instead contained enough force in each stride to flatten entire communities and destroy the basic corpus of a whole way of life. As the demon strode across the steel-towns and cities of the Midlands and South Yorkshire, he made his way purposefully towards the textile towns further North, allowing his feet to fall with the same devastating effect, one on either side of the Pennines. He straddled the backbone of England, the spine that had once helped to hold the nation up, gloating with murderous appraisal at the smashed industries oozing in ruptured tatters from beneath those huge, unstoppable boots. He reached Sunnybank Mills in 1982, closed them down, and—like a spider killing a fly but leaving it to devour until later—wrapped them in a cocoon of "FOR SALE" and "TO LET" signs pasted in vandalized windows; suspended on the web of uncertainty over future use of the buildings. Then he went off to plunder elsewhere before returning in April 1983 to feast on the wholesale destruction of the textile complex at his leisure.

Outside the post-apocalyptic style melodrama of an occasional TV news report, I had not experienced the sensation of the bomb of industrial decline dropping on my own area. But as textile recession reached its zenith, I saw the demon annihilate industry in my neighbourhood first hand. I saw that he came armed with a workforce of men and machines possessed, dependent upon his ruthless mission for their own survival to prevent themselves from falling victim to those huge, crushing boots. The demolition men were the vultures of industrial decline, swooping down on the stiff, silent corpse of Sunnybank Mills rotting in the warm spring sunshine, ready to tear chunks of their mill stone free, like the real-life birds squabbling over the corpse of the wilderbeeste buzzing with flies in the African sun. The disturbing thing was, I could have sworn I detected a look of malicious, evil intent surfacing on the features of the demolition men, lending an undercurrent of sadistic enjoyment to their carrying out of the sentence of death imposed upon the old buildings. I'm sure it was there, etched indelibly onto the faces of the workmen and the lorrydrivers as clearly as the tattoos on their forearms. But it was subdued, being kept in check, as if the knowledge of the wage-packet at the end of the week stopped their otherwise eager copulation of kill-smash-destroy-demolition from achieving an explosive climax, lest they perform the conquest too hastily and earn less money. The demolition of Sunnybank Mills was happening in broad daylight, plainly, ostentatiously for all to see. Although they were falling under the onslaught of a whim of cruel underhanded rage instigated by that towering demon of recession, their removal by the demolition contractors was the beginning to some extensive forward planning, based upon their experience of knowing how best to dispose of an unwanted building safely and quickly, whilst at the same time yielding the greatest possible financial return once broken down ready for resale. The demolition of Sunnybank Mills was, ironically, a commercial undertaking. It was the calculated mutilation of a massive five and six storied stack of West Yorkshire's legacy of redundant industrial architecture by an organized body of men whose expressions were, now that I really think about it, not so much those bound by a malicious evil intent, but more a fixed gaze, then a virile exploration by eye of the unwilling body of a textile mill; doubtless in anticipation of the final frenzied rape of destruction that would reach its collective climax with the exhausted withering into the earth of the mighty phallus, at that time still thrusting itself haughtily towards the heavens—the chimney, nearly always left until last during the demolition of a mill, defiant unto the end.

Sunnybank Mills closed down about six months after I'd looked up at them that cold winter's day when I put the dead cat in the dustbin. The C. & J. Hirst textile empire that had built and run them was compulsorily wound up by the High Court in London. They were one of the oldest established textile concerns in West Yorkshire, holding title deeds to the land the mills stood upon going back to 1649. At the height of their manufacturing output, the complex employed some 2,000 people. By July 1981, the workforce had dwindled to 270, and by the end of April 1982, after several depressing newspaper headlines and only a month before the end, a mere eight or nine people were said to be on the payroll, reportedly engaged in generally tidying the place up in the hope of a last minute reprieve. Immediately that the firm died, the extensive mill premises were bought by private property developers. In conjunction with the County Council, they were to invest half a million pounds, not in the demolition of the mills and the erection of new buildings, but in selective remodelling and the complete refurbishment of the existing complex, with the intention of turning it into a group of industrial units for small businesses. It was anticipated that a hive of ready built, cheap accommodation would attract new companies to the site, which had good communications links due to being only a few minutes drive from the M62. In turn, it was hoped this would revitalize the mills as working buildings and breathe new life into Longwood, the village which had thrived on Sunnybank Mills when they were the heart and soul of the area. Newspaper headlines in the *Huddersfield Daily Examiner* told that all was going well. They reported enthusiastically how the new property developers had already refurbished the mills' main office and administration block, and had even decorated them with original paintings by Bradford born painter David Hockney. All was going according to plan. Then suddenly, on April 15th 1983, the *Examiner* announced "PULL OUT KILLS LONGWOOD PLAN" above a photograph depicting a bulldozer feeding on one of the smaller outbuildings. The private property developers with whom the County Council had been so surely negotiating—despite no papers having been signed to secure the deal—had decided instead to abandon their project at the eleventh hour and purchase the gigantic Dean Clough mill complex that sprawls along a ravine across one end of Halifax, several miles away. There they hoped to establish a similar operation to the one which had been proposed for Sunnybank Mills, but this time in a concentration of buildings that must have been ten or twenty times the size. Dean Clough had formerly been the manufacturing base of the vast carpets empire of John Crossley and Sons Ltd, a name synonymous with the West Yorkshire textile town of Halifax, and whose mill panorama grew to such proportions it lasted for nearly a mile and in its heyday was said to be almost like a town within a town. The Crossleys' good fortune had grown from the humblest of beginnings and the family shared their wealth with the town that had bred them through an impressive succession of philanthropical gestures, aimed benevolently at the town's ordinary citizens. Consequently, much of Halifax was designed, planned, and erected with the Crossleys' money. In later years, after they amalgamated with another carpet making company, Dean Clough produced carpets under the auspices of Carpets International before finally closing down at about the same time as Sunnybank Mills in 1982. They constitute the biggest single group of textile mills I know of anywhere in the region about which I write. They are crammed into the bottom of North Bridge on the outskirts of Halifax town centre. To the rear they are flanked by glass roofed weaving sheds with saw-toothed skylights, each section angled the long side to the North to gain maximum daylight, testimony to the plethora of textile machinery that once roared beneath. A hundred years ago, Dean Clough employed close to 6,000 people. When the mills closed down they employed less than 500. One of the stalwart architectural legacies that had built the town was dead and fierce controversy gripped it. The future of these mills—the biggest group of such structures in the country and described by a local historian as one of the most dramatic industrial landscapes in Europe—remained uncertain, the hungry spectre of demolition loomed on the horizon. Today, because the redevelopment scheme which was to have been the impetus of survival for Sunnybank Mills has been successful, Dean Clough Industrial Park has been built, *rebuilt,* from the ashes of one of West Yorkshire's tragic stories of industrial decline into the success story of Halifax: a blueprint for the future of such buildings that now houses a multitude of small businesses, including professional services, manufacturing, craftsmen, caterers, computer firms, photographers, a restaurant, graphic artists, a library and art gallery, even the offices of a film company. The list goes on to over two hundred companies, with three quarters of the one million-plus square feet of the mill complex now refurbished.

The potentially adaptable resources that the abandoned Sunnybank Mills, and many others in the immediate vicinity of Huddersfield, offered, were not seized. The benefit of hindsight afforded by successful projects such as Dean Clough occurred too late. For six months after the noose had tightened, the Hirst's mills had stood, vast and domineering, an empty shell enshrouded by an aura of permanent repose, pregnant with an eerie, sepulchral silence. During the last full summer they were there, with skylarks high on the breeze and dandelion clocks choking the air and the sun shining full blast, that uneasy silence pervaded. If anything, it was emphasised by the stagnant heat of July and August; the fruits of a previous age now dying, one of its industrial powerhouses decomposing yet ripening for the slaughter at the same time, surrounded by the same unearthly flies-buzzing-in-the-air stillness you recollect in overgrown country railway stations, when you played *Japs and Commandoes* in between the willowherb sprouting in them on hot summer's afternoons, when you were a

Heath House Mill, Golcar

child.

When the property developers purchased the mills in November 1982, the stockpile of cloth and looms and all the other associated industrial paraphernalia that makes up the interior workings of a textile mill had been sold off straight away. Much of it had, ironically, been purchased by the managements of other mills in the area that were still in operation. Then the empty buildings had patiently waited, forlorn and wretchedly hopeful, until the bottom dropped out of the proposals to give them a new lease of life. Their countenance remained unchanged whilst the jury of decision makers retired to assess their verdict, ready to pass sentence.

The jury returned.

They had reached a verdict.

After careful consideration and deliberation over the wishes of another group of property developers who had since bought the mills from the original developers who first put forward the refurbishment scheme, they had come to the conclusion that old multi-storied buildings were largely impractical for today's heavy machinery and small businesses which needed easy access. Therefore, it would be in the best interests of all concerned that the sentence be death. Their decision was irrevocable and absolute. There would be no time for the mills to uncover fresh evidence to reopen their case; no time spent on a textile mill's Death Row to enable someone to come along during the last reel, assess their potential anew, and acknowledge the silent plea for life. The case of Sunnybank Mills was closed. Now Longwood was about to lose one of its biggest industrial teeth, as had the steel wastelands of Sheffield further down the county. And here, as there, there would be no anaesthetic to relieve the pain.

The demolition men moved in immediately the "PULL OUT KILLS LONGWOOD PLAN" was announced, so quickly in fact, it seemed as if they had been waiting eagerly in the wings. They came with their steel dinosaurs, their circus train of equipment, roaring into the narrow corridors of the Colne Valley millscapes, the executioners, arriving with the tenacity of a bunch of sweaty navvies coming to build a railway. Their lorries roared, hungry to have their bellies filled with the fresh meat of condemned mill stone grit. The demolition men were the new merchants of woollen and worsted death, ready to carry out sentence swiftly and efficiently and precisely. Initially, they had removed the roofing materials so carefully it appeared that the buildings might only be receiving a manicure after all. Burly young men with large calloused hands and a beery jocularity balanced on the topmost joists, fearless of danger. They swaggered precariously six stories up, showing off, their faces blackened by clouds of black lime dust, their lips pink, like miners back up from the pit. Groups of young spectators leaned against their bicycles on the pavements far below, waving obscene two-fingered gestures up at them. Then the pack of men and machines swooped, not on the kids who swiftly disappeared up the street to maintain a comfortable distance between themselves and the recipients of their hand signals, but on the mills. They swooped fiercely; sometimes, it seemed, frenziedly. There would indeed be no mercy. The vultures had arrived. Now the feeding would begin proper. Now the stone carcass would be ripped viciously apart. The mills' outer skin, as well as their skeleton framework of timber, stone flagged floors, and cast-iron pillars, would be exposed to the air, the joists the giant ribs being picked completely clean as the more succulent flesh was stripped away. Now the steel dinosaurs that had arrived chained to the low-loaders stirred. Their thick hydraulic limbs unfolded and the monsters rolled clumsily down from the flat trailers still drugged. They crawled slowly, ponderously towards their prey, of such weight their metal caterpillar-tracks left imprints in the road surface. Then their engines growled. Somewhere, Radio One blared tinnily like background music psyching you up during the opening few minutes of a feature film as the killer assembles his machine-gun, before the action really begins. Those shovels reared. The metal teeth glinted in the sunshine, shiny like chrome along the pressure points from the savaging of a previous feeding. Gear levers were thrust this way and that by those big calloused hands. Diesel fumes permeated the air as the dinosaurs snorted and the great hydraulic limbs flexed and the mouths lunged and *WUNCH!*—steel jaws from the future bit deeply into Yorkshire mill stone from the past. Whole lengths of walls cracked then peeled off, familiarizing the shape of a street to generations, obliterating it in minutes as they plunged into the billowing clouds of dust and smoke and textile history. More spectators milled, drawn by the crashing and the din, watching in awe, saying hardly anything, just staring. The demolition men paraded, grinning at young ladies and flexing their shoulders, enjoying the centre stage of attention. More obscene two-fingered gestures were waved by the impish young cyclists from further up the street. Dogs barked. Unsuspecting motorists turned their cars away from "ROAD CLOSED" signs miming silent abuse from behind their steering wheels. A few pensioners shimmered through a heat-haze of dust and smoke further down the street, like you see in a telephoto lens shot during a TV documentary. They nodded to one another feelingly, drawing closer together each time they spoke above the clamour, their arms folded. The telephoto lens panned away from their faces and refocussed on an infant sat on a blackened dry-stone wall, his face cocked to one side, squinting in the sunlight, picking his nose, dragging a big gilbert out, inspecting it for black lime dust, then stuffing it into his mouth.

And on Grove Street below, the lorries lined up, shovelfulls of scooped up masonry clattering into their metal trailers with a basso-profundo regularity that soon became irritating.

Over a period of weeks, I watched Sunnybank Mills slowly vanish, disappearing up the street in the backs of convoys of the lorries bloated with their rubble. Standing at the bottom of Church Street at the awkward junction where it merges with Botham Hall Road and Dale Street, next to the old iron railings by the end terrace house with the peculiarly enormous brick chimney stack, I would watch them struggle to the top of the steep little road where it blended with Thornhill Road to form Longwood Gate. Sometimes, I wondered how their trailers full of grease-ridden timbers and twisted steel girders and chunks of stone now on their way *out* of Longwood had first been brought *into* Longwood over a century before, when the noisy internal combustion engines taken so much for granted today were but a figment of some Victorian engineers imagination; and horse power didn't mean the speed with which a series of cylindrical steel pistons could vibrate up and down within a gas filled chamber, but meant four legs and a sweating pulsating beast; and for petrol you fed it with a bagful of locally grown oats and barley, not some processed gue imported from hot climes a whole world away on the opposite side of the earth.

All around me, man-made cliffs of stone were being blown to Kingdom Come. That

OVERLEAF: VIEW ACROSS MILNSBRIDGE IN 1987. All these mills are now largely vacant. The town lost a higher proportion of textile jobs during the Recession than any other in West Yorkshire.

APPROACH TO THE REFURBISHED DEAN CLOUGH MILL COMPLEX, HALIFAX

Approach to the Refurbished Dean Clough Mill Complex, Halifax

claustrophobic little back street corner—my favourite corner thereabouts because it used to represent the power and confidence of local industry merging at the focal point of my daily journey to and from the bus stop—had, up until then, been enclosed within the implacable solidity of austere mill building that frowned at you from all sides. Now it was letting in the sky. More and more of it as the weeks went by. Suddenly my house became visible from a perspective I'd never seen it from before. For the first time, I could see my old bedroom window curtains from the bottom of Church Street on my way back down from Longwood Gate, the smell of burning timbers drifting in the air making the comparison to returning to the aftermath of a bombing irresistible. In a frightfully short space of time, the whole area was torn to pieces in a vicious, unrelenting fury of demolition that exploded across the lower part of Longwood with as ferocious an impact on the skyline as the mills must have caused when they were first built.

I remember there were a lot of heavy, muggy days during the summer of 1983 as the mills were being pulled down. One clammy, overcast evening at about nine o'clock, I was hanging out of my back bedroom window, looking across the bomb-site. It was amazing that the row of old outside toilets behind our house had not been caught in the blast: they couldn't have been more than five or six feet from the rear wall of the mills' main six storied weaving block. Some cast-iron railings to the right of the privvies *had* been caught: the topmost spikes, about eight or nine feet from the ground, all mottled and pock-marked from a century of repainting, were bent at one end. There was that overcast summer's evening humidity in the air, the grey sky loaded with thunder and just beginning to turn a sickly, lifeless pale orange on its dark under-belly. There was a dead silence and absolute stillness that was so acute it could have been deafening. I was reminded of a famous clip of newsreel film of the London blitz. One shot shows a house which has been bombed and has a double-decker bus laid on its side amidst the rubble. The view in front of me of Sunnybank Mills looked exactly like the remains of the house in that old black and white film clip: shattered masonry heaped in enormous piles, skewered with beams of splintered wood and buttressed corners of interior walls protruding from cascades of crushed and powdered brick: electric junction boxes hung open, their innards ripped out and dangling: and everywhere smashed windows, particularly on the lower floors where the kids' stones could easily reach. The only splash of red I could see was a fire hose bolted to the wall of what would once have been a landing near a staircase. It stood out starkly against the glossy paintwork surround of cream and pale turquoise brushed over bare blockwork. Then a sound suddenly broke the turgid silence. It was a lone blackbird calling from in the rubble, up, down, along, in front of me, behind—I couldn't tell from where. It seemed to be half dazed, its chirruping slower at first, the last bird alive on a post atomic-war Earth which has just downed the last worm it found squirming out of the dust settling and knows it hasn't got long to go. Stupid as it sounds—for birds calling are supposed to raise our spirits, the psychologists say—a lone blackbird calling like that always seemed to suggest a pall of gloom and depression was about to triumph when I was younger. They only ever really seem to call like this in summer, at dusk, when there is the smell of freshly mown grass in the warm air, and the street lamps have just come on. If you stare, it is easy to become transfixed. The enclosing twilight plays tricks with your eyes and big areas of shadow look to be pulsating if you try not to blink. And the bird's mournful calling plays unchanging, a looped tape somebody has cunningly positioned at the back of your somnolence to try and hypnotize you with.

Whenever I hear a blackbird calling with this tone of voice at this time of the year, it either makes me think of eating fish and chips out of the newspaper whilst out walking with the girl I nearly married or else it takes me back to a summer's evening in 1968, when I can distinctly recall cresting the brow of a hill up the road where we lived and being greeted by a deep orange sunset and really registering the sound of such a blackbird for the first time. Their chirruping encourages you to feel like you would if you were looking at a photo-album filled with pictures of your family, who are all now dead, while listening to 'Greensleeves' playing on the hi-fi. The blackbird's monotonous chanting that humid evening when I was pondering the demise of Sunnybank Mills and the death of this part of my village was the perfect embellishment to the feeling the smashed ruins of this particular Athens of the Industrial Revolution were giving off: a nauseating sensation of it being the end of an era; or more exactly, the end of a chapter in what had been to me the adventure book of the environment of my upbringing. I'd now reached the end of that part of the yarn only to find the next chapter was missing. I could see it being torn out before my eyes and screwed up and thrown into the backs of the lorries by big steel sinewed bulldozers and diggers and cranes. Although I'd read the book many times and knew it well and knew that the houses and the streets and the hillsides and the church and the school and the allotment with the old enamelled bath which had been there for as long as I could remember would tell me that, several pages from now, the yarn continued much as it had done, those pages which were essential to understanding the book as a whole were going. From then on, as I walked the streets, I would always have to pull them out from the musty bookshelf of the mind, or read them with the gaping hole of that missing chapter. The only thing was, it wasn't a single chapter that was being shredded but nearly the whole novel. I was being *left* with a chapter, only vague and half meaningful without the basic plot that dictates the flow of the rest of the story around it.

It was easy to be cynical when considering the bizarre irony of the cottage converters and the estate agents and the builders converging on some of the mills' associated housing, clustered in terraces up the sides of the valley. Most of it was a product of industrialism—textile industrialism—as were the older pre-industrial revolution weavers' cottages dotted in and amongst. They, with their three storeys and rows of characteristic stone mullioned windows, designed to give maximum daylight to the upper floors when weavers had toiled on hand-looms within, had themselves been made redundant by progress and by the mushrooming of the industrial revolution, the arrival of the mills, and the factory system below. Now, as those big blotches of industry around which everything else had grown were being destroyed, the original houses were becoming fashionable places in which to live. They were being presumptuously antiquated, filled with mock stone fireplaces, exposed rafters which were not necessarily structural supports but hollow ornamentation: brass trinkets: photographs of the locality in generations past: superfluous details harkening nostalgically from between the modern comfort of the video, the microwave, instant hot water and central heating—and the high-speed reality of the lifeline of the motorway roaring five minutes out of sight over the hill, which the estate agents blurbs always cite after the descriptions of the dwellings and how they capture the spirit of mocking at a cottages horse-drawn past.

As the houses were being so lovingly 'modernised' up the hillsides, the mills that bore them were dying and being hastily swept away. On Sunday mornings the bells rang in Longwood church, as they still do; an impeccably Northern anthem as traditional to the sabbath up here as the roast beef and Yorkshire pudding most of the congregation would probably be going home to. Sunnybank Mills were in their death throes, being eaten away by progress just as they themselves had once been the progress eating away at what had gone before them. Now the world was changing again, readjusting itself with another of its periodic industrial upheavals. The vultures of textile decline, the demolition men, were scavenging below the church as its bells rang; scrounging every last nut and bolt, every last plank of decent wood, every last vestige of stone and metal that could be scraped free of its grease-impregnated textile identity and turned into resaleable profit.

Whilst the bulldozers' engines gurgled intermittently and masonry crumpled and acrid dust mushroomed into the air, the church bells rang from a tower paid for by the Hirst family who built Sunnybank Mills in the first place. The bells, too, had been installed by them, and there was the final kick between the legs of irony: the bells of St. Marks chiming, witness to trailerfulls of the mills grinding past in the lorries in front of them, spewing diesel fumes into the graveyard as they struggled round the bend at the top of the street. The mills had been the heart that pumped the lifeblood of purpose into the area. They had given the place its purpose, its buzz. Its life. Now that heart—or maybe more, maybe the area itself—had suffered a massive seizure. It had stopped beating and was stiffening with the rigour-mortice of traditional manufacturing decline.

Sunnybank Mills had been gaunt, austere buildings, part of an industry and a landscape and a folklore and the North, whatever its controversies, in the process of being meticulously removed and transported to the vultures' giant nest for sorting and re-distribution because nobody with any money or imagination wanted them.

St. Marks Parish Church, Longwood

2

St. Marks Parish Church, Longwood, stands at the top of Church Street where it merges with Thornhill Road and Longwood Gate. Strictly speaking, the church building is not on Church Street but a few yards off it, halfway up a narrow cobbled road called Church Lane. The graveyard is in two halves, three if you include the area of headstones around the church itself.

Walking up Church Lane, the church becomes visible through its cast-iron entrance gates on the left. Across to the right is another separate graveyard. A third graveyard is some distance away, across the main road at the top side of the church, behind the bus shelter and public toilets. The area just here is remarkably intact. The only obvious intrusion to what it must have looked like when it was built is a detached house that looks to have been built in the last thirty or forty years. Other than this, and the cars and various fixtures replaced in the facades of the rest of the buildings from the array of wares sold by todays giant home DIY stores, Church Street and the narrow lanes branching off it look much as they would have done at the time Sunnybank Mills were built at the bottom of the valley. Even the street lamps up Church Lane contribute to the period flavour of the immediate area and the visual balance that remains in and around the church's ornate black gates: they are the original cast-iron gas lamp standards, only the tops having been taken away and superseded by modern sodium chloride fittings.

The church steeple is a landmark from miles around, one of the few man-made ones hereabouts to be left standing. It is an ornate Gothic structure, slicing up from between the branches of the Sycamore and Ash and Elm that frame it. These trees virtually obscure the rest of the building in summer and emphasize the ruggedness of its stone texture and the starkness of the housing and the landscape surrounding it when they are devoid of foliage in winter. At the turn of the century, the trees would have been veritable saplings, or so they appear on the old picture postcard of the church with its recently built tower, photographed in the 1920's, in a book of views of old Huddersfield which I have in my possession. The church was built in 1877, replacing an old chapel that dated from 1749 and which served the adjoining areas of Quarmby, Golcar, and Linthwaite. Longwood was denoted an ecclesiastical parish in 1866. As I mentioned at the end of the first chapter, the tower was added by the Hirst family of Longwood, the textile magnates and creators of Sunnybank Mills being blitzed at the bottom of the street, who erected it as a memorial to Crosland Hirst and his wife in 1914. Crosland Hirst had founded the firm with his brother James in 1860 at Sunnybank, but the account books of a cloth finishing business started by Abraham Hirst on the same site went back to 1815. The company grew into a five mill complex with over sixty thousand square yards of floor space producing their speciality novelty tweeds that was to make the name "C. & J.'s" famous all over the world.

During demolition of the mills I was standing at the bottom of Church Lane one hot summer's afternoon, where it forms a crossroads with the top of Ballroyd Lane. At that point there is an awkward section of the steep road which narrows to a slight s-bend, before the junction with Thornhill Road at the top. Drivers from either direction must approach this bend with some care, as the number of collisions have helped testify to, particularly when cars come out from Church Lane and are completely blind to traffic that may be hurtling down from Longwood Gate. On this occasion, one of the demolition lorries was struggling with its heavy load up past the row of pre-industrial revolution weavers' cottages, next to the pub where the alsatian or some other such dog (I never actually saw what it was) used to explode into a fit of barking when you passed the yard housing it at the bottom of Church Lane. The lorry was straining to breast the tape of freedom at the top of the street where it levels out into Thornhill Road and away. Its cargo of disembowelled textile mill stank of old plaster and musty black lime dust. Protruding from the rubble in its belly was a steel girder machine-gunned with two rows of large rivets. It was instantly recognizable as being from Sunnybank Mills because of its buttermilk-and-turquoise paint scheme, as standard a pair of colours in mills around here as light-blue-and-cream was in railway stations during the 1960's.

As the vehicle approached the nasty bend, a red sports car suddenly appeared at great speed from the downward direction. The lorry braked sharply, slipped a gear, and ground to a halt. The young man driving the sports car was wearing mirrored sunglasses and a white sweat-shirt emblazoned with a reference to the masculinity of his anatomy. He weaved defiantly past and raced off down the street amidst a cacophony of disco music booming from within and a dazzle of ostentatious silver alloy wheel-trims flickering crudely from without. The lorry had stopped right in front of me, the jerk from its cough causing it to spill a few lumps of shattered Victorian and Edwardian brick out of its trailer into the centre of the road. There was a hiss of air-brakes and I fancied I saw a silent mouthing of obscenities from behind the cigarette wedged between the driver's lips. There was a split second—one of those frozen moments in time that last only for an instant—when your senses are bombarded by several different observations all at once, which you can remember in minute detail months later.

There was the hot summer's day filled with a breeze that wasn't fanning pleasantly, but irritating by blowing warm air rather than cool. I remember thinking that the pieces of bricks which had fallen out of the trailer had probably not seen daylight for a hundred years. They were encrusted with remnants of black lime cement and strands of floppy, dusty spiders' webs. The pre-industrial revolution weavers' cottages were standing where they had stood before Sunnybank Mills were even built, as they would continue to stand for some time yet; long after those big mills had completely vanished from the face of the earth. I was aware of the lorry's modular plastic control panel, visible through its tinted windscreens, and the padded contour seat the driver was sitting in. The shape of the vehicle's bodywork was so crisp, so clean cut and Of This Age, you could imagine how the enthusiastic strokes of the industrial designer's marker-pens on paper had helped dictate the eventual shape of the styling of his creation when the prototype was built in reality. In front of me was a stark contrast between the industrial concoctions from two distant generations: roughly cut stone, cobbles, cast-iron lamp posts, an environment planned and laid out by people in the age of steel bolted impudently against steel, where that futuristic lorry, where the simplest push-button convenience of today would, back at the time those streets and mills were built, be the most fantastic conceptions of H.G. Wells or a distant tomorrow.

Minutes earlier, I'd left my house down the road having been excited by music playing on my record player from a rock band who make sounds almost entirely through the utilization of sophisticated electronic instruments, computer programming, moogs, fairlights, and mini-moogs, produced from a studio deep in the heart of the teeming Metropolis. I was working in that Metropolis—or just outside it—during the week. I reached it at a speed of a hundred and twenty five miles per hour aboard a gleaming blue-and-yellow projectile called a High Speed Train, the design of which was as alien to the civilization that built the millscape I was standing in at that moment in time as the incredibly fine ten denier stockings my girlfriend had pulled onto her legs before I came out for the bus.

The moment ended and the driver of the lorry was wrestling with the gear lever. He located first gear and, with a groan of near animal ferocity, the big machine spluttered then lurched forward again, resuming its ponderous crawl to the top of the street. A cloud of blue-grey diesel fumes shot up from the exhaust pipe protruding behind the cab and appeared to leap into the graveyard alongside, dissipating between the finely chiselled handiwork of several generations of stonemasons. The fumes came out of the lorry's engine in a defiant snarl from the age of the micro-processor chip and the world of the plastic injection moulding. They were a final derisive spit-in-the-eye at the handcrafted, considerably more human looking four-pronged church tower watching silently from between the trees a hundred yards up the hillside above. The church had seen much in its time. It had grown as Longwood had grown, as the trees in its graveyard have since grown, as did Sunnybank Mills in the bottom of the valley grow. At the time the church tower had been put up, the mills had been alive, still in their relative infancy. They were the focal point of the lower part of Longwood around which the streets and the houses and the school and the people had expanded. By the year nineteen hundred and eighty three, the church was witnessing an uncomfortable puther of noisy activity that raged at the bottom of its street. The equation was being bitterly and ironically reversed.

I'd made that journey on foot up and down from the bus stop hundreds of times over the years. At that point in the topography of the landscape, there was a fascinating interrelation of mills and narrow lanes, ginnels, cobbled snickets, odd shaped houses with different sized chimney stacks and roofs almost on level with your feet, allotments, and tiny patches of original flagged pavements, cracked and sunken and not yet completely tarmacced over. Looking across to Wood Street from Church Street, you could see the old coal depot piled high with stacks of coke. It used to be a railway goods yard in years gone by, the classic siding branching off from the nearby main line, penetrating the heart of the industrial community below the steep back walls of the terraced houses adjacent to it. I should think the yard was built to bring coal to feed the mills and transport their cloth, being situated, as they were, immediately around it. The original coal drops remain, and look to be in use by road vehicles, but the railway tracks were long since pulled up, before I was even born, if the aerial photographs of the area which I have scrutinized in the local history library are dated correctly. Sunnybank Mills stood to the right of the coal yard. To the left stood Job Beaumont's Woodland Mill, directly below one of the old railway goods sheds that still stand. Job Beaumont's mill went into liquidation during the early 1980's and his six storied

Lindley Street, Milnsbridge, a fine row of Huddersfield terraced houses with roofline and doorways still intact

behemoth was razed to the ground at the same time as Sunnybank Mills in 1983. More terraced houses were visible behind the goods depot and the mill, steeply graded in bunches of half a dozen up a narrow sidestreet. From certain angles on frosty winter's mornings, with the sun rising above Crosland Moor on the horizon, the stepped profile of the house rooftops flowed into the big bulk of Woodland Mill and its chimney in a backlit hazy silhouette that conveyed yet another example of this area's amazing pockets of architectural shapes, summarizing what the rest of the industrial landscape spread out around it was all about. Now the houses look lost, like so many other isolated groups or single buildings around here, where what they were once overshadowed by has been taken away leaving an awkward open quality, with too much sky visible too near the ground, that isn't right. The houses look across the former site of Job Beaumont's mill which has been turned into a second-hand timber yard selling large quantities of Pitch Pine — a wood used extensively in the construction of West Yorkshire textile buildings. Another secondhand timber merchant in the area sends sizable shipments of Pitch Pine to the South of England, where the higher asking price for such excellent quality and beautiful, resinous smelling wood is more readily paid, before it is reborn—into handmade fitted kitchen units.

When we are young, the world is an adventure playground. Before the reality of adulthood and its accrued stresses and responsibilities grab us; before money; before an awareness of how money works, moreover, before an awareness of certain people and how they can work, everything is sacredly and naively sentimental. When I was young, when I was playing in my adventure playground, the mill village, the ginnels, the old cindered back yard, that adventure book of the environment of my upbringing when all the chapters had still been in place, the feeling of living the distance between our house and the bus stop gave off was so thick it was palpable: even if such cliched, well-established surroundings faced on to the modern old people's council bungalows across the road and Gary Glitter was belting out of the radiogram in the living room. It was all exemplified by the ever present background rumble of the mills, throbbing like the distant hum of the engine room in a ship, interwoven with the sound effects of a village going about its daily business. There was the sound of footsteps out in the street. There was the rattle of the chain from the block-and-tackle by which the bales of raw wool were hoisted to the upper stories of the mill, so often my alarm clock on schoolday mornings, as were the mouthfuls of obscene four-letter words interspersed with the chains' coursing, from the men shouting aggressively at each other with several floors between them. There was the spasmodic revving of lorries backing into the mill yards, and the swish of their roller-concertina doors being highered or lowered. At several points in the day, the shrieking of infant children playing in the schoolyard above the mills echoed around the entire neighbourhood. It was a curiously pendulous sound, especially on misty overcast days in winter, when it felt to oscillate upon the very surface of the air itself. There is something innately Northern about the sound of children playing in a schoolyard when you're walking around the old industrial suburbs up here. Hearing it is reminiscent of old British black and white kitchen sink dramas, where the factory worker and his wife were couped up in a cramped bedsit, and there was the constant noise of kids playing in the street outside, and the clinking of railway trucks being shunted together in a goods yard in the background.

Longwood school closed in 1984, another nail hammered abruptly in the village's coffin.

I can see it from my window, blackened and Victorian, as I am typing this now. For the first decade I occupied the bedroom, I couldn't see the school because Sunnybank Mills were in the way. My Father attended the school during the 1930's. Next to my typewriter I have a creased, sepia-toned school photograph of him and the rest of his class sat cross-legged on the playground, the little girls sat on an old fashioned wooden form behind them. They look to be about five or six years old. The girls are wearing sandals and the little boys are wearing black working boots, and short trousers, and their knees are dirty, and they could all be any number of the kids you see darting in and out of the dusty passageways on innumerable old photographs that were taken up here at the time. Their faces are innocent, undefiled, bubbling with young expectancy because they were still enjoying their adventure playground, yet to be lined by the years of toil they would no doubt grow up to endure. I'm turning the photograph over. On the back, an infant's harshly scrawled hyroglyphics achieved with a struggle—my Father's written in pencil—manages to say "LONGWOOD SCHOOL HAVE HAD THEIR PHOTOGRAPH . . .". I assume the missing word was 'taken'. His birth certificate, folded in an envelope with his funeral papers, tells me that he was born at No 92, Longwood Gate, in 1925. All that remains of the house and its adjoining terrace are the gate posts, blocked up with stonework a few hundred yards up the road from the school, facing Prospect Mills at the other side of the street. In 1987, most of the school's windows have been boarded up. Those which aren't have been utterly smashed by vandals. The playground is sprouting weeds round the edges and is covered with shards of glittering broken glass. Some bright-blue graffitti daubed thickly informs you that "SILLY IS A VEGETARIAN BASTARD". The building stands rotting next to the church. Below it and in front of it are great slopes of overgrown rubble that used to be Sunnybank Mills, makeshift wooden fencing erected where it all tumbles down to meet the road. I don't know where the little kids made in Longwood, Huddersfield, West Yorkshire, up North, go to school now, although I suppose they must be the young people I sometimes see crowding a special bus going to Paddock, a mile or so away, in the mornings. At least they still shout and cheer.

The last time the neighbourhood contained any semblance of a soundtrack that could be regarded as those of the industrious living, it was the dramatic noise of demolition. The stagnant air of hopeless despondency hanging over the former site of Sunnybank Mills and their immediate vicinity today had yet to catch hold. Before that, there would be yet more irony to endure.

I was discussing something of this with my Grandmother one Sunday evening when I visited her, about six months after the demolition of the mills had got underway. Prompted by a comment I made, she went into her bedroom—a veritable Alladin's Cave of relics and cherished mementoes from bygone eras — and emerged holding a slightly yellowing but otherwise mint condition copy of the *Huddersfield Daily Examiner* from July 8th 1968. She had kept that particular issue because it was a special supplement to the regular edition, published to coincide with the celebration that year of Huddersfield's centenary of incorporation into the borough. The paper was packed with historical anecdotes about the town, photographs, comments from the local notable and the not so notable, and lots of those interesting little facts you'd always wanted to know, such as the town's present superb library being opened in 1940, and its first municipal park being opened in 1883.

The whole of the back page had been given over to several people who came from the town, ranging from students and a youth organizer, to the president of the junior chamber of commerce and the mayor's wife. They had been given the opportunity to offer their own personal visions of how they would have liked to see the Huddersfield of tomorrow develop. Their opinions were augmented by the musings of some of the other inhabitants of the town, within the supplement itself. Overall, it presented an interesting cross section of opinion. Some espoused optimistically, and in one instance nauseatingly, towards a bright ferro-concreted future of pedestrianized shopping precincts festooning all corners of the town, escalators, the ubiquitous flyovers and ring roads, numerous multi-storey car parks, and of course, high-rise flats that would offer such splendid views for the part of the population that had to live in them. The population of tomorrow's Huddersfield was seen by most observers to be relaxing during it's shopping expeditions, lolling upon seats, surrounded by flower beds and landscaped areas on the piazzas, due to the increased leisure time that would be afforded by the mysteriously reduced length of the working week that must surely be coming, the readers are told. Presumably, this reduction in the length of the working week would be tolerated by employers who would still pay their employees the same affluent wages in the new age of prosperity as they had earned for the full week; now that machinery replaced the labour of the people for the rest of the week. You could visualize these citizens of the new Huddersfield, passing along the open walkways connecting the vast shopping precincts and the flower beds, gazing languidly across the bright townscape of Utopia where the sun always shines, where people, you feel, are all well behaved and celibate, beaming with the smiles of a perfectly proportioned architect's sketch, and who never allow a four-letter word to pass their lips or emerge from the nozzle of the spray can as they play with beach balls on the endless expanses of green where the dogs never hunch.

Other observers were remarkably accurate in their estimations of how the Huddersfield of the future is being made. Interestingly enough, they were offered by the youngest writers, then still at college. Some of them commented on the need for a theatre in the town, a controversy that simmers gently in the same press twenty years later. Leisure activity centred around the canal and marina were anticipated, which is materializing. The ugliness of the dirty old town would be swiftly erased by the sterile greyness and the contrived greeness of the new, although one or two of the town's commentators were of the opinion that some of the more impressive buildings around St. George's Square ought to be preserved, after sandblasting of course, and with pedestrianization; another premonition that looks like it is going to materialize.

"BEFORE THE ERA OF GLEAMING PLATE GLASS AND CHROMIUM FITTINGS" announced one of the headlines, superimposed in white type over a photograph of a new box-shaped development that was **'rising from the dust and rubble'.** Conversely, another writer on the adjacent page observed how all the windows of the little old houses she could see as she walked about Huddersfield had numerous different designs emblazoned within the panes of glass. She noted how the town's chimney pots and windows were peculiarly attractive to her (she was acknowledging character), concluding—and here is an astute observation, at odds with the general pebble-dashed notions being bandied around in numerous council chambers at the time and coloured with concrete and connected by flyovers and framed by contrived flower beds—that in the new Huddersfield, she could see the smaller, more comfortable districts with the narrow streets and the windy lanes, the stalwart terraces, no longer having the appearance whereby the constructional shape of every house had an individuality. She saw the onset of order and light, convenience, regularity, neatness, similarity (she was acknowledging the loss of humanity) taking their place in time. And she finished by saying that something would be lost in the town then, and something missed. She anticipated the present day realization that it is informality, spontaneous variety in texture, both in tone and shape, the subtle details in all the right places to draw your attention to the focal points and effect a way in which we perceive them, that pleases the eye in buildings and environments. As such, she made the most poignant and intelligent observations in the entire centenary supplement, but with a sensitivity to the pleasures of the senses that was embedded in a proper awareness for a proper reality.

The single most noticeable theme running throughout the supplement from all concerned was the general air of real confidence in the future of the town that it positively exuded. It was of course the prosperous '60's'. Man was about to embark on his first journey to the moon. The Prime Minister of our country at the time hailed from Huddersfield (about ten minutes walk from Sunnybank Mills as a matter of fact). Huddersfield was still making things on a vast scale with large workforces; its cloth still at the forefront of its industry and famous right across the world. Only now, twenty years later, can we look back at a yellowing newspaper and feel tinges of embarrassment at dated comments that seem to epitomize so much of environmental and cultured thinking in the 1960's. After a hundred years of official existence as a borough, Huddersfield was giving itself a well deserved slap on the back. It did this with an enthusiasm that was genuine and not in the slightest bit contrived, or painfully over patriotic, or intentionally ironic, but was made at a time when the town was healthy and booming with industry and near full employment. You can forgive the town of the day for its wholehearted optimism and applaud it at the same time.

In the 1980's, quite a few writers of letters to the *Huddersfield Daily Examiner* have lamented the loss of the town's superb Victorian market hall in 1969 (along with the recent felling of a fine 1930's cinema, the single most contemptible blunder the town's representatives have ever made). You still hear it discussed occasionally over drinks in pubs twenty years hence; aged residents pine for the open grocers' stalls from the living rooms of their new council tenements, they miss the cobbled, homely atmosphere of the Shambles and the informality of the old Packhorse Yard across the road. How could a group of supposedly intelligent, perceptive individuals assemble in a town hall chamber and seriously enthuse over the demolition of the market hall—one of the architectural focal points in the flow of the town centre's fabric—and the erection of the piddling little concrete box put up in its place? they insinuate. But reading through the centenary supplement, even watching clips from '60's news bulletins and going over back issues of local newspapers stored on microfiche in the reference libraries, you can see that at least such mistakes appeared to be born of a genuine air of optimism, and we tend to forget this in our savage condemnation of 1960's town planning from today's shrewdly pessimistic retrospective standpoint. (As a matter of interest, it is worth pointing out that some of the original contractors used far more than the legal level of calcium chloride to encourage quicker setting of the concrete. This has also helped a faster corrosion, but the original builders are not forced to pay out compensation due to either having gone out of business, or through

SPINKWELL MILLS, DEWSBURY, DURING DEMOLITION IN 1987, AND SINCE REPLACED BY A SUPERMARKET

being protected by intricate webs of legal immunization). The aerial photograph of Huddersfield town centre in the newspaper, the scars of large scale demolition still to heal over, seemed like it was part of a positive attitude towards the future, however naïve or truncated much of its detritus looks today. At least the blocks of flats some of the town's observers desired were born of a real movement; they had a desire to take the future by the scruff of the neck and shake it up and say they will change it and do it how *they* want to do it. The prospect of Huddersfield's new ring road, then at the planning stage and not destined to cut its swath for another three or four years, embraced the motor car (whilst talking about pedestrianizing inside the ring road in the same breath), even if by offering such outstretched arms the planners may have stripped away lumps of the town's character that should have been preserved, and uglified a good deal of it in the process, very likely without realizing it. Today, the same newspaper and much of the town's motoring population regard the town centre and the automobile coming together with a sort of surly cynicism. The well balanced and level-headed newspaper editorials consistently refer to the vehicles, not as the product of the internal combustion engine, but the *infernal* combustion engine. Everyone complains about the lack of adequate town centre parking. Everyone complains about the one-way systems, the congestion, the tailbacks caused by the simplest of roadworks during the rush hours. The pundits offer solutions. The government predicts that the number of car owners will increase by however many percent by the year 2000. I shop in Huddersfield town centre as little as possible, like many others. I complain about the number of vehicles, like many others. But I would find it difficult to exist without a car, like many others. We all curse and swear and say what ought to be done to solve it all—whilst not having to abandon our own individual set of wheels of course. Meanwhile, the obvious cause of the difficulty, that there are quite simply too many cars on the roads in too cramped a space in environments that were never laid out to accommodate a motor age, gets worse every year as car sales figures jump to their biggest yet. A portent of the snarling up that can occur transpired at Christmas in 1985, when Huddersfield's town centre became absolutely jammed solid with cars on Christmas Eve and all the major roads in and out were closed by police until the congestion had relieved itself. Back in 1968, such a glut of motoring must have been only a twinkle in the odd sceptic's eye.

Turning the pages of that old supplement, I marvelled at photographs of town centre streets now gone, or rendered grey and inlaid with glass and perspex, the layout of which I had completely forgotten since redevelopment but which came flooding back on confrontation with a picture. The men visible in the photographs had yet to be brainwashed by the flared trouser leg, the bushy sideburn, and the platform shoe. The women looked like my Mother did when I was at infants school; some wore those funny, oval shaped horn-rimmed spectacles like Olive did a few years later in *On the Buses*. Others wore those heavy looking overcoats which were usually that dark shade of green that is most unappealing on a paint card, with fur collars sometimes speckled with the pattern of imitation leopardskin.

Once I had hungrily scrutinized all the 'papers photographic content like a man eating his first visual meal after a seventeen year fast, I began to notice large graphic advertisements with which the supplement appeared to be crammed. Essentially, they were from local firms, most of whom gave the impression that they were thriving; many of whom were based in the town's traditional industries of engineering, chemicals, and,

THE DAWNING OF THE SECOND INDUSTRIAL REVOLUTION: SLAITHWAITE, IN THE COLNE VALLEY, NEAR HUDDERSFIELD

coincidentally, textiles; and many of whom had taken out larger than normal box announcements pointing out how long they had been established in the town, and wishing the populace of Huddersfield a happy and prosperous future. Many of these names continue to trade, albeit in some cases with a mere fraction of their former workforces of 1968.

It was while perusing these proud advertisements and trying to connect them with localities that I had since got to know well, that still existed, when I came across one of the biggest proclamations in the entire supplement. It filled the bottom half of a page and came from the textile firm of C. & J. Hirst and Sons Ltd, of Sunnybank Mills, Longwood. It pointed out how renowned the company was for the manufacture of its world famous Sunnybank Tweeds, besides expressing how honoured the company had been to have received the Princess Alexandra during her recent visit to Huddersfield to coincide with the town's celebrations. Here was the yet-more-irony-to-endure bit. I knew there were probably hundreds of such mills that had closed down, both before and since, not to mention steel in Sheffield, shipbuilding on the Tyne, and coal mining just about everywhere in between. The Hirsts' textile combine was but a single drop in that vast tidal-wave of liquidation. But as I had lived in the shadow of those particular mills for half of my life, experiencing first hand the transition from living in a place pulsating with the lifeblood of industry, to living in a place hung over with a pall of gloom and an infernal quietness in the air which took so long to adjust to, the announcement in the centenary supplement made by C. & J. Hirst and Sons Ltd had a special significance. Reading the advertisement, with its implication of a company healthy and prosperous, then equating it to the picture in my mind of the derelict, rubble strewn wasteland festering where the big buildings had stood outside my bedroom window, had as debilitating an effect upon the emotions as the effect of fingernails being raked down a blackboard has on the teeth. It drove home the changes that had descended, not only on my own neighbourhood, but Huddersfield and other parts of the Lancashire and Yorkshire millscapes on the whole. It may have been going on for the past fifteen or twenty years. I may have read that the textile industry in the North had been slowly winding down since the end of the Second World War, but Longwood and its companion town of Milnsbridge experienced an acceleration of this process towards the end of the 1970's and beginning of the 1980's to such a speed that for a time the brakes failed, and immense gaps opened up in the flow of the town's fabric that you couldn't fail to italicize, whether it had been gathering momentum for twenty years or not.

Looking back at the Hirsts' announcement in 1968 was, I can imagine, rather like the gut realization you get on looking back at old photographs taken on a bright sunny day of the house you grew up in, before it was blown up during the war, which you come upon suddenly, years later, when sorting through the junk in the attic. On examining the Hirsts' announcement, the irony bit even deeper when I read a short sort of verse they had incorporated into it, not only to emphasize their standing in 1968 as one of the major contributors to Huddersfield's world famous reputation for producing the finest cloth, but also the transition that had taken place in the structure of the industry over the hundred years since Crosland and James Hirst had set up their original business. The verse made reference to the fact that, before the onslaught of the factory system and the birth of the industrial revolution—spearheaded in the North of England—cloth had been woven on hand-looms in the upper stories of those weavers' cottages up the hillsides, where they could gain maximum light. These familiar, isolated groups of now very desirable three-storied houses, occupied largely by the fashionable middle class commuters of today, were the 'factories' in which textiles had first been produced before industrialism had blossomed in the valleys and grown into towns and cities below. The verse made a crisp acknowledgement of this and read as follows:

> THEN a row of donkeys waited each morning near
> Longwood Church for yarn for cottage hand weavers
>
> NOW in the shadow of Longwood Church at
> Sunnybank Mills, thousands of yards of fancy
> tweeds are manufactured each week and
> exported to the markets of the world

I looked at this proud declaration long and hard, seeing yet again in my mind the wasteland outside my back bedroom window that Sunnybank Mills had become. The amount of daylight that the demolition of the buildings allowed into the room was unnerving at first. Over a decade, you grow unconsciously accustomed to the light in a room and your senses adjust themselves accordingly. When it changes, you feel somewhat vulnerable and slightly nauseated. A man-made cliff-face of rugged stonework had kept my bedroom in near sunless isolation for as long as I had known, especially during the winter months, when the sun was much lower in the sky, and the room became so cold due to lack of direct sunlight steam actually used to rise from my clothes when I warmed them in front of the fire downstairs in the mornings.

Sunnybank Mills produced textiles up until the beginning of the 1980's, but the rot had set in some years previously. When I left school in 1977, I worked part-time in a small mill down at the end of our street, where my Mother worked as a Mender. By early 1979, the mill had closed down, victim of a crisis in the Middle East, the destination of most of the cloth I can remember 'perching', then rolling and packing up, after it came off the looms. My Mother considered trying to get a job in Sunnybank Mills, the obvious place due to its convenient location out the back door. But rumours had been filtering through the grapevine of local gossip that the mills were 'going down the nick'. In the summer of 1979, another of C. & J. Hirst's mills, Commercial Mill down in Milnsbridge, had closed down. Even while my Mother was still on the payroll of the mill where I worked, the rumour of Commercial Mill's imminent demise had added substance to the seemingly exaggerated theory that the Hirsts were struggling to stand on their last legs, and new stories would bubble to the boil. This went on over a period of months, possibly years, it's difficult to remember precise dates in the blur of distant memory, only feelings. A lady who lived further up our terrace had worked in Sunnybank Mills for many years (several generations of employees had followed each other into the mills over the years. One elderly gentleman lived in a house a few yards from the mill entrance and worked inside it for 60 years) and most of the rumours that circulated in our household were announced at teatime, when I came in from school, after my Mother had exchanged conversation with this lady in the street outside when they were returning from work.

I knew there had to be some strength to these rumours: the mills gradually stopped working through the night, and for the first time since I'd moved into my bedroom when I was a kid, I experienced prolonged periods of pitch blackness when I was in bed. Up until then, my room had been lit softly all night long by the glow from the windows of the mills outside. I'm sure I'd become dependent upon them, and the background beating of their looms, to send me off to sleep. Being without it was like being high on caffeine before you got into bed. When I'd first moved into the bedroom in 1974, the mills working throughout the night so close to the back of our house filled me with a tremendous schoolboy excitement. Sometimes, in my pyjamas, I used to lift open the window and lean out over the windowsill in the middle of the night and just listen to them and look at them. The row of disused outside toilets at the bottom of our back yard were lit by the mills' warm, florescent glow, and were so close to the main six storied weaving block, I'm sure the draught from the movement of the looms could have fanned your backside if you were sat in them when they were still in use. When it rained heavily, I could hear the water trickling and dripping with a loud slapping noise from the handrails of the fire-escapes, whenever I was laid awake in bed.

Looking back, it seems rather odd now. You search the depths of your memory and remember how you used to perceive such an everyday thing as the environment you existed in, but in a way you have since completely forgotten. Suddenly, you receive a fresh mental stab of recollection; for a split second, your brain seems to contract then expand again, as though under the impact of an electric jolt for the tiniest moment in time. For an instant that isn't even an instant you've gone back in time. You experience it at the most unexpected of times: brewing some tea and watching the rain splashing on the upturned dustbin lid in the yard outside: the play of moving sunlight across a familiar building that has remained standing: sudden smells of damp grass or cloth: dusk as you sit in the armchair and watch the living room slowly devoured by shadow, the orange playing of the streetlamp outside throwing the elongated trelliswork of the leaded-lights on the front window back into the house, and across the chimney breast. Things you noticed as a child which now hit you in the head with the same staccato punching to the senses as if somebody has prodded you in the memory and the back of your neck goes stiff. It's sometimes like this when I think back to hanging out of the bedroom window in the middle of the night so long ago. I was then on the threshold of adolescence, too young to be able to realize what I was doing or question the reasons behind it. The mills seemed to have a magical, almost hypnotic presence at night that seems impossible, even absurdly hypocritical to comprehend now, but which was particularly vivid at that time. It sounds ridiculous to say it, but the mood of the whole area could be affected by whether or not large textile mills were lit up and working during the night. Even if you were downstairs in the house watching television before you went up to bed, unable to see or hear them, you felt peculiarly contented, reassured—in the same absurd manner as hearing the vacuum-cleaner going downstairs when you were in bed on Saturday morning—if you knew in the back of your mind that they were there, functioning, keeping their strong arm of traditional manufacturing stability around the shoulder of the neighbourhood; keeping it alive even as it slept.

Pondering the little verse made by the management of Sunnybank Mills in 1968 brought all these feelings back with a rush. They'd begun to simmer again due to me having worked for some time and lived in London, then outside it, in a dingy bedsit in affluent

Windsor, only a few minutes walk from the castle and the Great Park. Down there I was high on adrenalin, fantasizing about the far future, designing and making spacecraft, vehicles, and buildings for the special effects on a TV series, living in a horrible room that had bed bugs and was owned by an extremely well spoken landlord who drove a four-wheel drive jeep long before they began putting the explanatory decals on the sides, and who looked like the cartoon character Fred Flintstone and had a chain smoking wife, whilst two hundred miles away, the bulldozers were tearing the brash solidity of my 19th century built hometown to pieces. During the week, Sunnybank Mills were a long way off, but I didn't need to be standing next to them to visualize them crashing to the ground. I saw them at weekends, which curiously accelerated the demolition, abbreviating the process of them being eaten away to some crazy time-lapse. On the rare occasions I didn't go back up North at weekends, I stayed in Windsor, laying in bed until dinnertime in winter to keep warm, surrounded by a tepid aroma of stale flatulence drifting up from beneath the bedsheets and yearning instead in some idiotic way for the sounds and smells of distant demolition. It was this contrast between living in two places at once, smelling two different airs, identifying the divide, suddenly noticing textures and sometimes even the very lowering of the air temperature itself as I got off the 125 at Wakefield when I came back up on Friday nights—stupidly obvious little things that I'd become almost oblivious to due to never having experienced the textures of the South—that sowed the seeds of this book and the endless wandering with a camera and a determination to register thought officially and observe textures of stone walls, mullioned windows, cobbles and overgrown ginnels in print, and just generally assemble it all between two covers to neaten it all up and place it in some sort of perspective and underline it, but intersperse it with the demolition and the concrete and the high-rise and the ugly new houses, to paint the correct picture as it really was.

When I had been perusing the old centenary supplement to the *Huddersfield Daily Examiner* from 1968 that night at my Grandmother's, and reading the little verse from Sunnybank Mills again and again, I'd already come back to live up here, and I remembered an old man I'd heard jabbering at the bus stop a few days previous to that Sunday night. I'd joined the queue when he was halfway through a tempestuous oratorical to the rivetted passengers, most of whom were of pensionable age, standing in the icy November wind, reflecting upon The Glory of Former Days. I'd taken the old man's knowledge of the mills we could all hear being torn apart below us to be an indication that he had, at some time in his life if not a major part of it, worked for C. & J. Hirst. His vehement condemnation of the dereliction befalling Longwood and Milnsbridge lead him off onto the familiar tangent of making slanderous references to the attitudes of the particular government of the day, its lack of caring about the North, the lazy affluence of the South, and the idleness of today's youth.

"Bloody young 'uns today" he said, "they don't know what hard work is".

"Aye" agreed the rest of the bus queue disdainfully.

"They've no bloody manners an' no bloody respect. I mean, look at state o' them idle sods who sits in this 'ere blasted bus shelter. They sit smokin', and they 'eckle yer behind yer back, and only t'other week, one of 'em spat on a bloke's back as he got on t'bus. They should put 'em in t'bloody army, that's what they should do wi'em; wi' whole bloody lot of 'em!"

OVERLEAF: LONGWOOD SCHOOL, CLOSED DOWN 1984.
Planning permission has been applied for to convert it into a residential nursing home.

PUNX

"Aye!" agreed the rest of the bus queue, less disdainful but beginning to sound increasingly like a choir. The old man was broadcasting to the neighbourhood now and nodding animatedly to punctuate his own observations. The kids he was referring to, as loutish as they were, were mostly still at school and not yet of YOP scheme or dole age.

He continued: "Aye, it's not like when we were kids, I'll tell yer. In our day yer had manners, an' yer respected yer elders, an' th' were more t'life than sex and bloody drugs. Aye . . ."

The rest of the bus queue were becoming decidely ruffled. There was the sound of feet crunching on bits of gravel on the spot. A frailish old lady plastered with make-up and with a voice like air being released slowly from the neck of a balloon joined in: "Aye, an' if yer knew what was best, you were frightened o't local bobby an'all, 'cause back then, he weren't afraid to clatter yer around yer 'ead if yer were up t'summat yer shouldn't o' been".

"Aye!" said the rest of the bus queue. They were now in danger of breaking out into an anarchistic mass of gesticulating vigilantes, ready to crush this modern phenomenon and threat to the status-quo. The old man started to say something else and waved his roll-up around before the words managed to get out, nearly dropping it in his enthusiasm to mobilize his troops. Then he noticed me and they all abruptly shut up. Even though in my twenties and theoretically beyond my period of loutish behaviour, I was frowning sarcastically like a man accused. This, in combination with my stubbled appearance, must have been enough to place me in the category of the young which they were venomously denouncing. They regarded me with the same uneasy, beady-eyed distrust as if I was the one they suspected of having just farted silently in a crowded lift. The old man broke the uncomfortable silence of the moment by moving back to the subject of the demolition of Sunnybank Mills. His manner lowered considerably, both in posture and in decibel, as he began to relate what he had heart about the mills through the grapevine. During the familiar street theatre rhetoric of a few minutes before I'd wanted to yawn in his face, but suddenly my hand was over my mouth and I was all eyes and ears.

He pointed out that, as they were being pulled down, the stone from Sunnybank Mills was being transported down South, at least that's where I think he said it was going. I didn't catch the name of the place but the reference to it was made with the average Northerners general tone of non-credibility to anywhere below Watford (this joke about Watford has always slightly baffled me. Despite the name of the company who have published this book, unconsciously, ever since I was a small child, I've somehow imagined that the South of England starts just below Sheffield and includes Wales, which must be an insult to the Welsh for which I wholeheartedly apologize. Funnily enough, the North of England never included the east or west coasts parallel to where we lived. The holiday resorts we went to such as Blackpool or Mablethorpe were not in the North of England, but somewhere flat and sunny with no ups and downs or aggressive buildings, which, again, somehow made them down South). Below Watford, the stone was being cleaned then shipped across the Channel to Holland, where it was being reused to build new flats or houses. This was the last comment I can remember hearing the old man make that day standing at the bus stop. He sounded to repeat himself a lot after that, his voice became garbled, then trailed off because I was no longer listening. I was glancing across the Colne Valley facing us instead. It disappears on a gradual incline towards the small milltown of Marsden five miles away, huddling below the bleak, windswept moorland at the end of the valley. Marsden is unique. It has legends of Luddites and murder during the turbulent days of pre-industrial revolution Pennine history, about which so much has been written. It has Bank Bottom Mills, built on the site of Ottiwells Mill, and which still has part of a stone barricade incorporated into its facade that was erected to defend the former structure against an attack by the Luddites in 1812. Marsden churchyard has in its grounds the grave of Enoch Taylor, a blacksmith in the village who, with his brother James, invented the shearing frame, a simple piece of machinery by which the woolly 'nap' could be cut from a piece of cloth by one man, replacing the jobs of ten hand-croppers. These hand-croppers, their livelihoods threatened by machinery, became desperate men in their attempts to fend off the threat of unemployment and starvation. They mounted a battle against the owners of local mills who installed the new machines, threatening them, and organizing raids on the factories by night when they broke into the premises and smashed up the frames. Twelve thousand troops were needed to finally suppress Luddism in the North of England, more than had been required to vanquish Spain in the Peninsula War, but not before William Horsefall of Marsden had been murdered for installing the new machinery in his mill, even if he had to **'ride up to his girths in Luddite blood'** to do it. He was shot and killed at Crosland Moor, overlooking Longwood and Milnsbridge, on market day, April 28th 1812. Three Luddites were hanged in York, others were transported, and a further five were executed for their part in the local Luddite disturbances. Bank Bottom Mills dominate the top end of Marsden and continue to thrive with the production of Yorkshire cloth, lit up in the dark with a night-shift that makes them the complete focal point of the town. They stand ominously at the foot of steep hillsides, flanked by ruler straight rows of terraced houses, watching over the rest of Marsden's rooftops like a brooding guardian. If you stand on Cop Hill, two miles before Marsden past Slaithwaite, and look down onto it on a sunny day, you are confronted by a panorama that graphically illustrates the confluence of the relationship between milltown and moorland in this harsh landscape. Marsden's uniqueness is punctuated by this view, a perfect balanced millscape. If Bank Bottom Mills were to go, or even only their chimney, this balance would be destroyed. When the town is backlit by the sun in the distance, the mills stand out in a misty silhouette with a plume of smoke gently rising from the chimney. Behind is a colossal precipice of land. It is the backbone of England, dwarfing the mill which feels so overpowering when you are stood down in the town, on the street in front of it, but which looks so miniscule from up there on the hillside. From Cop Hill there is only silence, broken by the occasional shrieks of a curlew, as they say, the rustling of wiry grass in the breeze, the clatter of a train out of sight in the valley below, and the vast expansiveness of the Pennine landscape itself, threatening to swallow you and romanticization and the little town up with it's overpowering presence. Where the Colne Valley ends and the backbone begins to swell, there is only bleak boggy moorland called Standedge (pronounced *Stannidge)*; then over the top and down the other side, similarly rural milltowns called Diggle, Saddleworth, Greenfield, Mossley, Delph; then the stone is left behind, like the Yorkshire accents, and you hit the red brick periphery of Greater Manchester as you pass through towns called Stalybridge, Ashton-under-Lyne, Oldham, and the sprawling megalopolis of the Mancunian tongue and Lancashire beyond.

These were the Lancashire and Yorkshire millscapes, or what were millscapes, I'd

---

OVERLEAF: MARSDEN '. . . Bank Bottom Mills dominate the top end of Marsden . . . flanked by ruler straight rows of terraced houses, and watching over the rooftops like a brooding guardian . . .'

thought that day at the bus stop, and I saw them all spread out—strung out—on either side of the Pennines, however botched and muddled and tampered with they might have been, as the old man told us of stone from one of them going across the sea to build houses for a different nation of people who had probably never even heard of Lancashire or Yorkshire, let alone tramped through parts of their rich architectural fabric.

It was a cold November day, overcast and biting. Through the bare trees that were creaking in the wind in the graveyard across the road from the bus stop, I could see the big black railway viaduct running through the centre of Milnsbridge. It looked strangely far off, diminutive and unimposing from on the hillside up there at Longwood Gate. It was only a silhouette through the dampening mist; a miniature bridge connecting two protuberances of land, with toy buildings spread out on either side as on a model railway layout. A noisy rook spoke a pedantic soliloquy like my blackbird had done during the summer. It seemed odd. Rooks nearly always call in muddled groups. I spotted the bird, a black dot hardly

THE FAR END OF THE COLNE VALLEY: MARSDEN FROM COP HILL, SLAITHWAITE

'. . . Behind is a colossal precipice of land. It is the backbone of England, dwarfing the mill . . .'

flinching, high up in the branches of one of the bare trees in the graveyard, its cawing mimicking the peaks and troughs of human moaning, as if it was taking the mickey out of us all because it knew what we were all thinking as we heard the crashing of dead mills being loaded into the demolition lorries below the church. A plume of smoke rose up from the scrapyard that occupies the former site of the railway goods yard which used to spread out at one end of that far off viaduct. Milnsbridge station had been built at the other end, before it closed in 1968: the railway running through the town was perched on such a narrow ledge above it that the builders couldn't get goods and passenger facilities on the same spot, as they managed in most other places.

Looking across all this, I felt a day around me that was inescapably Northern. I only ever feel that days are inescapably Northern between October and March and that the rest of the year pretends to impersonate somewhere else. The black dry-stone walling opposite, the terraced houses and scattering of old shops and the war memorial to my left, the accents to my right, they all confirmed this. They couldn't have been built, they didn't belong, anywhere except in the same landscape as that big black viaduct down below, and the undulating expanse of rooftops describing Cowlersley beyond. All these things screamed for attention at once like a sequence of moody shots in an old Pathe newsreel above sombre music and Standard English from London telling us how we must never be allowed to build such places again. All gave substance to the time and the place and in a flash, I saw the history of it play before me like another newsreel, but this time in the full colours which I knew so well, and speeded up so fast it went by in a second and Standard English fumbled his lines and came out sounding like *Pinky and Perky.* I also saw my hated predicament of when I'd lived in the overcrowded glut of the Metropolis down South during the week, where a friend of mine had recently taken out an extortionate mortgage for what had once been merely the downstairs of a semi-detached house, partitioned, the staircase sealed up, and now called a 'flat'. The same money up here would have bought her a detached three bedroomed bungalow with gardens, a double garage, and panoramic views: but would, of course, have only drawn the same rate of interest if placed in a building society.

This all came in an instant, another of those broody moments in time suspended, when the old man pointed out the destination of the crumpled stonework from Sunnybank Mills on its way across the sea to Holland. Maybe he was wrong. Maybe the stone wasn't going across the sea to benefit somebody else. Maybe he was relating a story which he had heard only tenth-hand, exaggerated as stories so often are as they filter through the network of gossip, telescoped together to leave only the dramatic bits to spin a good yarn. But one thing was for sure: the stone wasn't staying in Longwood, even Huddersfield. It might have been going to the South of England like so much of the Pitch Pine from so many of the other smashed Northern mills, which seems even more ironic than if it was all going to Holland. I wondered if it *was* yet more irony. I wondered if the North of England was destined always to be an irony itself. Then I wondered if I was just obsessed with using the word without really knowing what it means. I imagined the pieces of the mills we could hear clattering into the backs of the hungry lorries out of sight, being lifted onto pallets, cleaned and prepared, then craned aboard a ship. I heard the sound of dockland activity, and seagulls, then I saw Yorkshire mill stone sailing out to sea to be reborn as quaint, new little houses on the continent, with exactly the right amount of tile-bricked courtyards and purpose built

MILNSBRIDGE 1988: DIRTY OLD MILL TOWN . . .? *(turn to page 83). . .*

parking spaces and gaudy red painted herringbone valances to make them go straight onto the cover of *Architectural Today*. I saw good looking men and women moving into them with mouthfuls of perfect, pure white teeth, their hands resting on the shoulders of sweet looking little boys and girls, smiling together in the familiar bouquet of human happiness with a well fed labrador pup on the cover of an investment brochure in a building society, gushing with references to you and your family above tempting illustrations of cars, houses, holidays, hi-fi's, TV sets, laughter: the joys of all your goals and dreams come true at whatever percent interest rate between one and five years.

What did all this imply? Did it imply that the mills were being sold off cheap in a craze to dispose of them quickly at any excuse, to be rid of that dirty old town image of the North yet again, now there was another opportunity? Was there some other more elusive reason which I, in my ignorant comprehension of world economics, was unable to fathom out? Why was the stone being shipped across to Holland, or the South, or wherever, to build nice new houses? Why wasn't it put to better use in the place where it had been hewn from, weathering under the elements blasting down from the roof of the Pennines for the last hundred-odd years? Why were we just accepting manufacturing decline and kicking ourselves in the mouth by skinning our towns of their remaining structure and bits of orderliness, then apologizing to everybody on the news bulletins because it was the effect of the recession you know. At least then the mills would be giving something back to the environment and the people from which they had extracted so much.

Standing at the bus stop with that harsh, monotonous sound in the background like a metallic crash in a steelyard, each time a shovelful of textile mill was dumped in the back of a lorry by the bulldozers, had made me feel angrier by the second. I'd felt I had a right to feel angry; it was the place where I lived that was being gutted; it was me who was being aggravated by the constant banging and clattering of demolition; my sense of old established security that was being terminated; my back yard that was looking out onto a flaming bombsite. It was seeing those cold few minutes once more when I read the unsuspecting announcement of confidence and a future from C. & J. Hirst, in that slightly yellowing but otherwise mint condition newspaper from 1968 at my Grandmother's, that the pall of gloom descending into the neighbourhood began to shift into some sense of a perspective.

THEN in the shadow of Longwood Church at
Sunnybank Mills, thousands of yards of fancy
tweeds were manufactured each week and
exported to the markets of the world

NOW a row of bulldozers and lorries wait each
morning near Longwood Church where Sunnybank
Mills are themselves being exported to the
markets of the world

End of Chapter

3

My back bedroom window was originally of the old fashioned sashed type with leaded patterning on the glass that was installed in the little terraced house when it was built in 1872. The paintwork on the inside of it has been only two colours since we moved in, in 1974. When I first occupied the room it was a sickly pink, as it was on the back of the original panelled door through which you entered the room from the landing at the top of the staircase. During Easter 1975, we redecorated the room and the paintwork was redone using a brilliant white non-drip gloss. Twelve years on, this white has lost its lustre quite considerably and is in the process of cracking off around the glazing, due to condensation and the after-effects of damp which got into the room when a slate was blown off the roof by a strong wind, and which took me over twelve months to eventually get round to replacing.

I began redecorating the bedroom again in May 1986. I stripped all the wallpaper off this time, right down to the bare plaster which was a greyish-blue in colour. It was interesting to note the different layers of wallpaper that had been applied over the years. The oldest—the first above the plaster—probably dated back to the 1920's or '30's, and was by far the most attractive of all. It was a pale yellow in colour, with little red flowers that were not in the least bit gaudy like the day-glo reds and purples of some of the 'papers of more recent years have been. It displayed a very pleasing balance, and for a crazy few moments, I contemplated whether or not it would be possible to somehow steam all the layers off the walls above it, leaving it revealed again in all its former glory. I quickly abandoned the idea, but kept a sample pressed flat in a folder for posterity. The further forward you came in time, the more garish the wallpapers seemed to get. Looking at the papers materializing from the 1960's, as they did when I repeated the process later in the living room downstairs, there was absolutely no way in this whole wide world that they were as good as the older ones. By far the most hideous 'paper revealed in the bedroom was the layer that was on the walls when I moved into the room in 1974; it was as crude and naïvely insensitive as the sickly pink paint on the skirting boards and the window frames. I can't describe the stupidity of its graphics other than to say they harmonized perfectly with the overall crassness of fashions in the early 1970's. Although only wallpaper, it amazes me to think that horrible stuff was actually designed and money invested in its manufacture and worse, people bought it and pasted it to the walls of their homes.

When I started redecorating the bedroom in 1986, I left the job unfinished. The room is, at the time of writing, in use as a storeroom. The walls are still the bare plaster, pock-marked with bits of brown thistle-plaster where I filled in various holes and dents and cracks, and plugged scars left over from the time when I screwed a crude home-made shelf to one of the walls to display my collection of assembled plastic construction kits of war planes and horror film monsters. The room is crammed full of books, records, models, old clothes, a stepladder, and more books and records. It still contains the single bed upon which I lost my virginity. This bed is now bereft of sheets and is in use as a shelf, piled high with papers and numerous photographs.

We came to the house in November 1974. It was a tiny stone-built two-up two-down that cost £2,300 and opened straight onto the pavement. The entire floor area from front to back and side to side measured only twenty-two feet by fourteen. It had been modernized in that crude way which was a leftover from the wipe-easy craze when everybody nailed hardboard over original panelled doors and sealed fireplaces up. The overall interior decoration when we arrived was an uncompromising mixture of Victorian, Edwardian, pre-war, post-war, 1950's wipe-easy, 1960's eye-poppingness, and 1970's infantile yukiness, epitomized by that dynamic bastion of home decorating taste, the polystyrene ceiling tile. Thus you would ascend the dog-leg staircase with its stone steps worn into hollows by clogs under a carpet that had been glued into place in say 1970, whilst being surrounded by wallpaper from maybe the 1920's or even earlier (the staircase was so high, nobody could get any ladders long enough to get up to the ceiling and repaper it), noting the old panelled doors skinned with hardboard on one side and still the old fashioned dark-brown woodgrain paint effect on the other, then enter the bathroom with its 1960's tiles and early Armitage Shanks, the monicker upon which I always aimed my pee at when I used the toilet pot.

1974 was a time I can best remember as the age of flared trousers, platform shoes, tallocky hairstyles, bushy sideburns, women wearing knee-length white boots with massive heels and tinselley short dresses still hungover, shirt collars you could go hang-gliding in, purple and orange coloured cars, chequered jackets, Glitter Rock, power cuts, and the *Six Million Dollar Man.* When I first entered the back bedroom of our new little house, it was when I was wearing a pair of bell-bottomed jeans and some turquoise-and-blue coloured shoes with three inch heels as horrendous as the 'paper lining the walls.

The view that unfolded out of that sashed-and-leaded window was a lot different to what it is now. It was filled with Sunnybank Mills. Over the years, I would occasionally be inspired to photograph it, sketch it, and paint it. The buildings themselves rose abruptly, a mere stone's throw (more like a half-hearted stone's toss, as they were much nearer than that) at the bottom of our yard, immediately behind an old dilapidated wash-house, and were part of a gaunt procession of five and six-storied monolithic structures which began half a mile or so up the road at Parkwood, and trailed down into Milnsbridge (a few minutes down the road from Sunnybank Mills) where they bunched together on either side of that similarly massive and just as imposing black railway viaduct that produced, from certain angles, a juxtaposing of sheer architectural presence that was so blatantly an expression of the uncompromising power of nineteenth century industrialism, that was so classic a living testimony to Blake's worn phrase about dark satanic you-know-what's, it was almost a cliche.

Directly in front of my bedroom window was the apex of what I should think was a wool sorting shed. Along its roof were several rows of angled tubular air ducts resembling air funnels on the deck of a ship. They were bent like the knee-bend in a pipe, with a circular disc of metal on top which caught the wind and spun them skillfully in whichever direction it was blowing from, so as to channel fresh air into the clogged atmosphere of wool grease below. Shortly after we'd moved into the house, I was laid on my bed brooding about something (probably women) in the winter dusk, without the bedroom light on. These funnels outside suddenly began spinning crazily but silently at the blurred edge of my vision for the first time. I can remember jumping up, thinking instinctively that somebody was prowling along the roof of the mills, peering into my room.

Next to the wool sorting shed the main building itself reached up, six stories high, about twenty feet diagonally from my window. It did this with that familiar black-bulk-outlined-against-the-grey-sky-abruptness that so much of the industrial architecture around here did and still does, and seeing it in full on Grove Street often made me think of a man-made butte hacked out of millstone grit, even though in later years I was to realize it was made from Yorkshire sandstone. On the corner was the fire-escape, running in dog-leg fashion from top to bottom. It was painted in that dull maroon colour which would once have been shiny, a hangover from the 1950's. This colour proliferated on old buildings when I was younger, along with a dusty, aged shade of dark green, and peeling remnants of original mock painted woodgrain. You still come across odd ones today, incredibly ancient looking, with a dust impregnated, fly-blown quality, as though a high-pressure hose-pipe has been aimed at their facades blasting them with black lime powder from a demolition site. There are a few boarded-up shops in the inner city parts of Bradford that are like this, peeling beyond recovery; the old establishments of barbers or electrical shops or newsagents, aged and dejected, with yellowing net curtains hanging limply, the few remaining vestiges of the customs of a previous age when windows and their decorations were still in unity with the style of the overall building. You might spot the corroded remains of the odd enamelled metal sign that hasn't gone to the collectors or the museums, "PLAYERS PLEASE", "SENIOR SERVICE", or the faded graphics from advertisements hand painted on the gable ends of terraced houses proclaiming the desirability of "WATNEYS ALES" or "CAPTSTAN MEDIUM TIPPED CIGARETTES".

At lunchtimes, the weavers at Sunnybank Mills came out and sat on the old red fire-escape to eat their sandwiches and spit onto the glass roof covering a yard far below. When the mills used to work throughout the night, enshrouded by their blazing glow of florescent light and with the constant hum of beating looms, noticeably quieter than during the day, some of the men stepped out onto the fire-escape in the dark and urinated off the edge. Presumably, they thought the row of terraced houses beneath them were oblivious to their night-time ablutions. I imagined a fine spray being carried to the four corners of the wind on blustery evenings and made a point of always looking up above me if I went out to empty the rubbish-basket, just in case.

Beyond the immediate view outside my window, Sunnybank Mills spread out over a twenty acre site that included more five and six-storied mill buildings, adjoining annexes, warehouses and sorting sheds, connected from opposite sides of Grove Street by covered walkways that spanned the road. These walkways are a regular feature of mill building down narrow streets, resembling the old footbridges connecting platforms in railway stations. If I looked straight in front out my window, I could see the top section of a four-storied part of the mill complex that had obviously been built much later than the rest, poking up from behind a grey slated rooftop with another regiment of those air funnels along the top. I would have guessed it to have been built during the 1920's, but the *Huddersfield Daily Examiner* implied in its article about the "PULL OUT KILLS LONGWOOD PLAN" that it was in fact a post-war extension. It was this extension, the floors and interior walls of which were made from reinforced concrete, that seemed to prove difficult during demolition. For weeks on end, a JCB hammered away at the prefabricated

February Dusk, Slaithwaite

floors with a device fitted to its hydraulic arm called a *henpecker.* This henpecker was basically a pneumatic drill which vibrated much slower, but on a much bigger scale, than the usual implement you see roadworkers dancing about with, and its function was much the same. Progress was tediously slow, especially on Sunday mornings when you wanted to have a lay-in, but were woken by the henpecker at about eight in the morning. Because the concrete floors had numerous thin steel bars running through, as the henpecker chipped away at them, large chunks gave way under their own weight, suspended by the steel tendons to make fantastic sculptures in harsh sunlight.

I lived in that back bedroom for years and grew to know every nook and cranny of the buildings that loomed outside it with what I can only see now as a morbid scientific relish. Strange as it sounds today, back then I wouldn't have swapped it for a room with a view across green trees and fields or the ocean for anything. I can remember thinking this when I was too young to have been swayed by any of the pseudo-pretentious romanticizations that can take hold of your nostalgic impulses unawares, if you're not careful. The mills breathed the unmistakeable rumble of healthy industry into the streets that clung to them. Even now, I feel instinctively comfortable if I'm near big industrial buildings (yet I can feel unnerved walking through wooded countryside) but I have stacks of books spanning generations that repeatedly describe the 'ugliness' of these structures. Much as I try, I am afraid I cannot see ugliness in mills, chimneys, or long rows of little houses sweeping up hillsides that are generally regarded as being undesirable, even in this age of supposed conservation.

Recently I was photographing Slaithwaite (pronounced *Slath-wait* or *Slowwitt* to the locals) up the valley when some people walking past commented, very matter-of-factly, in the same way they would about the state of the weather, without stopping: "In't it bloody horrible". This confounded me, but it is a reaction I've often received from people in the street if I've been shooting anything remotely connected with the old industrial North; unless it is a railway station or a town hall. I could have tried to reason with them, but they wouldn't have understood what I was trying to say, and I would probably have ended up making a fool of myself under the circumstances. So I turned to Spa Mill in front of me. From that angle on Manchester Road, one of Slaithwaite's two railway viaducts runs behind it, bisecting the flow of the lines of the shape of the mill in a perfectly balanced relationship and co-ordination of perspective in that rough-textured-mass-of-aggressive-building-chimney-and-curved-solidity-of-viaduct way that is anything but horrible. In fact, the mill chimney is vital to the appreciation of the composition. I tried to get out of myself, to study it excruciatingly, straining to see it from a completely different perceptiveness. But the only horrible thing I could see, as reluctant as I was to admit it, was a new residential housing estate. Its weakness and blandness seemed to be emphasized all the more by trying to look at the old buildings from another, more determined standpoint. You simply couldn't compare the two. The new buildings weren't real buildings, they were cardboard looking makeshifts with all the corners cut and the details skimped, and yet—an incredible paradox — they fetch much higher prices on the property circuit. But old Slaithwaite, even the most mundane stone lean-to built onto the rear of the terraced houses in the foreground, had presence, weight, an immediacy of shape which seemed at once to harmonize with the spontaneity of textures, the naturalness of textures, the details, the sculptural sense of form that was all probably somewhat accidental, if only because it used

NEAR TROOPER LANE, HALIFAX '. . . a black dry stone wall . . . the mottled texture of repainted cast iron, the stout chapels . . . they possessed a character and interweaving that was only of this part of the world . . .'

to be the accepted norm.

It is odd how large numbers of the English people spurn drama in old industrial buildings and landscapes—for instance, you feel almost every Northerner mentally stifles a snigger when contemplating a mill chimney—but are living increasingly in sentimental imitations of decent buildings from the same, albeit generally idealized past. But curiously enough, the life force of the human race tends to thrive around drama. Whether it is the conflict repeatedly anticipated in the news, the competitiveness of sports activities, the instant sense of prestige that is acknowledged through the displaying of strength or physical courage; the predominance of a sort of comic-book masculinity with gritted teeth and dark patches under the armpits, even the nationally ingrained passions associated with the consumption of alcohol—all generally derive energy from, and seem to be connected to, modern society's powerhouse of driving speed and this inherent aggression factor, and therefore the drama which it absorbs as a civilization. But yet—and here's another paradox –a very large proportion of the people in this country, probably a good half, aspire to live in environments which suggest peace and tranquility and simulate the storybook epitome of Englishness and a fairy-tale country living, generally bound up with the traditionally pastoral beauty of nature, village greenery, and ducks and geese crossing narrow leafy lanes. That quintessential Ealing comedy which secretly tucks into bed the heart of almost every English man and woman, an idealized ruralness, somewhere between double-glazed mock-Georgian bow windows and the transfers on the sides of toasters depicting a farmer sowing his seed by hand, rather than by sophisticated microchip seed-drill. Cottage living, Merrie England, and Tudor beams are so ingrained into the collective English subconscious they can genuinely be seen as national characteristics, as important as the deep-rooted affection for flowers, the magnanimous passions for Royal births, hot climates, football, patio doors, and the increasingly disturbing pre-occupation with driving far too fast. In fact, as a small aside, of all these characteristics, undoubtedly the most accurate indicator to the social atmosphere prevalent in England during the latter part of the twentieth century can be seen by studying the country's driving habits, especially on motorways or at roundabouts.

All this links with another paradox, which is, of course, the progression of modern technology, now forever making a mockery of national rural sentiment. So stealthily has this process ingrained itself, you could convincingly argue it is easy to remain oblivious to the irony of fielded door panels moulded from plastic; or the mad scramble along the motorway to The City each morning to the air conditioned office chattering ceaselessly with computers; or the mad dash back at teatime to the idyllic untouched village "only a few minutes drive from major motorway networks", and the relaxation in front of the imitation log fire that is really gas but is so brilliantly engineered it looks, feels, smells and sounds exactly like the real thing. After the speed and the activity and the pace, why aren't we rallying to the battle-cry of a lashing rain or blustery gales?

It is a curious love-hate relationship, one which suggests further investigation beyond these pages. Looking at the environment which I experienced –which I suppose, in all honesty, never tried to be anything except what it was—the inter-relation between people and industry we lived in the shadow of, the throb of heavy machinery, the revving of engines, the rattle of the block-and-tackle, above all, the presence of the stiff architecture and the landscape itself, at the time it all seemed less forbidding, even homely. Most definitely of all homely.

Of course, looking back on childhood as I have been can be fraught with danger, primarily because an adolescent's perceptions are almost wholly sentimental (with a boy, his dominating preoccupation is to lose his virginity as quickly as possible) and such reflections later in life invariably recall key emotional situations, for example, those connected with sex or fighting. But children are not cynical in the mature sense of the term, and the more perceptive ones can make mental notes about environments which might be less biased by adult prejudice. Consequently, when I was a kid I was always voyeuristically aware of this curious knitting together of environmental characteristics around Sunnybank Mills, and also down the valley in Milnsbridge. The place was as unpretentious and uncontrived in its daily atmosphere as dandelions and buttercups are spontaneously beautiful in a field. Leafy residential suburbs were always alien to me, and I can remember noting this whenever I ventured into one. They were too quiet, like a never-ending Sunday afternoon when there was a deathly stillness to everything that I absolutely abhorred. Most importantly, leafy residential suburbs had no inherent character, no sense of relating to anything, no quality of being a genuine off-shoot of some other function. In a leafy residential suburb in Huddersfield—the typical post-war or modern type—I was loosely aware that I could have been in a leafy residential suburb in Greater Manchester, or Peterborough, or on the South Bank. They were universally alike, which was why when I stood in such places I did not feel to be standing in Huddersfield. There were none of its established regional-built characteristics breathing out with a strong self-identity. But the old places had this. They looked bedded in. Everything looked to have been done with a good eye. They were solid. Real. Strong. Worth looking at. Worth keeping. They flowed into one another in such an unconsciously delicious manner they almost became a sort of visual poetry, punctuated between each dimensional stanza by beautifully carved blackened gate-posts. And this was, and still is, the key to their appeal. *Pace* the apostle of the traditional town and village landscape who is actually being captivated by the natural, uncontrived manner by which ordinary domestic buildings tended to be erected before the commercial age took hold. For it is the lack of deliberate pretentiousness, balanced by genuinely superior natural materials, that is really latching onto the reasons why we consider pre-twentieth-century domestic architecture to be 'quaint', accentuated by the climatic weathering process, which with natural materials tends to be the exact reverse of man-made ones, with the curious exception of certain types of brick. A fishing village, like a cluster of pre-Industrial Revolution Yorkshire cottages, grew in a naturally organic manner, unconcerned with socially prestigious effect or big profits, whereas most modern housing is expressly laid out with a social purpose in mind, rather like ornaments deliberately arranged on a mantlepiece.

But the old places like where we lived were, you felt, regarded in a bad light, due primarily to social stigma. They were the butt of music hall jokes, unless they had been erected by the old municipality, in which case they were acceptable. As a result of this, you only ever really allowed yourself to be secretly aware of these sentimental observations. Even then, they were vaguely clouded. One half of you warmed to the area like a dog does to its master, but the other half was responding to social conditioning. By which I mean there was not necessarily any need to evaluate environmental standards because socially your perceptions had been manufactured for you by the effects of indoctrinating advertising, the constant atmosphere of the music hall joke hanging over your head, but more especially by television, which holds the unique capacity of being able to make something aesthetically ridiculous appear socially desirable. As an easily impressionable youngster, you still aspired to live in a brand new house as a matter of course, but you were not questioning the physical quality of what you desired, merely adhering to its principle within the social hierarchy, which had taken complete control of your acquisitive stupefaction. Therefore, although I enjoyed living in the small house next to the mills, cherished it passionately, even I remember being slightly embarrassed the first time I brought a girl home for tea; the way we steered her clear of the tiny kitchen because it was a tip with its rusty sink, and exposed gas meter in the corner covered in a thick mass of sticky, greasy fluff, and the bare stone walls from when it used to be a cold store covered in a hundred years' of gloss paint and distemper, and the single exposed light-bulb hanging in the middle which lit it. But I remember feeling precisely the same form of domestic embarrassment when I visited her house, which was brand new, but cheap, with all the associated trimmings in all the correct upwardly mobile places. Most of all I was embarrassed by the garden gnomes and the cropped lawn, because every single garden on the estate had them competitively the same–like all the houses up our terrace looked exactly the same, except we had no gardens, because they opened onto the pavement. But the view when I got back home and looked out of my bedroom window, the environment around it, the house itself, were unmistakably made in Huddersfield, in the North, and it encouraged a fierce, though unconscious sense of belonging. It was a scenario shaped almost entirely by the Yorkshire textile industry, and it had been done with some guts, some drama, some interest, some underlying meaning to it all. Even into the 1980's, it was the overpowering smell of structure in this part of the town's air. The most mundane of Victorian lean-to's, the ridiculously simple observation of how a black dry-stone wall butted up to the end gable of a more substantial building or end of a row of terraced houses, the mottled texture of repainted cast-iron, the stout chapels, even the old dilapidated railway fences smelling of tar at the top of cuttings and embankments—they were this visual sense of poetry and they possessed a character and inter-weaving that was only of this part of the world. They created a focal point that at once set it apart, gave it its own abrupt individuality, albeit beautifully utilitarian, whatever the controversies attached to it and what and who built it. And why.

At the end of our terrace was the ubiquitous corner shop. It depended on the tea breaks and dinnertime sandwich queues from Sunnybank Mills for its survival. They sometimes stretched outside the door, into the street. The men wore dark-blue overalls and boots that looked to be caked with oil from an engineering shop, but which were actually impregnated with wool grease. Some had bits of wool or 'weft' in their hair, and the women wore nylon overalls with bright-pink or turquoise or light-blue floral patterning, and used nail-varnish to stop the ladders in their tights from running. Above all else, the corner shop sold the best beef-dripping teacakes I ever tasted at only 13p a throw, because the Scottish couple who ran it always gave you plenty of gravy bits from the bottom of the dish, if you asked politely.

The shop closed down only a year or so after the mills upon which its livelihood hinged had died. The Scottish couple had been sharp-witted. They had acknowledged the rumours

Ballroyd Lane, Longwood

of impending doom and sold up and got out and gone back to their homeland while the mills were still in business and they could sell the property. Like so many defunct corner shops these days, it has received planning permission to be converted into a living room for the adjoining terraced house by the final proprietors. There is still an orange, enamelled "BROOKE BOND TEA" sign attached to the wall outside the door. It must be donkey's years old. Of all the things around here, the landmarks, the gateposts, everything you see so often you become literally oblivious to them after a while, that orange tea sign is one thing I looked at every single time I walked past it to and from the bus stop. Ever since 1974. I intend to get that sign. No way will I not get that sign. The shop had served its purpose when it bustled all day long, when the constant flurry of activity—the pace of the neighbourhood—was still there and made you feel like you were growing up in a place that was really alive,

TIME WARP: A BOLTON BACK ALLEY

rippling with a pulse of industrial energy that coursed like an electric current throughout it. Now, like the open space behind it where the mills rose, the shop is dead.

During November there is a peculiar smell in the air which I am only ever truly aware of during that month. It is a vaguely acrid, underlying smoky smell which falls halfway between burning cinders and the exquisite, musty smell of old books. I can remember a similar smell used to hang around railway bridges, after the passage of a steam train, when I was a child. But the bridge smell was warmer; the November smell is cold and damp as mist. I suspect the November smell is a result of leaves being burned after Autumn, mingling with the after-effects of fireworks or the smouldering embers of Bonfire Night which, despite it happening but one night a year, permeates the atmosphere the few weeks both before and after.

I used to relish the approach of this time of the year, because it seemed to harmonize best with the background rhythm and spirit of the environment. The November smell was, and still is, one of the special pleasures of the Northern landscape. Indeed, in winter, the West Yorkshire landscape possesses a quality that is difficult to find elsewhere. Most landscapes take on a similar quality in summer because of the bleaching-out effects of the high sun. But over the hills of the old millscapes in winter there is a faintly mysterious light that has an atmosphere all of its own, particularly on clear, biting days, caused by the sun being much lower in the sky. Vast chasms of jet-black shadow fill up the hollows and valley bottoms with a tremendous contrast, and in the late afternoons, the sun richochets off the tops of crags and hillocks like claw-marks raked in raw gold. Ice bitten cloughs complement the eerie light, remaining unlit throughout the daylight hours because of the swelling blocks of land; and the subtlety of frost fusing together footpaths and leaves, shading hillsides and railway sleepers. And on Monday mornings, the steam rising up from the valley in great billowing clouds, creeping up from those black chasms cramming the cuts between the lumps of population, as the remaining mills fire up again after the weekend shutdown.

As I have implied, to the youngster which has not been cynicised by the social and economic realities of adulthood, such pleasures appear in their virgin state, and it is these minor instalments of one's early life that really shade in perceptions and nostalgias much later. They are a necessary part of growing up, and of being grown up. I was aware of the inherent qualities of the Colne Valley's industrial-rural landscapes, but only whilst they were still in their, to me, ethereal colours. Especially in winter, to the extent that I actually used to pine for the November smell; for the clocks to be moved back an hour in October, because this early darkness at teatime seemed best to emphasize the living and working relationship between people, homes, and buildings, due to the plethora of lights. Part of the thrill of returning home from school on such winters' evenings was to revel in the very acute sensation that, as the bus passed along Manchester Road towards the harbour of mills lit up in the basin of Milnsbridge in the foreground, you were entering an environment which was indisputably *alive* in that bread-still-baked-in-the-town way, unique to an industrial area. Integral to the blending together of these things were healthy textiles, cold weather, and the November smell. The mills were the *raison d'etre.* They were the reason for the place having evolved in its *modus operandi,* something which did not change in the Colne Valley until only very recently. Cold weather made you appreciate the comfort of your own home so much better, or the exhilarating warmth of a large mug of coffee in a cafe after a walk, the condensation on the windows being an added ecstasy. In fact, the colder weather was the precise catalyst to homely cosiness. The gust of icy air blowing at you down a street on a December evening was important, not only because it emphasized the faculties. The secret to it—and this is common experience to all people who allow themselves to admit to their emotions—was the knowledge of the hot drink or piping hot meal waiting in the oven at home, and the doze in front of the fire afterwards—that sentimental base to which most of us subconsciously aspire. The shape of homelife—especially in the close intimacy forced by the smaller rooms of a working class home—always seems to fall into a more natural shape around the climate of winter, mainly because colder weather encourages the appreciation of other people's warmth. Look at Christmas. The real appeal of Christmas is not only that we exchange gifts and become gripped by a Georgian picture-card idealism for a couple of weeks (although, in fairness now, Christmas strikes you as being really embroiled in a furore of alcohol), but the association with snow. Even in countries which never see a flake of frozen rain at any time of the year, the greetings cards on sale in the shops invariably depict sentimental weather because of the way it encourages human beings to come mutually closer together around a warm fire of 'glad tidings and joy'. A tea-and-biscuit routine to life on a cold day is conducive to an intimacy almost impossible in humid weather. Festering outside a pub on a stinking hot summer's afternoon encourages a sort of blurred stupor surrounded by a cloud of stewing body odours, which has the effect of subconsciously forcing people mentally further apart. Winter is sexual because it suggests fewer nasty smells.

It is true that from a comparatively early age I have always disliked very hot weather. I do not suffer from hay-fever, but even when the pollen count is only fairly low, and particularly when the sun is extremely hot, I experience a 'full' feeling in the head and behind the eyes. So naturally, as a youngster, I hated and detested summer. I associated it with sweat, being too hot in bed, stickiness, eyes perpetually half closed, suspicious creeping smells, stagnant lethargy, and this annoying 'fullness' in the head, if I was outside for any length of time, if the temperature really soared. The sun is a marvellous antidote to life, but only when it is below a certain degree. A really hot summer seemed to deliver with it a string of infuriating discomforts, conspiring to prevent you from working or reading productively. Steamy hot days blurred the brain into inactivity and blunted the senses. They lacked the crisp sharpness of winter, which enthused you to something constructive, enlightened the senses, and showed colours in their true richness. I was accused of being morbid because I would leap about with joy if I got up in the morning in summer to find it throwing it down with rain. Rain was another exquisite pleasure of living in an industrial landscape, and still is. Wet rooftops. Glistening pavements. Chinese cloud effects colouring flagstones. Fresh smells in the air. Mood. And after a summer downpour, the sweetish taste lifting from the hedge-parsley tucked away down the unpaved backlanes. I was continually irritated by the generally accepted notion that a blazing hot summer was preferable to the living atmospherics of winter, and always felt that it was an obsession really mixed up with laziness and alcohol. During the winter months, Great Britain really exists in perpetual anticipation of a red-hot summer, like a huge family living in a street where it does not feel collectively quite at home, but with the reluctant knowledge that it knows it can never successfully remove elsewhere. Spring or autumn are probably the best times of the year in this country. Like most philosophies upon life ought to be, they come in moderation, comprised of the best elements from both climatic arguments. The first glimpses of spring, with the bluebells and dandelions choking the grassy embankments along the Huddersfield canal in the Colne Valley, are an inspiration. You don't have to convince yourself you need to climb aboard an aircraft to feel any sense of well-being, then experience some absurd jet-lag. The rat-race is only a manufactured joke, out of sight over the hills in the more densely populated parts of the country. And the quality of a genuine English meadow in late May. With its subtle scribble of buttercups interrupted by the occasional browsing horse, or a few Fresians scattered amongst the cow-slips, threaded between by meandering dusty lanes, the hedge-parsley pressed beneath spontaneous drystone walls—sheer poetry, albeit well recited by now.

As I have said, at the time I was living next to Sunnybank Mills, I was too young to be able to question these things with any sense of real subjective awareness. I was always aware *of* them, but because there had been no accumulation of experience later in life creating the need to place them into any kind of perspective, like most people, I never really questioned why. I knew vaguely that it was all part of this feeling of being constantly embellished in your movements, your domestic perceptions, by a glowing sensation that everything formed part of a spontaneous whole. Everything linked, bounced off each other, knitted back together, coerced one another into a multifarious but nevertheless singularly formed complete entity. It was the spirit of the place, and again it was this point about 'domestic perceptions'—like the tea-and-biscuits thing—which contained the essence of it. For if I think back to this period, it is a warm and intensely human atmosphere which chiefly springs to mind, largely untainted by any dreary social pretentiousness (always bubbling of course), just a plain, ordinary, in-front-of-the-fire living, modest and not greedy-manipulated into dog-eared submission, interspersed with the clattering of plates being washed in relatives' kitchens on Boxing Day afternoons, as you pointlessly pushed naughty sweets into your face. It was a rewarding atmosphere to breathe, provided you were sufficiently immersed in the child's unbelievably fantastic vision of the world to appreciate it all for what it was.

The enigma of the industrial North for people in the South seems either a mystery or a joke. One feels instinctively that it is a spirit which this part of the country has been trying to live down for generations. But it was a spirit that did exist, and I think I just caught the very back end of it, just as it was being computerized. It is a spirit that catches in the throat of memory every time I experience vague snippets of it elsewhere today—the warm aroma of boiled vegetables drifting from open doorways, a sudden mechanical noise, kids playing in those Northern school yards, mills lit up through the night, or the bursts of catty laughter from textile women, with their clean, soapy-smelling sexyness and dumpy breasts. Such sentiments tug away at the furthest reaches of the consciousness as they would if they were quick cuts from some long ago guilty happenings. It is pointless to dismiss such feelings as unimportant; to try and somehow sneeringly intellectualize about ordinary sentimental impulses, desperately pretending to be some mathematically calculating automaton, when one is in fact merely a human being.

It is a curious but very awkward dilemma as to how one reconciles one's thoughts upon all

UNCLEARED FORMER SITE OF SUNNYBANK MILLS, LONGWOOD, EASTER 1988, five years after demolition of the textile complex. At the time of going to press in January 1989, clearance of the land has at long last been announced with the aid of a central government grant, and there is now speculation of a courtyard housing development.

In the middleground of the shot is the awkward junction where the corners of Church Street, Dale Street and Botham Hall Road merge, '. . . my favourite corner thereabouts because it used to represent the power and confidence of local industry merging at the focal point of my daily journey to and from the bus stop . . . In a frightfully short space of time, the whole area was torn to pieces in a vicious, unrelenting fury of demolition that exploded across the lower part of Longwood with as ferocious an impact on the skyline as the mills must have caused when they were first built . . .'

By the time this book appears in the shops, the area will probably have been landscaped.

these social ingredients now. As regards what I have been discussing over the previous few pages, the infernal problem is that one can only acutely perceive such things with the documentarist's detached sensitivity, in which case the essential substance is lost due to preconception. Sometimes, I've been walking through parts of, say, Blackburn or Bradford, on one of those gloomily grey, bitter cold winter's afternoons, and experienced jolts of them all again. It immediately forces an introspective, one of those peculiar frozen moments in time where, for an absurd few seconds, you feel like a visitor from another planet and the film camera of the mind spontaneously kicks itself into motion. It is like being pole-axed. There is one street in Bolton, just one street, which has the same atmosphere I have been suggesting earlier. It's all red because it was made from brick over there, whereas mine was a sort of blackish beige because it was made from weathered stone. But the sound, the feeling of muffled back alley isolation, is exactly the same. The alley in Bolton is cobbled, whereas mine was muddy and contained a lot of green at the base of the walls of blackish beige because it was overgrown; but the close proximity of houses to mill, and the parallel layout, is identical. And the sound. It is a pocket of the industrial North that is absolutely untouched, as it was when it was originally built, a perfect film set. The last time I stood in it, suddenly wallowing in my own morbid nostalgia, the heavens opened and absolutely saturated me to the skin. I just stood in it with my camera set up on its tripod and let the rain run off the end of my nose, onto my lips, faintly salty in its taste. I watched a pile of soft dog muck on the worn flag-stones next to the cobbles slowly pulverized into a hideous sickly brown porridge by the torrential downpour. The sound of the mill over the brick wall, and its presence, held that back alley as surely as if it had discharged it from its own bowels. I wouldn't be at all surprised if the mill, and the other I could see down at the end of the alley, had been producing computer systems components rather than cotton now. I was soaked to the skin, and was reliving those simple atmospherics all over again. But today, it is impossible to perceive it the same as back then; the way the scene unfolded outside the bedroom window and beyond during a blinkered youth. Reality is too realistic now, and it hangs like a dead weight around your brain when you are moved by such authentic 'locations'. The real world impresses itself nauseatingly upon the emotions, along with what the mills and such environments really represented. It provokes an infuriating mental tussle, blocking you in the mind and making you feel like a great big hypocrite, especially when you aim a camera on such scenes. It is not a question of absurdly idealizing the past, but try to deny any sense of attachment to these places and it smothers the impulses that help to maintain the very way in which you think. I was photographing a cobbled street by a back alley off the centre of Halifax, and two old blokes passed me, and one muttered under his breath ".. Allus photographing t'bloody poor areas ...". He wouldn't be marvelling at the relationship of cobbles, sashed window, gable end. It made me question the reasons I was standing there very hard, pathetically enthusing over filters and shadow and sunlight, and it made me feel sick for a moment. It didn't alter the fact that the old guy felt I was an intruder, whether I could acutely identify with the environment or not.

The hold of the local mills over the environment, over our row of houses, was absolute. Although you accepted them without really stopping to sit down and fully realize it, you noticed every single sound or smell they gave off, particularly if something changed. When they closed for two weeks during the Huddersfield textile holiday in July, the place seemed empty, a bit lost. It was suddenly too quiet and sombre. The mills represented power back then. The people inside them were actually *making* things, not shuffling bits of paper about. Their places of work had majesty, you walked past them in the same frame of mind, and felt as diminutive as if you were walking past an ocean liner moored at a timber jetty. This sense of permanence the buildings could evoke to the place was amplified by their sheer size. They oozed an immovable solidity. They couldn't be dented. I'm sure nobody who grew up living next to a big group of textile mills, however disinterested in it they might have been, could fail to be aware of its presence. They may have hated what they perceived to be its ugliness, or they may have loved its rhythm of light and sound, but they could not fail to be aware of *it*. Having said that, I was taking a photograph of Fox Mill in Oldham last year, and some children rushed up to me in a bundle and asked me why I was taking a picture of the rubbish on the overgrown wasteland in front of it. It never occurred to them that I was photographing the building that so utterly dominated everything else around, and they'd come out of the narrow alley behind the adjacent terraced houses, so I assume they lived there. When I said I was taking a picture of the mill they all reacted with genuine surprise. They stood back and gawped at it for a few moments, as if it really was the first time they had ever set eyes on it. Their conclusion was unanimous: what on earth was I photographing that bloody thing for?

Perhaps, looking back to when I was young, I can sympathise to an extent with those kids in Oldham. Even though there was an energy surrounding the mills by our house, you were carried along with it to the extent that, after a while, you became conditioned, even oblivious to it. As with any major change to your everyday environment, you only really become acutely aware of it after it has happened.

The demolition company that came in and shattered the tail end of this reverie went bankrupt before they finished the job. As a result, if I look out of my back bedroom window today, I am confronted by a vast expanse of uncleared, derelict wasteland.

Immediately below the old outside toilets and bent cast-iron railings at the bottom of the old cindered yard, piles of twisted metal, shattered bricks, rotten beams, shards of smashed concrete tangled amidst their infra-structure of steel rods like bags of prefabricated knitting, a smattering of rubbish dumped deliberately by human hand, are gradually becoming interwoven with patches of green and, in summer, the inevitable pink of willowherb, swaying in groups in the breezes like sea-weed moving in slow motion under water. A yellow sign, erected by the council, used to proclaim that the penalty for dumping rubbish would be £200, but this disappeared a long time ago. One Sunday a couple of years back, I was peering out of the bedroom window and saw a rather decrepit transit van pull onto the wasteland. To my astonishment, a group of rough-looking men climbed out and began to unload what appeared to be an old asbestos garage with great haste, hurling it into the rest of the mill wreckage. They were dumping it illegally, under a hail of abuse from the lady next door to my house, who was hanging her washing out in the back yard at the time. The men quickly leapt into their vehicle and sped off the rough ground, the van buffeted about on its suspension as it careered across the bumpy furrows like something out of a chase sequence in a BBC drama serial, in that staged, too-far-from-the-camera way then tend to shoot such things. A cloud of dust lingered for a few minutes after the van had gone. If you

Residential Housing, Manningham, Bradford

look hard, amongst the decaying industrial effluent, you can still pick out pieces of the garage and other piles of rubble that are of domestic rather than industrial heritage. One evening during winter, I was walking back down the cobbled lane from the off-license up Leymoor Road and saw an old car in the process of being dumped upside down on its roof. The next morning it had gone.

Through the middle of all this dereliction and festering decay runs Grove Street. It used to have the mills' post-war extension built on the far side, and the main six-storied weaving block, sorting sheds and some offices on the nearside, in front of my bedroom window. Because these structures have gone, Grove Street doesn't look like a street at this point along its length anymore. I always associate streets as being lined with buildings, so now it seems more like a road. It is encroached upon from both sides by the rubble. Although in theory a road then, the pot-holes and lumps of tarmac that have been dolloped into position without being steam-rollered flat by various road works units over the years brings such cynically inspired phraseology as 'dirt track' to mind.

Over at the opposite side of Grove Street, more scruffy piles of rubble climb the foot of the hillside in great flat, jagged shards and lumps, leading up to the old boarded-up school a few hundred yards above, and the church hidden in the trees over to the right. This place is crying out to be used as a location in a film set after World War Three. A few piles of burned out cars from a scrapyard dumped in the middle, some tyres burning out of sight behind some chunks of concrete to create the black smoke of the drifting, silent aftermath, some unearthly synthesized sound effects and a filter over the camera lens, and there you go. Perfect. Further over to the left, directly above the bombsite, there used to be an enormous tangle of undergrowth and blackberry bushes and nettles, spreading across the hillside below an old petrol station that still retained its original metal pumps. In 1985, this undergrowth was landscaped. Bulldozers were brought in, and everyone down the terrace thought the site of Sunnybank Mills was going to be cleared at last. But no. Only the undergrowth above it; harmless, natural, built up slowly over decades with the genuine bedded-in quality that only nature and the passage of time can accomplish. It was landscaped then seeded to leave it with the awkward, contrived look that 'landscaped' areas always have. There was nothing wrong with the undergrowth which was there, nothing at all. It was what was below it, immediately below it, actually butting up to it, that needed landscaping, but it seems there was some controversy over exactly who owned the former site of the mills. Despite this, money was spent. And although it is going on five years since Sunnybank Mills were demolished, and three years since this landscaping above the remains, the land still hasn't been cleared. Rather infuriatingly, houses are being built in the adjoining area described as a 'quiet residential area' not a minute or two's walk away, in green fields. But nobody has been enforcing the reclamation of this wasteland. It ought to be imperative that developers are forced to utilize available derelict space economically first, to tidy up the big holes in the village first, to create a uniformity with what already exists, to consider the requirements of people already living here first, before digging up green fields. There is actually a piece of land about three hundred yards from the site of the mills—it was the car park for the mills when they were standing—that is up for sale as "RESIDENTIAL BUILDING LAND". The most noticeable thing that strikes you about this quandary is that these pockets of land invariably become available where there are incumbent views. Some of the people in the streets nearby would stress that their views are generally regarded as being unimportant, even though the *Huddersfield Daily Examiner* has reported the repeated complaints of the local residents around the old site of Sunnybank Mills over the past few years. They would stress that theirs are just grubby little terraced houses which can make do with a view of blatant refuse and the tryouts for a post-war nuclear holocaust race. It is the continuing story of the saga that has transpired since 1974 outside my back bedroom window.

So I've covered every inch of this mess with my camera, for posterity, for this book, as a salute to the other ten thousand places between here and Newcastle or wherever else such shoulders of big manufacturing industry have been trodden into the landscape—before they are eventually grassed over and this aspect of their demise is completely forgotten about, only lamented over in the new museums. The despicable thing is, my creative impulses are aroused when I wander about it, humping my camera on the end of its tripod on my shoulders (it's a big 6x7). It's the drama. The contrast. As I said earlier, it's what makes us tick. You can make a form of art out of the mills even after they are dead. I contort into stupid positions, altering the length of the tripod's legs, changing filters and lenses, splayed between lumps of concrete skewed in the rubble, looking back over my shoulder all the time at our old house, a poignant reminder of the perspective it has all now been placed in, past, present, and future.

And the church tower above.

When the bells have rung if I've been contorting on Sunday mornings—remember, this rubble was once full of people whose products gave the owners the money to build that tower as a memorial to one of the two men who started the firm a hundred and thirty years ago—you can feel the irony hanging in the air. You can cut it. The atmosphere is so thick it is turgid.

And the smell of damp, dead, musty buildings' entrails, slowly decomposing under the ever changing sky. This is the only memorial that has been left to the generations of people who worked the mills.

To the left of my bedroom window, about five hundred yards away, the original Sunnybank Mill, built by Crosland and James Hirst as a finishing business before the firm grew, also stands decaying. Along with a three-storied mill building and some offices at the other end of the site, near the old coal depot, it is the only mill building as such to have survived the demolition. It is a four-storied construction that looks older than most of the other mills did around here. It has a small cupola clocktower on the roof, but the faces have gone, leaving only a hole right the way through. It is asking to be turned into some kind of wool textile museum, which the Colne Valley desperately needs—and the building is only four of five minutes' drive from the motorway. It is also the type of building you could see being converted into a cottage-style restaurant, with mock Georgian windows, and the menu fastened to an internally lit glass box on the wall outside the door. Grove Street runs underneath the mill at one end, where the building forms an arch over the road, its main architectural feature[1]. You can imagine how diners seated at their tables would find such a position most appetizing. Perhaps the two ought to be combined. At the present time, it is a

[1]since the time of writing, a council lorry clipped the arch and this end of the mill collapsed.

vandalized shell with blue plastic sheeting along the entire length of its roof because the demolition men took all the slates with them. I've lived here for years and years, but I can't remember whether they were stone, or grey Welsh. The building has not been demolished because it is listed by the Department of the Environment as being of historical and architectural importance. I suppose I can see some of the reasoning for this, but it seems absurd that a final, incongruous vestige should remain, when the rest of the complex—the real substance of it—has been destroyed, much of which needed less work than this one to make it rehabitable. It seems to have been typical of the piecemeal listing of buildings in isolation, rather than entire groups, chimneys, outbuildings and all, before the major rethink in this town several years back. The after effects in a lot of places, a majority of the industrial towns, is to leave a botchy, patchwork quality with crude contrasts which seems to be the accepted norm in our present day urban landscapes.

The building is somewhat controversial, like the rest of the mess, having been part of schemes to convert it into luxury flats, new factory space, and now even an indoor swimming pool and leisure centre. It broods at one end of the bombsite, its ground floor windows sealed up with breeze-block, until somebody decides what to do with it.

To the right of my window, the piles of rubble sprawl up towards St. Mark's church. The church bells continue to ring on Sunday mornings, irony day, and also on Thursday evenings for some reason. The tower watches over the former site of the mills long after the demolition men have gone. Below the tower, the main office and administration block of the mills still stand, a couple of hundred yards up Church Street. They are of a slightly more elaborate architectural style than the rest of the complex was, as you would expect of a building serving such a purpose and housing the various Hirst offspring over the years. They must have also been listed piecemeal, like the original Sunnybank Mill across at the other end of the bombsite. For a number of years after the demolition had finished, these offices stood empty, "TO LET" signs enquiring of you to telephone a number miles away, in Otley near Harrogate, if you were interested. Today they are occupied by an organization that helps rehabilitate young offenders. Although serving a constructive purpose rather than falling into decay, because of what they used to be built up against and actually connected to, they seem lost and utterly incongruous without the wholeness of the former, like a guard's van that's lost its train.

I've always found the ringing of church bells somewhat nauseous and sombre. Thus, when they ring in Longwood church on Sunday mornings now, for me they are the perfect sardonic catalyst to the general air of depression and aftermath of industrial disease suspended over this part of the neighbourhood. They emphasize the sense of despair the bombsite gives off. Doubtless, if and when the wasteland is eventually cleared or built upon, this feeling of despair, this air of being unprocessed fodder ripe for moody shots in the TV documentaries about the decline of the North's traditional manufacturing base, will dissipate. At present, in 1987, the former site of Sunnybank Mills lays rotting, literally. It stands or rambles obtrusively, whichever, silent mouldering testimony to a loophole in the law that does not enforce demolition companies to finish the job if they go bankrupt in the meantime, because Sod's Law prevails, as always. And Sod's Law has been pursuing me now for about twenty five years, and I have not the slightest doubt that, by the time this book finally gets into print, the mess will have been cleared, or else one of the schemes for the land which are reported from time to time in the newspaper will materialize. This is unimportant. What matters is that at this moment in time, in 1987, this is the story so far; a five year yarn which is the rotting postscript to one of Huddersfield's most well known textile concerns, and it needs cataloguing for posterity.

A year or so back, another demolition company came and tickled the site. Over a number of weeks, they seemed to be pushing rubble from one end to the other, behaving with the characteristics of weird gold diggers, desperate, burlesqued, scrounging the remaining steel girders encased in the remnants of shattered prefabricated concrete that formed the foundations of the mills' post-war extension. The bulldozers went away almost as quickly as they had come. The row of terraced houses overlooking them were disappointed for a third time. The bombsite will probably rear its controversial head in the local press again, as it does from time to time, when some councillor has his photograph taken standing with a handful of the local populace and pledging, with a serious face curiously and absurdly at odds with the genuinely strained expressions on the fan of faces around him, to do something about it because the faces have seen rats running about again.

Over to the left of my window once more, above the original Sunnybank Mill, the chimney of Prospect Mills stands proudly, a final remaining icon, occasionally belching steam, reminding you with so much more irony above the scar that was Sunnybank Mills below, that this was, and still is, a textile region of the old industrial North. It reminds you rather more positively than the tapestry of ruptured textile industry displayed at its foot.

Times must change, as they say. Time marches on. And we are told we must and should look towards the future without dwelling too deeply on the great industrial past. Nevertheless, it is important to question the reasons for the peaks and troughs in these vast economical upheavals, whenever they occur, to remember the fiscal shifts they represent. This being so, perhaps the Sunnybank Mills bombsite shouldn't be cleared at all, but left as it is and turned into a bizarre open air museum, so that in years to come, parties of school children can be brought round during their history lessons and shown what the industrial devastation that reaped its deadly harvest across the face of many communities in the North all those years ago was all about.

Blow-torched Girder which once held up Sunnybank Mills, with St. Marks Churchtower watching in the background

Cliffe End Dye Works from Quarmby Clough, looking across Milnsbridge
and up the magnificent Colne Valley

PART TWO

4

Through the mill windows the sun was the colour of Braine's Demerara rum. It was a weakening but still bright autumn gold, hazy with a subtle enveloping mist, diffused even further by the frosted glass all around me. There was that sharpening chill to the air, not so much a chill as a cool undercurrent, which only happens at this time, when the leaves are preparing to vacate their branches and I realize that my favourite time of year, winter, is poised just around the corner of November, waiting ready to leap.

Below me was the ever-present hum of the hustle and bustle of Market Street and Savile Street. The panes in front of me vibrated lightly, a near imperceptible rattle, as a bus turned out onto the main road. The rush hour was beginning and I could hear the clatter of hollow aluminium scaffolding being dropped to the pavement by the man from the gas board, who had been doing something or other at the wall of the mill for most of the day.

I was sitting down to type these words at a dusty workbench on the second floor of a massive six-storied textile mill that was completely empty, except for the small businesses that had moved in on the two floors below me. There was a fresh apple-core next to my typewriter, beginning to tan. I played with it between my fingers as I swayed back and forth to observe the way the orange orb of the sun undulated through the ripples in the glass. I dug my thumbnail into the core, and where it collected, I flicked the residue across the room and saw it stick to a window before sliding down into some off-cuts of wood.

I say I was seated on the second floor of the mill, but to me it was the third floor. Commonsense suggests that if a floor is a solid base upon which you are standing in a building, then the first row of windows in the mill should be the first floor, but it isn't, it is called the ground floor. The first floor is the second row of windows on top of the first, like the upstairs in a house. My studio, which was behind the third row of windows, was on what is called the second floor, even though, as I have said, to me it should have been the third, if you see what I mean. People who have been to see me have often walked into the premises of the textile company underneath—the faint vibration of whose machinery I could feel on the soles of my feet as I sat there typing then—their commonsense telling them, too, where the second floor ought to have been. Regardless of this apparent anomaly in architectural vocabulary, what I did know was that I was high up, and when I eventually got round to having all the frosted glass windows replaced with clear glass, a panoramic view would be revealed of slated rooftops, numerous chimney stacks, saw-toothed workshops and weaving sheds, the few remaining mills, their even fewer remaining chimneys, and the exquisite, bumpy uneveness, the natural spontaneity, of cobbled yards, back alleys, hen-runs, dilapidated sheds, outside toilets, sheets of rusty corrugated iron made into fences, steep snickets, ginnels, and the entire confused higgledy-piggledy of a packed little industrial landscape that was, even then, several years after the gutting of much of its original sprawling industrial belly, inescapably a glimpse of the power of textiles in Victorian Yorkshire and the way in which it raped the people and the earth to feed its insatiable lust for wealth.

I was down the road from the site of Sunnybank Mills in Milnsbridge, a crammed industrial suburb approximately two miles from the centre of Huddersfield. It spreads out in the basin that is the commencement of the magnificent Colne Valley proper, its little terraced houses trailing down into the town at the Morley Lane end, off Manchester Road, in horizontal rows, blending with the compact shopping area down Market Street in the bottom, at either side of the River Colne. It is ringed nearly all the way around by the steeply rising Pennine uplands and challenges anyone with an interest in such old established places who sets eyes on it to immediately set about exploring it. From where I was sat, I could see Manchester Road at the other side of the town, running like a shelf below Crosland Moor along the edge of the bottom of the hill; its moving four wheeled dots flashing in the gaps between the buildings. If you follow Manchester Road for about twenty three miles, it eventually takes you to the city, by way of plunging through the former cotton spinning capital of Oldham en-route. Unlike some such roads which start on the outskirts of a town, professing to be called the name of a place a considerable number of miles away, but which peter out or blend with a road coming at you from the opposite direction that sometimes, incredibly, is named after the town you left behind in the first place, this Manchester Road will take you all the way from Huddersfield to Manchester. You cannot, if you follow the sign posts correctly at the brief intersection of motorway and flyover along the bottom side of Oldham, possibly get lost. It provides a colourful journey, and I use this road, the A62, every time I drive to Manchester. If you are not already familiar with the look of the old Lancashire and Yorkshire millscapes as they are today, and wish to be enlightened, to see their confused hotch-potch of old and new in the gratuitously rambling inner cities; the rural windswept moorlands dotted with tiny clustering villages, pubs, farms, cottages, electric pylons; the deep set milltowns linking the focal points of the complete picture, drive from Huddersfield to Manchester on Manchester Road (or better still, walk it) and you will see it all. Along this route, you will see essentially the spirit that the photographs accompanying the text in this book have tried to convey, one way or the other. You will see the place as it looks in the 1980's, coming to terms with the prefabricated, computer, and remodelled road junction age, not always as it looks on the neatly framed street scenes of a nostalgic yesteryear in the prim and proper museums. You see it, with all its stark contrasts and misdemeanours, the Lancashire and Yorkshire millscapes that are, in places, so near perfectly intact it is as though you have stepped through a time portal, or the place has been plucked out of a past century and dropped in front of your eyes to tantalize your sense of wonder with How We Used To Live. A few minutes later, you can be standing in a grey concrete wasteland of near derelict high-rise barracks, another futuristic set piece from a science-fiction film, thrown up into the Northern landscape from a post-apocalyptic vision of some far distant state controlled hell where people are stored to service The Big Machine. More often than not, you find yourself standing in a garish, uneasy truce between the two. *Old and New.* Each overlapping into the other's territory from the perplexed irresolution of the which-direction-to-turn-next dilemma of today. *Old and New.* A few short phlegmatic coughs of genuinely thoughtful attempts at combining the practicalities of one with the existing aesthetic balance and confluence of the other. *Old and New.* The latest state-of-the-art slick advertising graphics pasted on billboards bolted to the end gables of old terraced housing or the sides of crumbling mills. *Old and New.* More ghettoes of terraced housing, Victorian and Edwardian vehicles with new engines fitted and a quick respray with doors and windows manufactured on computerized lathes and routing machines. *Old and New.* Ring roads and bypasses filled with the aerodynamic shapes of today, swinging over the odd remnant of a cobbled street next to a mill by some rough ground with an old bent cast-iron street lamp base straight out of Lowry.

And above, virtually wherever you turn, the unchanging Pennine moors.

The A62 is a good way to see it, playing in either forward or reverse. You will have the road more or less to yourself as well, because everyone else piles predictably onto the motorway. If you go that way, all you see is a glut of speeding vehicles pumped up high on their intoxicating elixirs of hurry and aggression, endless tarmaccadem, and a lot of inhospitable moorland.

Milnsbridge is only a few minutes' drive from the M62 motorway and this omnipresent moorland. Its main claim to fame is that of being the birth place of former Prime Minister Harold Wilson, born at No 4 Warneford Road, Cowlersley, on the 16th of March 1916. The other, of course, is its long association with textiles, the trade that is almost singlehandedly responsible for the predominantly 19th century battered looking town that remains today and which, upon its abrupt decline, was almost singlehandedly responsible for its destruction as a major manufacturing centre as well. The town is said to take its name from a 13th century water-powered mill and the bridge that stood alongside it. The mill I was sitting in as I drafted this, towers over Savile Street, and it was the Saviles of Botham Hall, just up the road, who are thought to have established the 13th century mill, for the grinding of corn, on a site that is today occupied by the new supermarket. The former site of Sunnybank Mills rots a few minutes' walk out of Milnsbridge, through the viaduct, at Longwood behind where I was sat.

Longwood is like Harold Wilson's Cowlersley, in that it is difficult to determine exactly where it starts and where Milnsbridge stops. As a result there is a thick band that constitutes the dividing line between the two that can regard itself sometimes as one or the other. The two places don't really stop and start but blend into each other, as do most suburbs on the outskirts of larger towns. Our house, whilst nearer to Milnsbridge than Longwood centre itself, was at Longwood on the postal address. The railway station that used to be in Milnsbridge got it right by calling itself "LONGWOOD AND MILNSBRIDGE" because of the close proximity of the two, even though a place called Paddock looks noticeably nearer to Milnsbridge than Longwood at that point, and even though Longwood was written first on the station nameboards, despite being further away than Milnsbridge, where the facility was built.

The mill I was sitting in is called Commercial Mill. It was the first of the old C. & J. Hirst textile empire to cease making Huddersfield cloth during the summer of 1979. After it shut down, the machinery was stripped out and it was put up for sale. It was bought the following December by the current owner and landlord, to rehouse his growing air conditioning manufacturing company, which at the time was situated in the old Co-Op bakery up at Longwood, but which is now firmly established on the bottom floor of the mill. He refuses to

DERELICT FARM NEAR DENSHAW, ON THE MOORS ABOVE OLDHAM. A common sight until comparatively recently, most have now been converted into fashionable commuter dwellings within easy reach of the motorways.

tell me how much he paid for the building, but I assume it to have been a relative bargain for such a colossal amount of space, particularly when you consider that he only intended to use the bottom floor for his own purposes, but could afford to pay for a further five empty stories, and adjoining outbuildings, under this premise. In body, but certainly not in spirit, he looks to me like he was always destined to own a mill; the typical mill or factory owner, transported through time from the pages of a Dickens novel into a modern businessman's suit. He is what my mind imagines a Mr. Pickwick might look like in one of those BBC videotaped serials with the creaky sets and the sound of pencils dropping off camera that they show at teatime on Sunday afternoons; but with less of the stomach padding and no knee length stockings and without the buckle-up shoes. There, any cliched resemblance to the mill or factory owner prowling his factory terrifying barefooted children, or a whimsical eccentric stalking the English countryside abruptly ends, blurrs in the melting pot of modern appearances and terminology, then emerges as today's small factory owner of comfortable means, the combination-locked attache case, telex and fax machines, and the fast drive to meetings along the M1 or M62 in a plush Ford Granada—but still as a member of the old fashioned Freemasonry nevertheless. True, he owns a mill, as hackneyed or as symbolic as that might once have been in these parts; and I'm sure this must continue to give anyone with any real perceptiveness or sense for the dramatically ostentatious a good kick up the ego as they descend with the traffic flow into the valley each morning from their nocturnal residential roosting place, and see their stone built fortress looming into view, the focal point, utterly dwarfing everything else around with a kind of segacious scowl, if buildings are capable of such a thing. But this landlord has not presided over this, or any other mill, whilst it produced the traditionally Northern yield it was erected to churn out. He is one of the new generation of mill owners, like the proprietors of the Dean Clough Industrial Park over in Halifax; the type of business entrepreneur who moves into a redundant textile mill because they have generally gone for a song and, if perseverance and a littie creative

A Street Corner in Oldham

initiative are employed, can provide vast amounts of lucrative space very cheaply, while maintaining some of the original architectural flavour of the area.

Since he took Commercial Mill, the adjoining outbuildings opening onto the mill yard—covered by a glass canopy similar to the more austere roofs erected over large Victorian railway goods sheds—have been sandblasted, and window boxes crammed with healthy geraniums and crawling ivys line the stone 'sills around the sides. Many people entering the yard for the first time comment on its pleasant atmosphere, the mellow playing of mottled sunlight refracted through the glass roof during clear weather. The outbuildings have seen a fairly regular turnover of tenants, one or two of whom have used the low-cost premises to start their companys before moving on to expand, and have included health food manufacturers, bakers, a leatherworker, duvet manufacturers, electronics people, and on the top floor of the proper mill building itself, a chap growing mushrooms, would you believe. Apparently, the skylights and humid atmosphere so high up were ideal growing conditions for vegetables, and his soil has been left behind, covering the entire surface of the top floor and helping to insulate the rest of the mill below. At present, the outbuildings are occupied by an engineer, a craftsman making the finest quality handmade furniture to both traditional and contemporary designs that I have ever seen, a carpet wholesaler, and a group of Indian clothing manufacturers who work all the hours under the sun. The original mill office at the front, the stone flagged passage through which the former employees manoeuvred, ready to clock on and make Huddersfield textiles, is today occupied by a building design consultant. Along with the above mentioned Indians, the only aspect of textiles that Commercial Mill is involved in today happens on the first floor, where a small husband-and-wife-run company employs about a dozen local women in the rolling of balls of wool—for the home knitting market.

The three floors above my studio are all empty. They still smell strongly of grease and the enclosing mustiness of textile manufacture nearly a decade after it ended. It never ceases to amaze me how you can walk onto empty floors in a mill such as this one, devoid of everything but the thick cast-iron pillars holding the rest of the building up above you, and continue to feel the presence of textile production—its ghostly after-taste—going on all around you. Even though you are standing in a silent tomb long since grave-robbed by the scrap metal merchants and machine breakers to leave an eerie void, the looms' hold on it lingers, presumably this is because the pungent aroma of grease-impregnated timbers and flag stones encourages your imagination to see and hear what is no longer actually there. Aside from this immediately noticeable effect upon your sense of smell, subtle, forlorn clues to the building's previous use remain, like the bits of old machine parts on the floor in the corners, a few old cardboard bobbins, clocks on the walls with the hands frozen at a time long since expired, or ancient nameplates from local machinery makers, like them, long since forgotten by the recent scavengers, gathering dust and becoming matted with spiders webs on the thin stone windowsills.

At one end of the floor where my unit was built, an accumulation of old office furniture with horse-hair seats, planks of wood, beams, crates full of what look to be oily cogs from engines, even a belt-driven pillar drill, gather dust and are becoming increasingly speckled with splodges of white deposited by the pigeons that perch on the metal light casings hanging from the ceilings above. Everything but everything is caked in a layer of what

Trooper Lane, Halifax

seems at first glance to be dried oil. It is not oil, but years of wool grease, dulled almost into a hardened resin. "NO SMOKING PAST THIS POINT" signs, written in both English and Urdu, confront you on the landings in the stairwells, at the entrance to each floor; a warning to the highly inflammable atmosphere the grease and cloth generated within.

Inside the doors, by the first window on each floor, old brown bakelite telephones, so thick with the after effects of grease you can scrape it off with your fingernails and roll it into tiny balls between your forefinger and thumb, are bolted to the walls. A sequence of half faded initials, written in fountain-pen ink alongside ivory pressbuttons under the ornamented receivers, give clues to the different parts of the mill the overlookers would once call up. Goodness knows how they heard themselves speak above the din of crashing looms. When I worked at the small mill at the end of our street it still operated using old machinery. Each time people used the internal telephones with the weaving shed clattering in full swing, they frowned feverishly, one hand pressed tightly over one ear, jerking their heads this way and that in a peculiarly painful looking silent pantomime, constantly mouthing "What?", "Eh?". Balls of black fluff, actually the scraps of raw wool that litter the floors of any textile mill like shavings in a joiner's shop, are scattered throughout the uninhabited parts of this enormous building. You find them mostly on the wooden floors of the upper three stories (the first three are stone flagged from wall to wall like vast indoor pavements) that creak and groan ominously as you walk across them, but which the landlord assures me are as safe as houses, or as safe as mills I suppose. These old wooden floors, absolutely saturated with grease that gives them the shiny colour of black treacle-toffee, are peppered with balls of this strange black fluff, although they are becoming fewer in number all the time, because the pigeons that have got into the mill use it to make nests in the rafters. The fluff wasn't originally black, but white; this is due to the fact that as it has been kicked and trodden about the mill over the years, it has become mixed with dust and grease. On blustery days, high up in the top stories of the mill, the wind howls feverishly against the windows, managing to find its way into the building through cracks and empty panes, or up the stairwell tower. Then these balls of black fluff roll about with a will of their own, as if in some ridiculous miniature parody of bushes blowing about the streets of a ghost town in an old Hollywood western; pitiful references to a bygone era in the history of Commercial Mill that only ended in 1979.

As you step gingerly about the empty part of the mill, the same respectful, slightly sinister manner about your actions as you would if stepping between headstones in a graveyard, you come upon the tortured carcasses of dead pigeons rotting in the stairwell; their breasts curiously imploded; their eye sockets empty and black; entombed within a vast monolithic structure into which they flew to roost and build nests from black fluff, but were unable to escape.

Like the ever present stench of dead textiles all around you.

In the view of Milnsbridge from above Manchester Road, Commercial Mill is the large square building directly in front of the viaduct. You can see it on the photograph opposite, along with Longwood climbing gently up the valley behind, towards Prospect Mills' proud chimney, standing out against the skyline like an exclamation mark at the end of what used to be an arrogant architectural sentence. Most of the harsh words that made up the sentence have been rubbed out, with an abrasive ink rubber at that, so the surface of the paper is grazed and damaged. Sunnybank Mills were originally visible behind the viaduct, below Prospect Mills' chimney. The church steeple you can see slightly to the right at that point is St. Mark's church again, the steeple which was built by the Hirsts when their mills thrived to the left of it. In the middleground of the shot, the mill with the black chimney is Holme Mills, the one that is on the front cover of this book, but taken from down there, in the street outside. You will notice the white patches along the walls where an adjoining part of the mill was demolished some years back, after the long established textile company that built and owns it vacated the building and moved into purpose built, modern single-storey premises across the road. This is another dilemma that ageing textile mills must face towards the end of the 20th century, even when the company that makes cloth inside them is still healthy and strong. The company in question here was faced with a crisis during the mid-1970's whereby it either had to modernize its production plant quite significantly in the face of increased foreign competition and rising energy costs, or else risk an impact against its standing in the international market. The company management quickly established that to adapt the existing five-storied mill and attached outbuildings and sheds—built during the Victorian age—to modern factory standards, would be impractical and costly; the most obvious problem being that posed by the weight and stresses and vibrations

. . . OR PROSPECT FOR A BRIGHTER FUTURE . . .?

from today's high-speed machinery. Thinking towards the long term, they decided it was cheaper, and more practical, to abandon the old buildings and take the opportunity to re-evaluate proposals first mooted some years previously, by designing a completely new production plant on adjacent land which they owned, custom designing it around an in-at-the-one-end and out-of-the-other type of one level set up.

Many of the other photographs in this book were taken somewhere within the field of view encompassed by the one just mentioned. Commercial Mill might look diminutive and far off from this distance, but some indication of its domineering size can be gleaned if you scale it to the roof tops of Market Street and the streets immediately in front of it. Close up, the building is a six-storied man-mountain of stone. It stands on the corner of Savile Street. If you are waiting at the bus stop outside, if you crane your head and look straight up, you can sense something of the remorseless power that shaped what you can see remaining all around—there was a great deal more to it once—especially if it is foggy or pouring with rain. On the postal address the mill is said to be on Savile Street, but the longest wall that is in shadow faces onto Market Street. Savile Street is named after the Saviles of Botham Hall again, the builders of the 13th century corn mill that would have stood to the left of Commercial Mill. They also owned much of the land that this part of the town was built on.

Amazingly, Commercial Mill is not listed as being of either historical or architectural importance. I say amazingly, because it seems rather incredible, when you look at the flow of the landscape into which it falls, and the unique relationship around here that it holds of rubbing shoulders closely in that big-square-blotch-of-building-bisected-by-horizontal-line-of-aggressive-viaduct way, that it is not deemed as important to preserving the structure of Milnsbridge, especially when so much else in this area *is*. What is left in this one photograph, wretched and dejected and which, admittedly, only has real pictorial significance when viewed from this angle—but which is the angle most people approach the town from and which a cleverer Huddersfield would have cleaned up and promoted long since—is such that, if one more mill were to be removed or even only truncated, the town's last scrap of visual identity would be lost forever. But that Northern milltown stigmata blemishes any form of realistic perceptiveness of the value of such a grouping of buildings, of such a small town, its importance to the foundations that made Huddersfield as a whole.

Whether industrial landscapes are your idea of impressive spectacles that please the eye depends largely upon the individual. A panorama such as the one I am discussing here may therefore either excite or depress, but its capacity to incite such responses depends, fundamentally, upon what aspect of awareness you are at; upon taste; but most of all I think, if you hold affection for a place and harbour an all important sense of history which enables you to penetrate through the grime and neglect and decay, and perceive the potential it contains, whilst noting your own participation in it's ongoing story. It is these last few points that shape my every thought and sensation every single time I stand in the Colne Valley. Every remaining cobblestone, every stone step, every street corner always in the shadow of the hills on the misty mornings, every chunk of the incredible viaducts which straddle Milnsbridge and Slaithwaite, register, bombard the senses. But it is an appreciation that is only one that comes from an acute identification, familiarity, emotion, linked by memory, although I do often wonder if it is an over sensitivity to the environment to be so aware of it. Whatever it is, over the past few years, whenever I've cut through a side street or a ginnel and come upon one of the old mills being demolished or truncated, I have experienced precisely the same feeling of huge, empty, unnecessary loss as I do when watching a whale being skinned and gutted on an arctic harbour front on a documentary on TV.

To the best of my knowledge, Commercial Mill is the only remaining big mill building in Milnsbridge that is not listed as being of architectural or historical importance (and yet it happens to be the best, and the most impressively sited), and therefore cannot be demolished. So, considering those which are listed, this must be conservation within the town. But is it? Conservation orders such as these prevent buildings from being mindlessly and insensitively pulled down, and anything that does this, that parries against the predictable whines about how these acts stunt economic growth, has to be worthwhile, if only because it gains some time. If the shaping of towns went completely unchecked, scepticism tells you the all-consuming machine of redevelopment would devour everything conceivably demolishable, and what would be regurgitated into the English landscape would probably resemble an immense urban wilderness comprised of corrugated tin and plastic houses trying to look like Tudor England in the 21st century, but with the mock-Spanish verandas and the computerized bedspreads, all done in the worst possible taste utilizing the lastest quick-cheap methods of the day that technological progress and economic growth have provided at such competitive, knock-down prices. This is nonsense, exaggeration, but is of course the direction in which we are slowly, inexorably heading, and which must be the reason the entire frightened conservation movement came about.

But conservation orders that merely prevent buildings from being demolished full stop; that offer no viable solution and that are not part of an overall national strategy—in other words, and ever the classic punchline: those which have no realistic financial backing—are not the answer. In places such as Milnsbridge there ought to be a uniting of needs combining national prestige in historical assets with the requirements of commerce that comes midway between the two parties—the conservationists and the people who want to remove a building—but ultimately, as always, and another classic punchline, the chief responsibility, the guidance, has to come from government, and so long as there is a lack of genuine sensitivity there, in other words a lack of vision, a lack of direction, preserved buildings that nobody is prepared to invest either thought or capital into will slowly decompose, caught on the spider's web between two tangled philosophies, until the only serious alternative which remains is demolition.

Perhaps it is an impossible solution that can never be truly achieved. Perhaps no compromise can ever be realized in anything, simply because if there are two pros and cons of powerful determination, the realistic solution—compromise–does not materialize due to it requiring the most determined, intelligent, objective approach to make it work. Economic growth must remain of prime importance, but the implication generally seems to be that it is impossible to control the economy, hold it in check whilst steering it forward in a considered but fundamentally intelligent manner, and that because of this cultural integrity must be sacrificed simply because it costs too much money. Such an equation exists only because of the inherent weaknesses due to lack of inspired guidance which lies at the root of this philosophy, so the argument shows signs of inevitably disappearing up its own backside in the end anyway. And it is generally accepted nowadays that the Victorians, the Edwardians, were better architects and engineers than the equivalent practitioners of

CELLARS CLOUGH MILL AND CANAL NEAR MARSDEN

today. We harken nostalgically to the days when they 'knew how to make good buildings', and conveniently forget the living conditions of a great mass of the population of the day, which must have had some relevance to the price structure of the economy, to building standards, at that moment. The truth of the matter is that back then, the Victorians and the Edwardians didn't have to contend with the mentality that does not have any requirement for a genuine aesthetic morality, but is forever trying to cut corners to compete, mainly because the apparatus had not yet been invented with which it could do it. The genuine craftsman still pulled the strings. The man of substance who was only as good as his last job imposed his will on environmental standards, because it was in his nature. The army of machines was still an army of men.

If Commercial Mill was listed, the landlord might be able to obtain grants to improve its facilities, convert the unused upper floors into workshops, offices, studios, more rentable premises, more new blood for the prosperity of the town, but he cannot, simply because it is financially unrealistic to consider such refurbishment, much as he would like to do so. Another mill further up the Colne Valley from Milnsbridge, at Linthwaite, has been refurbished with the same degree of success—although on a much smaller scale—as Dean Clough in Halifax in chapter one. It houses over fifty businesses, but has been refitted with a combination of private and public money, which suggests both parties were capable of incentive. The landlord of Commercial Mill told me, when I took my unit in his building, that the amount of rent I pay as only one small source of income would be almost negligible as monetary input for the size of the premises on its own. He merely wished to put some new life back into the old place. He has regular enquirers who see the notice pinned on the wall on the outside of the mill by the bus stop advertising space to let. Huge paper letters, pasted behind the windows of the upper floors, proclaim boldly to the town and passengers hurtling by in the trains across the viaduct, that there is space "TO LET" inside. A steady stream of interested potential tenants are shown around the mill but, on confrontation with open empty floors filled with nothing but rows of cast-iron pillars and the aroma of dead textiles and squadrons of startled low flying pigeons, turn away because they, like the landlord, cannot afford to have to invest in the building of their own units, indeed, do not feel obliged to have to, even if the rents are cheap, and even if they could afford to do it. They usually need the space quickly. Space in Commercial Mill is measured in pence per square foot. I remember pausing on the footbridge at Slough railway station a few years back to study a poster which I'm sure encouraged new businesses to take root in Berkshire from **'as little as £25 per square foot'.** If Commercial Mill was situated further up the valley, it would be eligible for grants, due to being further out in the countryside and away from services, and due to falling under the umbrella of COSIRA—the Corporation for the Siting of Industry in Rural Areas (?). Because Milnsbridge is not situated there (even though it is near essential amenities, has good facilities of its own, and is only a few minutes' drive from a motorway) a vast amount of untapped potential business space that could help to contribute to the rebuilding of the prosperity of the town and the retaining of what is left of its butchered architectural fabric, lays empty, or has already been razed to the ground in pursuit of quick prosperity elsewhere; gradually being squatted in by tenants of the winged and feathered variety whose only contribution to the flavour of the mills is the fetid aroma of their acrid white discharges. Instead, there is talk of demolishing what is left of the town

---

OVERLEAF: INCREDIBLE ARCHITECTURE: UPPER INDEPENDENT CHAPEL, HECKMONDWIKE

even now, at this late stage in the assault upon its old battalion of stalwart buildings, and now that Britain is booming booming booming. If you've taken the trouble to keep a keen eye on the developments being made in this part of Huddersfield, the genuinely positive, sensitive, far-sighted developments, the only safe conclusion you can arrive at is that nobody in any position that matters really gives a damn about it any more. At least environmentally, this old industrial suburb stagnates. And as it is the environment which does indeed shape our dreams, our morality, and our lives, it clearly represents an indication of the way in which money is the inevitable governing factor of the environment, and dictates the way in which we shall live in it, and of course, what quality that environment shall be; even whether or not it must be run down or ruined as part of that process. In certain places, that is.

Elsewhere, however, the story of West Yorkshire's industrial regeneration has taken a firmer grasp of the derelict situation. Small towns such as Sowerby Bridge over near Halifax have been capitalizing on redundant industrial buildings and are supposedly on the verge of being 'reborn', along with numerous formerly run-down and enormously rambling suburbs. Much has been accomplished through conservation, despite the ludicrous anachronisms inherent in this generally selective approach to town planning (why, for instance, are incongruous concrete roof slates allowed to deface stone buildings? Builders are buying old terraced houses round here to 'improve' by systematically stripping the original stone slates deliberately to sell them in the South, due to the higher profit margins. A competent planning authority would ban such monstrous activity outright, yet it represents only another example of the way in which the North of England is exploited for the benefit of the South. Such actions *are* banned, but only in certain places). All this connects with the growth of another industry which has taken a real hold in West Yorkshire over the past decade, namely tourism. The industrial North is marketing itself vigorously, and is said to be attracting visitors from all over the country, even the world, keen to explore the millscapes. *Raison d'etre* places such as Milnsbridge are, paradoxically, closer to the spirit of the old industrial North than the tourist areas will ever manage, and this even after the Recession and the generally accepted notion that the area's old established black image—which secretly lies at the root of the nostalgic appeal of its tourism—has now gone forever.

Milnsbridge possesses a genuine workaday atmosphere, representing a typical old industrial suburb in the North of England during the nineteen eighties, both in the spirit of its people and its environment, and equally importantly, its commercial status (all of which I shall touch upon later). The basic feel of the town can be found in suburbs all over the North, and probably all over the built-up urban areas of Great Britain in the quintessential human sense. A major difference environmentally is that the story of the wrecking of Milnsbridge's industrial and architectural presence is the classic story of the potential jewel in the areas's heritage crown—*the* jewel—being destroyed before the place had time to realize that tourists from outside might want to come and have a look at it should it be successfully marketted, drink in tea rooms, and reminisce upon Ye Olde Yorkshire Life; and also that the potential existed for it to adapt redundant floor space should there have been an overall national strategy devised at the very outset of the years of Recession to effect adaptation to a changing economic climate within the industrial areas.

But this point about the town having potential for tourist development needs some qualification, for my own beliefs about the devastation and subsequent run-down feel of Milnsbridge are rooted in the very substance of the town's visual character, which is seen as being especially gloomy in the eyes of many local residents, particularly because the place is situated in the belly of a valley, and which has the psychological effect of making it appear somewhere rather morbid and inaccessible, like a steelworks crowding the bottom of a hillside city. Moreover this geographic visual quality is bound up with the fact that Milnsbridge contains little 'quaintness', which is an essential ingredient if a town is to exploit tourist potential, coupled as this almost invariably is to the potentiality for a place to become more residential. Milnsbridge is comprised almost entirely of straightforeward mill terraced housing, outbuildings, weaving sheds, and mills. Outside the characteristic up-and-over terraced houses appealingly stacked up the hillsides of picturesque Hebden Bridge, I have yet to see such apparently featureless mill housing become desirable on the property circuit. Which links to the next point, one of the underlying themes permeating nearly all tourist areas and a particularly sensitive one, but one which needs acknowledging if you are to appreciate certain other underlying tendencies which relate to it, within the overall social structure of our society.

The Colne Valley, at the foot of which Milnsbridge spreads out but in discussions and newspaper articles about which the connection is hardly ever mentioned, is without doubt a veritable gem amongst the magnificent landscapes of West Yorkshire, little known outside the area. And as Huddersfield goes, the valley is by far the least tampered with environmentally in terms of those incongruous new housing estates which scatter Northern hillsides like so much garish DIY confetti; so much so that on more than one occasion I have heard it described, perhaps unfairly, as the only decent place left that is worth living in round here any more, largely free from the influence of the *poseur* and associated mannerisms and accoutrements. At the moment, the canal which runs the length of the valley is in the process of being revitalized with a view to its reopening, primarily for what is seen as some tourist and boat based leisure potential, although this is likely to remain at the top end of the valley, or the Upper Colne Valley as it is generally referred to in feasibility studies. Whether tourism can and will take hold, is perhaps speculative at the moment. Tourism largely infers—if you look at Holmfirth, Hebden Bridge, and Haworth which are West Yorkshire's prime tourist attractions—tea rooms, antique shops, up-market fashion boutiques, antiquarian booksellers, and a few museums. In other words they cater for a particular wedge in the market which is really centred around leisure spending just above the average where, for example, it is expected and not quibbled that a cup of tea and a buttered scone might cost twice the price they would in the average plastic laminate-clad cafe along the wide main roads slicing through inner city suburbs. Thus, the usual tourist indicators have not really begun to appear in the Colne Valley at the present time although, if the canal is the success it is supposed to be going to be, they might well begin to do so. Again, it is difficult to predict, because it seems to me that tourist areas develop through an almost unconscious process of their own until, suddenly, they are huge tourist draws. Some potential for this in the Colne Valley does undoubtedly exist, but so does the potential for prosperity to increase in a more industrially based context as well. If you speak to some of the older inhabitants of the valley, they tend to reject tourism because they see it as an indication of another trend of tourist areas, this being the disproportionate growth of house prices and the proliferation of 'comers in'. They see tourism as potentially a dirty word, fearing the original soundtrack of the valley—comprised of the sound of beating looms—being replaced by the same sounds, but playing on looped cassette tapes in museums surrounded by sepia-toned photographs instead, embellished by poignant quotations from the memoirs of Owd Tyke. They are also perhaps apprehensive of the potential of the valley to turn itself into a 'desirable area', which means it might have one foot rooted firmly in the property market, which all desirable areas throughout the nation, from the Cotswolds to the Lake District, adopt as the mainstay of their cultural and environmental in other words investment appeal. Ultimately, they fear this might push the original inhabitants and their families out (see London's docklands). The potential for this to happen in the Colne Valley, at the top end of the valley, also undoubtedly exists, and its rejection by the more established residents is fully understandable. Recently, one of Huddersfield's leading estate agents opened a branch in Slaithwaite, which might be an indication of the genesis of a gradual movement in price increase direction what with the recent absurd explosion in property prices nationally, although in the Colne Valley this movement seems to have been only marginal in comparison to the fashionable Holme Valley over the hill. The 'comers in' argument is probably the oldest argument in the population diversification book. No one likes to feel their own personal spaces are being threatened or being edged towards something else merely because of the effects of financial status, least of all people who have been established within a given area for a great deal of time, and least of all their offspring, who might be subsequently priced out. I well recall the village where my Grandmother lived when I was a child being populated by newcomers on the chalet-type housing estates which sprung up during the 1960's and '70's, and their venomous rejection and instant dismissal by many of the older established residents who had grown up there and felt the place and the pubs to be their own. It is possible, then, that the Colne Valley might face something of a dilemma, and maybe not too far in the future if tourism begins to really take off, although I can't help having my doubts about this somehow. Industrial expansion or tourism, or both? And if tourism, is the underlying motivation to exhibit to and provide a country playground for people from elsewhere; to capture *their* imagination and fervour? Is it meant to initiate a feeling of camaraderie and identification for those already living within? And if those already living within say they are quite happy with the strong community camaraderie and the feeling of identification as it is thankyou-very-much, does this mean the promotion of a Northern Area as a *Northern Area,* a place for tourists, is completely bogus, and that more pressing human matters are inevitably bypassed as a matter of, say, house price increase course? Are these areas then *Northern* any longer? And just what *is* Northern? Does such a comment, riddled with sentimental innuendo, bear relevance in today's cosmopolitan and multi-racial world? Does it not imply strong regional differentiation? Should this not be avoided? Shouldn't a collective attitude be encouraged rather than the polarized continuation of native bodies that regard territories as their own? Such questions not only relate to people already established within an area, but also to the bodies of people which might begin to move in. The observation poses fundamental questions that strike at the very heart of the make up of our society, and which are far too complicated to consider here.

I am not condemning Yorkshire's tourist towns as I have probably spent as much time in the tea rooms and antiquarian bookshops there as anybody else, but as a small aside, I do sometimes question what precisely it *is* about them that appeals, whether they are *Northern* any longer, whether this does in fact have relevance any more, when I have indulged in 'afternoon tea' with the odd lady friend and felt very conscious, even mildly embarrassed, at the thought of being a tourist. What I have been aware of is that these West Yorkshire tourist towns provide a base for families and couples from which to satisfy the basic necessity of eating before spending money, walking, holidaying, or enlightening themselves historically in museums. This must not be sneered at, for so long as the human being has need for recreational activity, so will these facilities continue to exist. And what tourism definitely does do is preserve the environmental structure of these towns, and this rich Northern essense upon which they draw must, I assume, be part of their attraction (it certainly is with Haworth which, despite the teeming multitudes of an average weekend, maintains an almost eerie Victorian presence, oozing the gloom of death in its incredibly atmospheric graveyard where the wind forever cuts between the headstones as though blowing out at you from between the pages of a Bronte novel). But I suppose it could be argued—as indeed it has been—that these places are only Northern in a kind of semi-manufactured, semi-idealized sense, and that in the intrinsic *human* sense, to which they invariably relate as crucial to the substance of their sentimentalized appeal, they are not Northern any longer. But anything that puts the Northern towns and old industrial villages constructively on the map has got to be of some significance and if it tidies them up, promotes the harmonious design of new buildings and provides more income for the economy of the area, this has to be even better. But what of this all important Northern essence that bolts together their appeal? What is it, and what has it evolved from?

It has evolved in a most bizarre and unconsciously ironic manner from what you could term 'the real North of England', which silently looks down from the sepia-toned photographs on the walls of cafes and bookshops, and which shades in the background to the towns' storybook charisma. To understand this, you have only to remember that this is because Northern conservation has developed from what is, in fairness, essentially a middle class idealization of what were working class conditions and environments, customs and occupations. The 'real North of England' does still exist, several generations on, but in a fragmented, contemporary, post-industrial manifestation. Although it often blends almost indivisibly, it is immensely reduced as an overall unit. It is embellished with food-mixers, unemployment, Carolina front doors, high-rise blocks of flats with incumbent social problems, an annual migration to Benidorm and Tenerife rather than Wakes Week to Blackpool, and with cassette-players pumping House or Scratch in a few misbegotten scrag-ends off the town centres in places such as Milnsbridge, Blackburn, Bradford, Colne. These people are the descendants of the faces now nostalgically filling the books full of old picture postcards. But they go largely unnoticed in their unchanged cobbled backstreets aimed down at the few remaining mill chimneys at the bottom. The few remaining gasps, provided you avert your gaze from the nearby motorways teeming with articulated trucks, and ignore the bright perspex frontage of the old corner shop, now transformed—its windows crammed full of gritted teeth and bulging biceps—into a video library. And who would deny the people living in this other North of England the opportunity to sit in decent tea rooms, to shop in reasonable fashion boutiques, to enjoy the odd museum, to enjoy a co-ordinated and aesthetically encouraging strategy in the way their living places are thought about and laid out? Does not the fact that fraying, neglected towns and suburbs exist in one place and well-manicured tourist towns in others indicate some greater overall failing? It is a question you are forced into pondering solemnly as you stop to pause at row upon row of little terraced houses on the one hand, and the incongruous new supermarket at the other side of the corroding cast-iron railings, on the site of the old railway cutting now filled in, on the other.

However much you may or may not dismiss the tourist areas, well kept, neat, tidy, co-ordinated, plenty of new cars and fresh, clean smelling people, publicized, healthy, and essentially prosperous with little if any indication of suffering or contemporary under-privileged conditions, do they not comprise the basic ingredients under which *all* Northern towns, villages, and old industrial suburbs ought to be able to exist today? The way they ought to look in this softwared, post-industrialized, supposedly civilized age in which we now live? Well, do they, or don't they?

Seriously consider this from a variety of angles and it is then that it becomes possible to perceive something of a deeper significance behind the term *Northern Tourist Area.*

Within the marketted tourist areas there exist definite policies and guidelines for the way in which they are developed; a process of thought which tolerates aesthetic balance in the environment beyond the blandly functional, considers it as essential to the desires and requirements of the inhabitants. They are planned, there are even restrictions on the way in which they are *allowed* to develop as living and working spaces. They are controlled environmentally in an inspired manner, both from within and without, and are considered similarly in a commercial sense as well. Why does this basic criteria not generally exist in other *un*desirable areas such as Milnsbridge, or the crowded backstreets off the centre of Oldham? Why does planning for people in a socially and aesthetically concerned, i.e. overtly environmentally conscious manner, generally speaking maintain an inevitable connection with its guiding factor, property prices and speculation? Why does it seem to go hand-in-hand with an area becoming 'desirable'? Again, the questions antagonize monumental arguments rooted at the very core of our country and our society and, again, are perhaps too complicated to consider at the moment.

The aesthetically disgusting new supermarket that was erected in Milnsbridge a few years back, the eyesore of the town with its corrugated tin and bland prefabricated design, built on the site of the old Larchfield Textiles mill, would have been laughed out of Holmfirth, Hebden Bridge, or Haworth before it had even got to the first public consultation meeting, if indeed it had been allowed to get that far possessed of such an embarrassingly banal appearance. The building in its present guise would never have been permitted. Why? Why *was* it permitted? Why was it good enough for the people of Milnsbridge? Why are similar eyesores being built which are good enough for the people living in certain parts of Bradford, Oldham, Blackburn? More monumental questions begin to bubble. At least Halifax got the same supermarket chain to house itself in a very pleasing building indeed, not long after the heap was thrown up in Milnsbridge; but then Halifax now appears to have its head on its collective conservation-as-a-starting-point-and-guideline-for-future-development shoulders, at least in the town centre which is a space that can be enjoyed by most of its citizens. Halifax has a few absurdly incongruous modern eyesores of its own, but what it does have is its original Victorian market hall, almost a carbon-copy of the one that was insensitively demolished in Huddersfield, and it is vigorously marketting its appeal and actively restoring it, whilst Leeds, only a few miles away, astounds the citizens of that city and even HRH The Prince of Wales with its bureaucratic stupidity as it prepares to demolish its own magnificent Victorian market hall, despite tens of thousands of signatures and one of the most respected voices in the land backing them up, that refute such an idiotic action by a mere handful, and after such publicly outraged blunders elsewhere. The obvious questions swell up from the mass of confusion, whether or not we ever learn; if we ever listen.

I began to seek out 'real Northern places', market halls, the tourist towns, the leafy residential suburbs, the inner city areas, of the old Lancashire and Yorkshire millscapes, because it is essential to study them, experience them, perceive them, talk to them, listen to them, smell them, before you can even begin to formulate a serious opinion of the type of society and the type of country it is in which you wish to live and to which you ought to contribute a vote as a conscientious matter of course. Inevitably, such criteria must take into account your own preconceptions, nostalgias, and sentimentalities, and it is a coming to terms with these initially, and an acceptance that you are human and that you may or may not like what you find, and may even have to challenge it, that is vital to the germinating of a *considered* opinion beyond that of your immediate little glass bubble. The tourist towns represent only one aspect of this multi-faceted post-industrial landscape in which they are situated, and you have to consider why it is that they have come about, but also the yardstick they might represent. I explored the ordinary post-industrial places, photographed them, because they represented the continuation of the basic small-back-bedroom-in-the-terraced-house feeling with which I could identify, from when I was a kid at the tail-end of pounds, shillings, and pence. A spirit which seemed at once genuine and uncontrived, and wasn't spending all its time and energy keeping up appearances. There are obvious contradictions inherent in this observation, but it seemed to represent an essence perceptible *at that moment in time.* An essence which, walking about their changing equivalents of today, appears could only really register when it was inextricably connected to people who were manipulated or even exploited: and to people who often made things manually as part of that process, not that *this* has changed. It seemed the best, albeit a slightly confused place now, in which to start when I came back up from London, Windsor, the leafy residential suburbs of Buckinghamshire, and decided it would be for good.

Oddly enough, as much of the industrial North has been flattened, so the obsession with emulating the past which disgorged it has blossomed. All across the surrounding hillsides cottages and pubs are becoming decorated with painted cart-wheels or salvaged cast-iron bolted to garden walls. Dummy gas lamps are planted in front of Scandinavian-type or mock-Spanish bungalows. West Yorkshire terraced housing is becoming speckled with imitation plastic accoutrements, imitation roof slates, treacly-coloured hardwood doors, flimsily authentic new 'heritage homes' crossed with balsa-wood sham-Tudor, aluminium patio doors. Even big shopping centres inspired by Victorian arcades in some of the larger towns.

THE INNER CITY: WEST BOWLING, BRADFORD. GUIDEBOOK NORTH OR THE OTHER NORTH OF ENGLAND?

And here it is that you come back to something I mentioned much earlier which all of these things are inextricably bound up with — the accursed progression of modern technology. Hence, all around you unfolds the agonized spectacle of commercial reality desperately struggling to emulate nature or the hand of the craftsman, trying to appease the current national vogue, but within a disposable budget caused by the structure of economic necessity. It seems a bizarre mockery if you take a stroll around some of the run-down areas which still retain relative authenticity. You wonder why it is that as the old industrial landscapes have withered, so we should strive so dynamically to mock the age that bore them (Is another characteristic of the English that the present somehow never really becomes desirable until it becomes the past?) And what with home DIY now a staple ingredient of the economy, an Englishman's home is probably closer to being his castle in the truest sense of the word, more than ever before. Sentimentality is big business, quite often MADE IN TAIWAN, or Rumania, or China. Alternatively, it is possible to buy British by procuring your own locally made imitation Victorian plastic front door which, unlike the original, needs no painting, no maintenance, and will supposedly last forever, which means door and window manufacturers must be gradually, inexorably doing themselves out of a livelihood. So speaketh sophisticated modern technology. So speaketh the dawning of the second Industrial Revolution. You can be forgiven for considering the whole, vast, incredible irony of it all; for occasionally raising your eyebrows cynically when studying the advertisements encouraging you to purchase your very own plastic Victorian conservatory; or when folding out a tourist guide with the little pictures of canal locks, and mill chimneys, and sheep, but with particular emphasis on the diagrams of the motorways describing the fastest way to get to the places where Yorkshire's rich industrial horse-drawn heritage can best be enjoyed, a fun day out for all the family. This is England in the latter decades of the twentieth century, the anachronistic England, the England of Old, the England of New. The England of Old, the traditional England loaded with beauty and charm and surrounded by an eternal bed of daffodils, framed by rose gardens, glistening with steaming Dartmoor ponies drinking at the hillside pools on a sunny winter's afternoon, interwoven with cathedrals and Shakespeare and the Royal Crescent at Bath, mingling with the thatched roofs and pan tiles down the steep Shaftesbury lanes, and the ivy covered Sussex cottages, and Hadrian's Wall, and silent Summer Sundays, and tea rooms, and Corinthian columns, and Chesterfield furniture, and glittering pageantry, and sleepy grazing Fresians, and now the formerly gloomy towns and cities and villages of the old industrial North, firmly embedded on the map of prestigious national heritage.

Then the England of New, the England tolerated for the other five days of the week, the England of bijou dormitory villages surrounded by more daffodils and rose gardens, but at the end of commuting tentacles to and from the motorways. The England of colourful corrugated tin sheds springing up on the sites of long-demolished industry. Sheds and warehouses which are supplying and importing, wholesaling and distributing, the servicers providing the components, above all, and rather despairingly, the new England which is apparently quite content to seek spiritual fulfilment by merely making money from money that is making money from money. And for what purpose? A revival of economic performance and the restoration of real national pride, or merely a self-satisfied short-cut to that particular kind of individual prestige value? One really does have to wonder.

Technological revolution, commercial reality, dirty concrete, British history, British sentimentality—all exist simultaneously, going on beneath the surface of individual lives, binding forces forever pulling in opposite directions, endlessly aggravated by the surface tensions of a violent computerized and tarmacced and cellular telephoned reality.

Once again, what this really represents is the reluctance with which a rapidly advancing technological society embraces progress; the two-tier making up of its emotional landscape, now forever juxtaposing the lure of improving material comforts against the desire to remain attached to a copper-kettled and frilly-curtained living. Although my own appreciation of the North of England has to allow for the same blending together of anachronisms, and is born essentially of growing up here, it simply is not possible to conceive of a milltown as being dirty and ugly when the type of memories you associate with it are largely those of a rewarding upbringing; of living in a home, not a house. This is something commentators from outside the industrial areas, who have long commented upon their traditional dreary ugliness, obviously have little conception of. It is therefore impossible to deny this hold of a place because of the background knowledge of cruel exploitation generally associated with Victorian industrialism—whether your home is centrally heated now or not. This is not to condone it by any means, only to remember the framework from which one has evolved. Part of my eternal dilemma is the knowledge of suffering that went on in many of the buildings in West Yorkshire, each time I aim a camera at them. But to deny the pleasure of the texture of Huddersfield sandstone in autumn sunlight because of the attitude of an economic philosophy strikes me as being like denying love for one's own mother because you don't like the look of her face or, moreover, because you know you were an illegitimate child, or something along those lines, thoughts pushed privately into the back of your mind. Any ordinary human being generally finds this impossible to do.

Once, when I had been photographing a mill at the top end of the valley, a wizened old man asked me what the devil I was taking a picture of a mucky bloody old textile mill for.

JANUARY DUSK OVER THE POST-INDUSTRIAL PENNINE LANDSCAPE: In the foreground, middle-American Oldham. In the mid-ground, 19th century Oldham starting up for the night-shift, and through the haze in the distance, the skyscrapers of Manchester and the urban sprawl of Lancashire beyond.

He was as aghast as those kids were in Oldham. I told him I was shooting it to try and capture the look of the valley now, for a book I was writing. "Nay, lad", he said. "Thi' war evil bloody places. Thi' gave folk rickets, warped bones, an' malnutrition. Bloody sweatshops they were, an' thi' should pull the buggers down, 'cause they were full o' meaness and exploitation". I agreed they were, although I didn't know if this applied to mills in the Colne Valley. Did I know about exploitation he asked me, what with my fancy expensive looking camera? I told him that, as absurd as it might sound, even in this age where the overall British social table manners have largely softened so to speak, I did know about it, and that the experience had had a profound impact on my life and ironically had made me look at my own part of the country more acutely than ever before. I told him that my Grandmother and my Mother had worked in the mills nearly all their lives, and that my Father and Grandfather had started out in them in Milnsbridge as well, and that I would have probably done so myself, if not for the fact that an economic crisis had prevented me from taking a full-time job at the mill where I was working part-time in 1979 at a time I was desperately sick of what seemed to me then the largely futile rigmarole of a soul destroying education. The old man got off the bus and disappeared into a January fog, and I've never set eyes on him since. But his point of view needs to be observed, for it is shared by thousands of others who feel precisely the same. Few people who are passionately advocating the preservation of Yorkshire's industrial heritage have actually worked in the mills. It is an attitude largely developed through nostalgia of a different kind, idealism, romanticization, forever embellished by an aromatic compound of bowls of pot-pourri in craft shops and fashion boutiques, mingling with the smell of FRESHLY GROUND COFFEE SERVED HERE, but the fact remains that it is working.

I have before me a clipping of a letter from the *Huddersfield Daily Examiner* of a few years ago. The correspondent comments upon an article about Huddersfield's grand buildings recently printed in the 'paper at that time, and he reminds us that the money that paid for their erection came largely from exploited and underpaid workers, many of them bringing up children in back-to-back basements with stone flagged floors uncarpeted. The same correspondent goes on to relate how, only a few decades ago, he was carrying out some work for a local millowner who asked him to slope the windowsills at an angle, so the employees would find it difficult to sit on them at dinnertimes. It is a worn topic now, but is a topic that should never be allowed to completely wear away. Perhaps this is another reason why the mills should be regarded with some form of respect instead of ridicule. Maybe it is another reason why places such as Milnsbridge ought to be preserved more enthusiastically, woven into contemporary ways of life, because it is important to remember that it was as a direct result of the deprived conditions suffered by millions of workers a century ago, and less, that resulted in the social changes culminating after the Second World War; inevitable changes which had to transpire as a result of the failure of *laissez-faire* capitalism, and which formed the basis of the standards of living we have taken so much for granted ever since.

Anyway now, as I have described at some length already, Huddersfield and the rest of the Northern towns proclaim they are becoming proud of their rich industrial heritage, so much of it only so recently gone, and are placing preservation orders on the botched muddle of remnants and encouraging the growth of tourism as a staple industry. In certain places.

Better late than never?

WINTERS DUSK ON A WET SUNDAY AFTERNOON, MILNSBRIDGE, 1987

5

A few weeks later, I was walking down into Milnsbridge one afternoon during a blustery, wet spell of weather. The rain was gusting across the grey sky in great swirling blankets, giving the steep hillside at the far end of the town a diffused look, as though it were being molested by a thinly enclosing fog. Television aerials were wobbling in the howling wind, and the flag pole on the roof of Lloyds Bank down Market Street was vibrating so fast it looked like speeded up film. My grey polar anorak was sodden with wet, and I could feel my tatty red pullover absorbing the moisture underneath and my shirt sticking to my skin and my shoes squelching as if I was treading grapes. I had been out taking photographs, or attempting to, and was taking a short cut down a footpath which runs from Lowergate, under the railway line, and down the side of the railway embankment to reach Market Street at the bottom. At that point—as you come out from under the railway—the former arched entrance to Longwood and Milnsbridge station is visible on the left. It is defiantly walled up at the top of a slope. The only other indication of what used to be there are a few weeds sprouting from the remnants of number four platform—should you decide to use them as a marker and leap from a passing train.

To the left of the footpath, steep groups of terraced houses trail down to Armitage Road, their back gardens and shared yards a compact wilderness of rickety outbuildings and uneven stone flags and dustbins. On the right, the railway embankment gets gradually higher as the footpath falls further away from it; a few bits of heavy wooden fencing made from old sleepers with the tops cut to a point stand out in a jagged outline, against the sky, as the railway runs onto the viaduct. Just here, you feel to be manoeuvring yourself through the archetypal Northern ginnel: Commercial Mill blots out the sky at the bottom, next to the viaduct. The only thing missing is the mill's chimney, demolished some years back. But here is the Northern essence; what walking to and from the bus stops when I was at school was all about. You can see it as the location for shooting in another of those old black and white British kitchen sink dramas. You can see a Joe Lampton visiting an Aunt Emily in a Dufton. He's just got off the train at the station when it was still open at the top of the path. He comes down the cobbled slope from the ticket office and passes a solitary gas lamp standing out against the background mist at the head of a steep flight of worn stone steps. As he walks up and past, he throws his cigarette butt to the ground and WE TRACK WITH HIM. He exhales the last mouthful of smoke and pulls his overcoat collar up around his neck and jogs off down the ginnel, the mill chimney when it was still there at the bottom smoking in the top corner of our picture, the rain coming down in the same sort of lashing bucketfulls. There is the WHISTLING AND CHUFF-CHUFFING of the steam train as it pulls out of the station and clatters across the viaduct in the background, but then the vision echoes away down a long corridor and we STOP TRACKING AND HOLD as the angry young hero running off to the rest of a film that probably came from a book gets further away, smaller in the frame, then fades out and vanishes. Contrasty black and white film from the past becomes caught in the projector and the jumping about unpredictability of spontaneous imagination. Colour was turned up, the rain was still falling, but the sound of the train that passed me above was the slick *whooshing* of a brand new blue-and-grey Sprinter Unit belonging to a futuristic film, with a hero relaxing calmly in its modular plastic, bulletting into the bowels of a giant shopping complex deep in the heart of a glass megalopolis.

I reached the bottom of the path and turned into Market Street, by the secondhand shop on the corner. It was a stark contrast to the reactions galvanized into motion up the path a few seconds before. The sound of numerous car tyres swishing past on the wet road surface greeted me like a door being opened from one age into the next. The rush hour was beginning again in Milnsbridge. I could see and smell the latest in sleek car designs moving through it and congesting it in a cloud of carbon-monoxide fumes, at the junction at the bottom of Savile Street outside Commercial Mill. Many of the machines snarling up the flow had probably been made by robots. By progress. By fantastic computerized concoctions whose powerhouse was contained in a single micro-chip that I could sit on the end of my finger. The powerhouse that had fed Commercial Mill across from me was a three-storied enginehouse filled with massive cast-iron cogs and gears that wheezed and thumped on a diet of coal and steam. Many of the cars seemed blurred, not from speed (they were crawling too slowly because of the traffic clogging the flow that was waiting to turn up Scar Lane) but by design. I should imagine this was from the necessity to reduce wind resistance in the mad rush to achieve 0-90mph and to go faster faster faster and to raise blood pressures and short tempers and obscene two-fingered gestures in as few a number of seconds as possible.

There was a good looking middle-aged woman driving a brand new BMW in front of where I was standing. She was immaculate. Her hair was just beginning to grey but she oozed a lustrous, crows-feet-around-her-eyes sexuality. She was the aging actress, the wealthy executive's wife, indefatigable, slender, groomed by a lifestyle of good living who turns every bloke on who looks at her, regardless of his age, with an immediate Tap Room lust. Her features said she was perceptive and intelligent; her's was the art of subtlety in body language, of taste, of sensuality. I couldn't see her legs from where I was stood but I knew she would be wearing ultra-sheer stockings and her skin would be so good she could still get away with it. She glanced at me with my muddy clothes plastered to my body from the rain. My excitement at composing photographs of a milltown in the wet earlier in the afternoon instantly evaporated, seemed pathetic, as animal instincts came to the fore. I felt ugly and dejected. She was thoroughbred and unattainable, and I was the scraggy wet mongrel cowering on the pavement with it's tail between it's legs, getting turned on by taking pictures of dirty old buildings. Reality snapped abruptly back into place, as it does when the escapism of your 'intellectual standpoint' is suddenly jolted out of focus by lusty decadent desire. To regain some self-composure, I hefted my big Manfrotto camera tripod up as though I were a cybernetic warrior scowling with a heavy machine-gun and a pronounced bottom lip on a poster taped in a video shop window; then I stepped out deliberately in front of her lithe bonnet. I thought I could feel her cursing at my impudence on my back, but I didn't look at her. It had made me feel like a man again, even if it was predictable and immature and posturing and meant to be seen as gently extracting the urine out of masculinity. As I reached the opposite pavement I realized I was way out of my depth, a scruffy dog again. She hadn't even flinched. She was too elegant to trouble herself over such trivialities. Her entire countenance said Class, *real* Class, not in the petty social heirarchical sense. Or maybe I was wrong about her altogether. I could have sworn I saw the edges of her mouth turn up ever so slightly, as if she knew all about posters in video shop windows and pronounced bottom lips. But it was dark. I felt like I'd just been outbidded in an auction, and the piece I'd come specially to secure had slipped away from me forever and there would never be another chance. She moved off with the traffic wearing the BMW as though it was nothing but an expensive form of *Eau d'Cologne,* and that's what sticks in my mind about her: she wasn't driving the car, she was *wearing* it, and it fitted her as naturally as a five hundred quid pullover.

Some of the other cars were shaped like a kind of elongated tear-drop, as though they had originally been much squarer but had become rounded at the edges like well handled bars of soap. Others were wedge-shaped and flattened at the front, their headlights mere slits like demoniac frowns which would have been more at home zipping between the concrete of Los Angeles, or twisting through the air in an outrageous stunt during a James Bond film, not driving through a Northern textile town in England that looked as if it was built on a human scale. All the cars under a few years old had black plastic where bright chrome once used to gleam, as did my own car parked round the back of Commercial Mill. The narrow curving wings and almost naive looking smiling chromed radiator grill of my Uncle Terry's maroon Ford Anglia are things of the past, reserved only for the very up market of British executive cars today. The leather upholstery of my Mother and Father's old Ford Popular that smelled like the highly polished sitting room at a distant Aunty's on Sunday afternoons, when I was a child, are now only the nostalgic enjoyment of classic car enthusiasts, or more of the up market executives. The dark duck-egg green of our old Austin A40, or the squat, heavy expression of the blue-and-white Triumph Herald we had in 1966 with the thin chrome beading between the colours—always the thin chrome beading—are only vague recollections of times gone, like the simplicity of outlook during childhood that rode pillion to all of these. Gone too is the bulbous shape of an old Austin A30 which I helped a coal wagon driver do up, before we bought it from him for about eighty quid. It was the first car I ever drove, on waste ground when I was eleven or twelve, but is now a dark-green memory parked in one of the dim recesses of the mind. It's whining engine that sounded like cars do in vintage episodes of *Mysteries of Edgar Wallace* currently being shown on television late at night; the echoey metallic sound that rang throughout it when you slammed the doors; it's simple chromed radiator grill shaped like a louvred toilet seat—all are available only from the picture library of when-you-were-a-kid. Some can be taken out in full colour, but the reception is slightly fuzzy, the sound not quite crystal clear. Paradoxically, I can see the time the A30 lived in—but not the A30 itself—as pin-sharp Box Brownie snaps of what seems now to have been the largely black and white world of the 1960's, captured in fraying photo albums; the edited highlights of Uncles and Aunts and Mums and Dads standing on front doorsteps holding babies; or of seaside holidays spent at Mablethorpe and Sutton-on-Sea when, even in my time, life moved just that little bit slower and looked just a little bit less prepacked. Does anyone remember when, before cars had conventional indicator lights, a small orange finger flicked out of a groove in the bodywork between the front and back side windows, and lit up to indicate which direction you were turning in? And in some cars—our A30 for example—you turned a beautifully crude bakelite knob in the middle of the top of

ABANDONED CHAPEL NEAR SLAITHWAITE, SINCE CONVERTED INTO A HOUSE

the dashboard? It sounds crude, almost absurd, looking at the pseudo-computerized LED dashboard of my own car today, but somehow, no matter how practical the simplicity and operational capacity of the technology of their equivalents today—and nostalgia freak in rose-tinted spectacles or not—there was something a bit more human and believable about the old indicators; more of a connection with the workings of a mind than those of a machine—like the shapes of TV sets or the flat coloured packaging of domestic goods, and chromed headlight surrounds and the shapes of the cars themselves that looked like they had come out of the same design school as *Stingray* or *Supercar.*

I stood under the concrete bus shelter in front of Commercial Mill to shelter from the rain. Night was closing in, but it was still light enough to see, through the gaps in the passing traffic, pine furniture in the window of the bedroom shop across Market Street, interspersed with flashes of vivid red upholstery and what looked from there to be tempting offers of instant credit or your dream home.

The men walking the street were clothed largely in oily overalls or casual clothes which were no doubt imported, like my own sodden garments stuck to my body. It must be the price, you know. Hardly a worsted jacket or suit was to be seen—the street would once have been full of them, probably made within the town itself—except possibly on the backs of some of the pensioners, two of whom were standing at the corner of Armitage Road using their walking sticks as extensions of their forefingers to underline what were very likely to be venomous denunciations of how they saw the state of youth and their country today. Their flat caps and dull grey gaberdeens made them look like they had stepped out of an old photograph of Rochdale railway station which I once saw in a book, taken in the rain in 1957. Photographs are an amazing thing, yet like our everyday electronic gadgetry, we take them so much for granted. Unlike paintings and sketches which are only ever a semblance of reality, photographs capture everything, exactly as it is (except when you tamper with them in the darkroom). This is why I find photographs can always genuinely arouse a real sense of wonder, whereas paintings never do, except when they are abstract, when they tap into the deepest, most raw subconscious emotion. Figurative paintings are not real. They may suggest a certain mood, but a painting of a street scene never holds me in the same way that a photograph does. You can immediately identify with a photograph, relate acutely to its recording of texture, shadow, movement, because it is real. A photograph can be a documentary record, a window into the past, a perfect facsimile of the present, until, inevitably, that too becomes the past. Those two blokes who were captured on a railway enthusiast's window into the past at Rochdale station in 1957—a big steam train was in the centre of the picture, but it's what is going on in the background which really captivates –might have been going home to cramped red brick terraced houses at the other end of the town, before it was demolished and remodelled and turned into a sector of an East Berlin (there are seven blocks of high-rise flats, visible from miles around, nicknamed locally the 'seven sisters'). Or the men may have been relatively prosperous and have been going home to detached villas, with drives and gravel and manicured lawns and Romanesque figurines urinating into garden ponds. If they were just figures on a painting, it would be difficult to identify with them, because they would only be marks made with a brush. But on the photograph they are real people making real reflections on the wet stone beneath their feet; frozen in a moment in time, their backs to camera, anonymous citizens of a Lancashire cotton town with the rain shining on the wet cobbles, and a soot black town hall clock-tower sulking in the background. The station must have had a dozen platforms. It had a latticeworked glass awning and was busy with people and porters and barrows and luggage and gas lamps and wet edging stones and black walls and brylcreamed hair and "PASSENGERS MUST NOT CROSS THE LINE EXCEPT BY THE BRIDGE" and little pointed fingers on boards gesturing towards platforms three and four for trains to Bolton, Blackburn, Accrington and Manchester. Rochdale station in the 1980's has been pruned back so much, it looks as wretched and humiliating as the cheap looking galvanized metal sections the council have put up on top of the concrete street lamps down our street.

A pimpled youth came round the corner from the same footpath I had walked down by the railway a few minutes earlier. He was carrying a large cassette player—culture term: Ghetto Blaster—issuing synthesized drum-machine beats looped with a whining voice that sounded like it had an interminable stammer. He loped past the Indian and Chinese take-aways and received doubtful expressions from the two old men from the 1957 photograph of Rochdale station. They paused for a moment to study the youth as he passed them, lowering their walking sticks at the precise second their conversation was interrupted by mobile discotheque 1987 style. When the youth had gone past, and he had his back to them, they shook their heads despondently then started nodding in such a way that you knew one of them was making a reference to double-breasted jackets and big band ballroom dancing in the 1940's, and how they'd never dared to have walked about like this in their day, when sex and the promiscuity of youth always seem to have been things of a shiny condomed future.

I decided to go up to my studio in the mill and see if the modern piece of technology called an answering machine had brought me any work. As I stepped out from under the bus shelter, I saw a council man pushing a bright-yellow plastic dustbin on wheels, sweeping the gutter outside the Freemasons Masonic Hall. He has done this in Milnsbridge for as long as I can remember. There was a little child, probably not yet of infant school age, standing outside the butcher's open doorway, a few yards away from the council man, waiting for his Mother. She was visible inside the shop, gesturing to pies and livers and stewing meat and ground up pigs guts dumped in bloody heaps on silver trays beneath a row of lethal looking aluminium meat hooks suspended in the window. She could have been about twenty-five, but was more than likely a good seven or eight years younger. Her features were anxious, even though she was smiling at the butcher, and her complexion was pasty and ashen from a synthetic diet, sort of hardened at the edges like somebody appears when they are trying to rub the circulation into themselves outside on a bitter cold winter's morning. Her hair was too silver streaked for it to be the natural colour, and her dark-blue jeans were brand new, unfaded from washing, and so tight fitting they could have been sprayed on to deliberately emphasize the curvature of her sinewy buttocks and thighs. Her kid standing outside had the slightly wild, dilated expression of being weaned on a high energy diet of artificial food, fast moving television, and stroboscopic pop video. He was clutching some kind of 'robozoid' toy that must have been manufactured to tie in with the latest science-fiction film containing computer generated special effects set in galaxies far, far away in a time yet to be born.

A double-decker bus pulled up at the bottom of Savile Street. I was caught in the hoard of people it deposited who jostled with half a dozen more who came out from under the old concrete bus shelter with the corrugated asbestos roof around the corner as it stopped. As they filed on board, there was the noise of money being slipped into the open mouth of a waiting receptacle, then the *click-clunk* followed by a faint chatter as the coins dropped into an armour-plated cash box underneath as the driver punched the machine that spat out the ticket which even told you the time of the day. There are no bus conductors on the buses in Huddersfield any more: the driver has a little mechanical one with no face and no arms and no legs and no character that sits bolted to the dashboard by the side of him, reeling the tickets out in immaculate, unerring automation. Speed, efficiency, machines, automation, less human participation, keep costs down. The bus's axles needed oiling as it swung out into Market Street, a big green-and-cream coloured mechanical monster that took the full width of the road up and advised the approaching traffic to slow down and let it get out or else. The little kid was still outside the butcher's when the bus had gone. His Mother had come out into the street and was lighting a cigarette with her back to the wind. The kid was

ROCHDALE

oblivious to her. He was too preoccupied with the metallized plastic robot in his hand. I got a better glimpse of it: it was all red and white and chrome; the type of toy that no doubt originated in a fully automated factory in Japan, and was of the sort that changes into an aircraft when you twist it's head arse-over-tit. He was looking at it then, weaving it past his eye, mouthing silent sound effects to himself as it transported his imagination up from Market Street in the heart of an old Yorkshire textile town in 1987, off to some distant planet in the future where the sky is red and a devilish robotic supervillain plots the overthrow of the earth with an army of faceless, mechanical employees. I wondered how he perceived Milnsbridge, his home turf, I wondered if he lived on one of the narrow side streets up Morley Lane above the canal. Or maybe his house was on the big council estate up Scar Lane, where my Aunty Marjorie still lives, now widowed. Or maybe he was one of the kids who kick a football around in the road further down our street, from the very first day the clocks are moved forward at the start of British Summertime, and whom you nearly drive over at least three times a week as a result. I didn't know, it didn't matter, and I felt conscious of standing and staring at nothing in particular on the street in the pouring rain.

I went into Commercial Mill and opened the door at the bottom of the musty stairwell tower. A woman from the textile company on the floor below my studio came out of the door wearing flip-flops and a lovely smile. She jumped and said I'd nearly frightened the living daylights out of her as I yanked it open in front of her. I caught a whiff of her scent as she passed me, the exquisitely arousing female smell of soap flakes and clean hair. The door handle is a piece of real leather hide half an inch thick, stapled to the wood and the paintwork is peeling and the bottom corner, opposite the side hinged to the frame, is frayed and rotten. The door slammed shut with the speed of a jackhammer: the wind blows up and down the tower when it is blustery and you have to be on your guard. I climbed the worn stone steps. You can't use the lift, because it was deemed unsafe by the Inspectorate of Factories in 1982 and besides, the exercise does you good. The walls are painted half turquoise and half cream, like most mills were inside in this area, and continue to be. Up to the first floor, the air smells cleaner, sharper, faintly warm from the industrial heating mushrooming into the stairwell each time the door of the textile company is opened, mingling with the smell of cigarette smoke lingering occasionally, new knitting wool, and the sound of Radio One coming out from the crack under the door. Past the first floor, though, the smell becomes abruptly musty, colder, stagnant, an underlying smell of stale pigeon crap assaulting your nostrils. I unlocked the door to my studio and saw the little green diode flashing on my modular plastic answering machine in the darkness. Somebody had wanted to speak to me and had left a message because I was out walking in the rain and eyeing up beautiful women driving BMWs, and hadn't been there to take the call. The machine enabled me to make a more economic use of my time, to apparently increase the amount of time I had at my disposal, to be in two places at once. I listened to the message then switched on my record player. I removed a circular vinyl disk from a cardboard sleeve festooned with pictures of cobwebs and screaming faces and wild eyed young men and women wearing torn clothing and spiky hair. I placed the circle of vinyl onto the turntable, turned the volume up loud, and activated the machine by pulling a plastic switch toward me. Immediately, a stainless steel and black-plastic arm obeyed the electronic signal. It disengaged itself from its housing, swooped towards the turntable, which was now revolving, and sat down on the outside edge of the record. There was a brief sort of revolving silence from the speakers, interspersed with a few vague crackles, then a cacophony of synthesized drum machine beats looped with another whining voice that sounded like it had an interminable stammer exploded across my studio, blasting out so loud the soundwaves threatened to activate the sprinkler system hanging from the ceiling. "IGGGG-NOOOORRE THE MACHEEEEENE. .!!" screamed the voice, via the twelve inch remix from an original recording first heard courtesy of John Peel. That was the funny thing. No matter how hard you tried, you couldn't ignore the machine. I was depending on one to excite me and turn me on with music as surely as somebody sticks a tube of tightly compressed tobacco leaves into their mouths and ignites it and inhales the vapours.

When the music had finished, the traffic out in the street sounded unusually quiet. I looked around my studio and made a quick mental observation of the images pinned to the walls that stimulate me. As a kid, I was obsessed by special effects in film and TV. It was all I lived for. The first spacecraft model I ever made was sat on one of the workbenches. I lifted it up and waved it past my eye, like the little kid had been doing with his space model down below in the street. It had that I-made-this-about-ten-years-ago-and-have-come-a-long-way-since-then look to it. I remembered the enthusiasm with which I'd dirtied it down, the way I'd put the exhaust marks around its boosters. I have a video cassette at home, which I am unable to watch because I don't yet possess a video recorder (videos can distract you into a routine of lazy leisure rather than the constructive activities of reading, writing or photography) which has some 16mm film footage transferred to it that I shot with a friend of mine called The Jembo, later to be known as the Guy with a Thick Man-like Neck. During the college holidays, we used to go into a little industrial film studio and shoot our own special effects as professionally as possible. We built the sets, the models, lit them, and shot them, and felt very enthusiastic about having it processed at the same lab as Yorkshire Television's news footage, before they switched to tape. We shot the spaceship I was holding in a miniature forest made from dwarf conifers. We rigged an air hose that blew dust up from underneath it as it lifted off—suspended on micro-fine wires. Gradually we built up a show-reel of special effects footage and cheekily made appointments to go and see the special effects film people we'd idolized during childhood. We filmed sets with model cars bouncing about, rockfalls, spaceships, alien planet surfaces, and used the results to obtain employment in the film industry. I looked at the model again and remembered the enthusiasm that built it. Recently I watched the video show-reel for the first time in about five years. I was staggered at how good it still looked. The model cars we filmed driving about—ripped off from *Thunderbirds*—actually blow clouds of dust up from underneath as they move along, because we built air cannisters into the chassis; and they bounce on their suspension, they have scale *weight*. I've contributed to the special effects on some TV series since then, films, and a lot of commercials, but these simple effects shot by a couple of kids—kids that now seem so far off—stood up as good as a heck of a lot of the professional stuff I've been involved with. After watching the video-tape, I fished out the dozens of behind the scenes stills that we took of our sets and models. It was a different pair of people who shot that original film footage. The two people on the photographs, grinning in the hungry young way we did the summer we went off to be dishwashers at the Butlins holiday camp in Skegness, had a vision, and no one, absolutely no one, was going to stop them seeing it to

---

OVERLEAF: HAZY SUMMER ATMOSPHERICS OVER SLAITHWAITE DURING THE 1980s

fruition. I remember we once filmed a rockfall. As it all tumbled down the miniature cliff face we'd built from plaster and polystyrene, it hit the camera lens in a great ball of dust and smoke; the trees in the foreground bent and shook in scale due to the way in which we filmed it. When we got the footage back from the lab, we assembled in the little viewing theatre at the film studio where we shot the effects, along with a few of the blokes who owned the place. As our special effects flickered up onto the screen, and we saw it, it looked so good, so utterly professional, we actually jumped about on the spot and instantly erupted into a torrent of foul mouthed expletives, as film people tend to do when what they have shot looks good on the screen. The blokes just looked at us. We were practically going into orgasm. We watched it again and again. Enthusiasm. Such energetic enthusiasm embarrasses us both when we look back to it now—and Jobber will swear at me over the 'phone for including it here—but it was a different pair of people leaping about in the viewing theatre back then. For about three years we were constantly high on adrenalin. It's amazing the power it gives you to knuckle down and do things. I'm convinced that you have to be green to have this. One ounce of cynicism, one ounce of maturity even—a certain kind of maturity—and it would be shattered. Such is the mental scenery of youth, like a play with cheap paper backings.

Needless to say, at school such talk of this 'model thing' was usually dismissed as being immature. You were generally regarded as being in cloud cuckoo land, a fantasizer, a dreamer. Thus, school was largely meaningless to me, because I was uneasily aware of it trying to thwart my subjective impulses. To learn of the way a pebble displaced volume in a beaker of water felt to me to be the real immaturity. I'd realized it did this when I was very young, when I used to lower myself into the bath, and it seemed pointless to go through a laborious, painfully obvious simulation of such an absurdly simple experiment in a physics' classroom, and then draw it and set it down very neatly to prove you were developing feathers and turning into a parrot. It seemed a simple example that illustrated the absurd gulf existing between the academic and the creative; the domination of the philosophy which measures success, intellectual capacity, through merely theorizing a pre-set scale of answers to any given problem. What used to really bug me in a mathematics examination was that there was only one answer to each question, only one possible solution, and if you were incapable of finding your way through the tangle of numbers and multiples and square roots, this was in some way indicative of ignorance and lowered your credibility in academic circles. If you were inclined to sit down and draw and paint and sculpt and photograph instead, it was never noted that this might suggest perceptiveness, observation, analysis of reality; that writing may be a means to display a hunger for enlightenment through the spontaneous expression of questioning and ordered thought, and the yearning to really *understand,* which is what really stokes up the internal fire of any genuinely creative person. As I remember it, the educational system conspired to turn you into some pre-determined unit that you did not wish to be, which is why it was difficult to come to terms with it, and which is why I find it incredible to believe I then wasted two years at sixth form college. Art college was better, because at least, in theory, you were all on a similar wavelength; but best of all, you were exposed to intelligent creative lecturers with whom you could indulge in provocative and extremely stimulating arguments. The ability to be articulate in ones thought and to express it clearly seems far more important to me than knowing whether or not two and two must always equal four. So I used to scive a lot from school and become immersed in books and the study of film. When I ought really to have been doing homework, I used to teach myself how to construct stories and film scripts: how to write. I sat down in front of the television set whilst an episode of a TV series, or a film, was showing, and made continuous notes, rather as a typist does under dictation. I developed my own shorthand (this was before the age of home video, and I couldn't afford a decent tape recorder) and scribbled down every single happening on the screen as it occurred. After the programme had finished, I went upstairs to my bedroom and wrote out the entire story to the film neatly, like a story, in exercise books I obtained from the storerooms at school. The finished stories—which were really what the industry calls *treatments,* whereby no dialogue is written except perhaps the odd key word, but only action and the flow of the narrative is described—read like prose outlines. In this way, when I should have been revising for mathematics, biology, and physics, I was able to break down and analyse the way in which film was constructed, the way a hook is created at the beginning of the American imports to hold your interest and dictate the flow of the rest of the story before the opening credits, the way the whole film was divided up into acts, the way it was paced, the bouncing and rebounding of sub-plots, the establishment of characterizations. I still have these books of finished episodes written up into stories. They are some of my most cherished possessions. The date at the head of each insertion tells me they were the work of a fourteen or fifteen year old kid. Again, the enthusiasm comes across, feeding on the *genuine* desire to learn and achieve and participate in.

I thought about the council worker I'd seen about half an hour earlier outside the butchers down on Savile Street. As a kid, what had he fed on? He would probably tell me to shut up about what I fed on, because I've no idea what I missed. He had cut his teeth playing with a big tin-plate *Hornby* train which had that painted-on-detail look to it, which you wound up with a big key. He doesn't reminisce nostalgically over TV programmes, because when he were a lad, there weren't any. You played outside in the fresh air and didn't get under your Mother and Father's feet. *Thunderbirds* and *Batman* and arse-over-tit toy robots were things far, far away in a time yet to be born; but his days were good days, like my days were good days, just like the days of the little kid outside the butchers open doorway will be good days when he gets older. And so it goes.

In 1987, in that time now born, the council man's barrow is not timeless like he is, but is a product of the high-tech, mass production methods of manufacturing today. He used to push an old metal dustbin round that was fixed to a trolley, which I'm sure was painted maroon with HUDDERSFIELD DISTRICT CORPORATION written in gold lettering on the side. It was probably made by hand, or at least with hands not very far away. The trolley he pushes around today is a one-piece plastic moulding, probably made by a robot, or a vac-forming machine, or both. It is as much a reflection of this age as enamel plated "CAPSTAN" signs screwed to gable ends were of his. The thing is, since the pall of black smoke belched out by the mills hung menacingly over the town, since gas lamps glowed then were superseded by concrete replacements powered at the flick of a switch from the National Grid, since the railway goods yard up Scar Lane ceased clinking and shunting and grassed over, since *Thunderbirds* and *Batman* exploded from black and white television screens the first time around, since my Uncle Terry's maroon Ford Anglia, then flared trousers, then platform shoes, then shirt collars you could go hand gliding in—right up to the yellow plastic dustbin the council man was pushing and the little kid's Japanese toy robot and sleek cars with plastic bumpers and cheap decals in 1987 have come, gone, or are still with us, the big mill I was standing in had brooded throughout it all. Likewise, the Freemasons Masonic Hall next to the butchers—with its thrones and rumours of bared legs during strange initiation ceremonies for new members—continues to fill several nights a week with the owners of more up market cars parked ostentatiously along Lipscomb Street; as it will have done since the stone plaque on its corner was cemented into place exactly one hundred years ago in AD 1888.

I leaned against a workbench and told myself that I really ought to sweep all the mess up off the floor: bits of wood, off-cuts of perspex, shards of plaster, a few shrivelled applecores and a disgusting black banana skin next to some cans of emulsion paint over by the door. But I couldn't be bothered. Like when you are making your own bed, there are always more important things to do other than tidying up. I looked up at the walls around me. They were Northern walls. Incredibly thick, rough hewn, mill built walls. Like the walls in our kitchen had been when we'd moved into the house up the road in 1974, their natural texture was hidden, obscured by more than a century of whitewash and repainting. The windows must have been ten feet high. The floor was made from paving stones—real paving stones as they used to make pavements from, and which give me chill-blanes on my feet when the weather is frosty. They were, like the wooden floors of the upper stories above me, covered with a dark, impenetrable layer of grease from the mill's original textile function. Since they had all been butted snugly into position, there have been two world wars. My Grandmother, now in her eighties with a lifetime spent working in the mills behind her, would not be born for another twenty or so years. The Wright Brothers flew. Movies arrived. Le Corbusiers theories brainwashed a generation. Neil Armstrong took his famous first step. *Thunderbirds* and *Batman* have been repeated several times; the bubble-gum cards that tied in with their original release, along with *Matchbox, Dinky,* and *Corgi* toys, have become sought after collectors items, exchanging hands for considerable sums of money, especially if they are boxed or in mint condition. And about twenty tall mill chimneys have been erased from the map in Longwood and Milnsbridge, and nearly as many mills. Even when these above mentioned products from the modern world first appeared, and smoke abatement acts got rid of the pall of smoke that hung over the town from the old, and we'd never had it so good, the textile industry that built the town declared its presence with something more than the sum total of its few remaining mills today: most of which have their top five stories empty and are saved from the slavering jaws of the bulldozers only by being listed by the Department of the Environment.

But life and the town goes on. What remains, neglected, unfashionable, is essentially what was built at the time the enormous mill I was standing in was constructed all around me. The basic fabric of Milnsbridge has had its big ligaments torn, its innards ruptured. The book remains, a hardback edition at that, but with that annoying, floppy, loosened quality to the spine as you try to read it caused by the incongruous gaps where the most important chapters have been removed. In places, it teeters towards a semi-derelict look, but with top-of-the market executive cars parked and gleaming on adjacent ground. Oddly enough, this part of the Colne Valley retains those original bits of natural informality which I cherish:

weeds and dandelions growing under walls, the overgrown footpaths and canal bank with their wildlife, knobbly wrought-iron railings, the softer focus given by all of these things where they have not been artificially tidied up and seeded. However battered this town has become over the past few years, it maintains an original spirit. But what it does need is an injection of money, proper money, money with a real, solid sense of vision; it needs a body of people to sit down with a sense of conviction and decide they are going to preserve what little integrity is left of this one small suburb that was made in Huddersfield. That is all it takes; genuine commitment, but there are other gulfs that exist than the one I identified between two different philosophies when I was at school. Meanwhile, it carries on towards the next century. Cosmetics are applied, taken off, then re-applied to suit the trends and tastes of the day. New designs of cars fill the streets in ever increasing numbers, those from each new decade looking more and more alien in style to the texture of the environment they inhabit from the last. The years slip by. One decade overlaps into the next, then suddenly we are all ten years older and commenting on how quickly time passes the further away from childhood you get. That little kid who'd been standing outside the butchers, already formulating his own perceptions and living his own experiences that he, too, will be able to recall from the picture library of when-you-were-a-kid by the time he is no longer a kid, wasn't even conceived when I'd constructed that model spaceship I was holding in my hands. Two people, then still at school, had yet to mate. Bodily fluids had yet to intermingle to set the chemical reacton which generates the spark of life into motion. In so short a space of time, new life emerges from the womb. Doctors and nurses cluster around a hospital bed and yank a blood covered screaming mass out of the body of a female organism, to be hosed down and grow up to live in the same environment as hundreds of others have done in Milnsbridge, Huddersfield, West Yorkshire, up North before him and will do ahead of him.

Perhaps, in twenty years time, he will reach a point where he feels inclined to go back and dig the garden over, for whatever reason. Perhaps he will look back to the charms of his Uncle So-and-so's old Ford Sierra or Vauxhall Astra as he steps out into an electrically powered hover-car to take the short glide down the laser-rail into the town, which by then will have been completely demolished and replaced with yet another gigantic domed shopping complex. Will he marvel at its crowded open malls, its plastic mock-Tudor, its escalators and glass bubbles carrying the overawed clientele up the walls, its tinny background music, its plastic vegetation that looks like—always so it *Looks Like*—it is real, but isn't, and wouldn't grow there, but is meant to *Look Like* it does, to make the Saturday afternoon out *Look Like* it is somewhere more desirable, as long as it doesn't look like the somewhere it is.

Will he reminisce over what life was like as he grew up in an old Yorkshire milltown? Will he gasp at the size of the railway viaduct, now visible even more since Commercial Mill was pulled down, and sandblasted, and incorporated as the centrepiece into some kind of international garden festival? Will he yearn for a walk outside the dome of warmth and happiness up to Pole Moor, in the wind and rain, if only he could motivate himself to stop relying on the hover car to carry him everywhere, now that his arms and legs are withering away into useless fleshy stumps through an ever increasing dependence upon a push-buttoned existence? I doubt it, just as I doubt that Milnsbridge will be turned into an imitation of somewhere it is not. Like me, that little kid is better off thrilling to the umpteenth repeat showing of *Thunderbirds* or *Batman*, or playing with toy robots that change into aeroplanes when you twist their heads arse-over-tit.

The Industrial Landscape Transformed: Municipal Lawns and Royd Mill, Oldham

PART THREE

6

Days, weeks, months: they flit past. Time goes on. The light powdering of snow over the mess that was Sunnybank Mills melts away one crisp morning full of sunshine, but lingers in the harsh shadows under the walls. 1987 becomes 1988. Winter becomes early spring. Only twelve years to go now until the start of a new century. Twelve years ago it was 1976. It seems like it was only last week, only a few days since the famous dry summer.

Time. I've been fascinated by the passage of it since I used to peer out of my back bedroom window when I was a kid and observe the changing of the light of the seasons playing across the surface of the mills. There must be an immense egg-timer somewhere, as outrageously oversized as one of the cliff-hanger props out of an old episode of *Batman*. I eat my dinner in a local cafe nearly every single day. Over the past year, I must have consumed about 300 brown teacakes and drunk about 30 gallons of coffee and mashed about half a hundred weight of potatoes and crunched my way through more than 20 lettuce. Time. My Mother and Father adopted me at six weeks old from a 16 year old girl in Liverpool in 1961. I seem to remember being told I was conceived accidentally in the old Liverpool 8, and I know I was born in a hospital in Wigan, although I've never bothered to check this out by going back through the records and searching for the strange sounding name I was born with. The other day I was looking through a book full of old railway photographs taken in the North West, and there were some photographs of stations in Wigan and Liverpool taken in 1961, and shortly thereafter. Time. Looking at the photographs, they had that immense-goods-yard-filled-with-hundreds-of-dusty-railway-trucks quality. Going by the papers I have folded in an envelope, my blood-Father was 21 years old and employed on British Railways in the engineering shops. The cars on the photographs have the chrome beading between the colours; there are railway lines visible set into cobbles like tram lines; there are pictures of deep black cuttings with brick sides and the gable ends of terraced houses poking over the tops. The towns' layouts on these photographs have yet to develop the awkward open quality that some of these equivalent locations have today; that botched ugliness of immense car parks and old cobbled roads suddenly chopped in half by a new ring road, and incongruous walls of concrete bunkers thrusting up next to garish perspex tubes and silly pink and yellow triangles, and the overall hotched-potched makeshift look which nobody seems to be able to do much about. Time. Looking at some of the shots in the railway book, looking at the advertisements with their simple layouts and bold but charming headlines on the station buildings and bolted to the ends of houses, looking at the detail still inherent in much of the street and platform furniture, the relief detail and segregation of panels upon the heavy cast-iron bridges which give a sense of shape and proportion, it is difficult for me to comprehend that I was actually somewhere in a few of those photographs nearby, or just off them. It looks to be a different world. The steam trains in the foreground of some of the pictures are dirty and oily and belching steam. Another picture depicts a little locomotive trundling alongside a greasy black fence made from sleepers, with grass growing between the lines in the foreground, and a row of dusty terraced houses shooting off the photograph immediately to one side. The distance between the nearest front door of the end terrace house and the steam engine looks to be about the same as it was between my bedroom window and Sunnybank Mills. But the occupants of that end terrace house probably abhorred the sounds and smells the engine gave off, and probably rightly so. The buildings visible on some of the other photographs relate to one another harmoniously; they relate to the very fabric structure of the layout of the environment, the whole environment relates to itself, the windows and doors in the buildings relate to themselves. The ugly, dappled uneveness you see in so many places today is barely discernible. But there is dirt and grime. Despite this ingrained filth, you can see, if you look through it, that there is quality; you can see that the window frames appear integrated into the totality of the structures, the totality of the overall whole, as do the doors, even the textures of the cobbles and leftover gas lamps and latticeworked wrought-iron and chunky buttresses holding up bridges. There is an interweaving and a visual balance, whereas much of the details added since to these buildings which have survived have that crude stuck-on-afterwards look.

Have you ever stopped, half closed your eyes, and imagined a ring road development built as the Victorians would have built it? Have you imagined the banal modern footbridges made like old railway footbridges, with trellicework, rivets, emblems? Have you imagined sturdy stone or good brick in place of bland dirty concrete? Have you imagined the tall lamp standards with their utterly featureless expressions down the central reservations but made from cast-iron instead, with detail, chunkiness, interest, craftsmanship? Suddenly, the principle of ring roads obliterating sections of towns doesn't seem half as bad if it looked right. It is not necessarily the principle that is wrong, but the hopelessness of the way in which they are executed. But better than imagining all of these things above, have you imagined a society which had the confidence to design *completely new* street furniture, with the same inherent attention to detail, the precocious declaration of design skill, that was just as good as the Victorian or Edwardian or Georgian details we are busy imitating today when we do manage to make good street furniture, but is something entirely different? All this looking back for inspiration is all well and good (I do it myself), but slavish imitating implies a terrible lack of confidence in what we are capable of achieving in the present. More than this, you need to get to the bottom of why it is that we lack the direction to grab such a problem by the scruff of the neck, acknowledge previous inspirations and previous mistakes—or more importantly the underlying reasons for previous mistakes–before you can forge ahead with something else new, but better still than all previous comparisons.

The world in those pictures in the railway book is not a world I foolishly yearn for, but there are certain aspects of it which remain today, and which have been recorded on photographic film for posterity, that strike me as being far more environmentally stimulating than a lot of what exists far beyond these mill windows from where I type at this moment in time in the late twentieth century.

The late twentieth century.

Time.

Time does indeed look as if it is beginning to yearn nostalgically for the contents visible on some of the pictures in the book of railway photographs that connect me with the beginning, the very genesis, of my own time. So much so that we are looking at other such old photographs besides the railway prints, and copying what we can see. We are also beginning to put up some buildings that look really very good indeed, along with a great deal which still look very bad. Some of these new buildings relate to the old styles that are there. They imitate their details, even would you believe, their balance and sense of proportion. In some parts of Lancashire, such as Wigan and Bolton, new buildings are finally beginning to get their act together. There is nobody who receives more pleasure from experiencing these tastefully restored environments and new structures that mimic almost exactly the old, that re-erect authentic looking gas lamps, than I do. There is a new housing development—actually a group of three-storey flatlets I think—nearing completion at Thornton, on the outskirts of Bradford. It is absolutely superb, one of the best, most visually pleasing new buildings I've seen. It is made from stone, real stone, not that awful synthetic looking pretend stone which is really cast concrete formed in stone moulds. It has the details, the corbels under the guttering, and is one of those rare instances where a large expanse of green grass in the foreground actually works and sets the building off, because the designers have utilized a stone fencing—although cast imitation—to frame it, rather than just letting it bleed onto the pavements and footpaths as was customary in the 1960's and '70's. They could have been built a hundred years ago. But that is both the development's strength, and its weakness. *It could have been built a hundred years ago.* In other words, there is nothing new about it. But it is excellent. It is refreshing to see such well thought out new buildings. I stood outside it with my companion and we both exclaimed aloud. But there was that niggling doubt in the back of our minds that, somehow, whether we liked to admit it to ourselves or not, it could be seen as some form of regression. If not regression, then a displaying of a terrible lack of confidence in what we are capable of devising in the present to our own new designs. There you are, you see, the eternal dilemma: emotion versus nostalgia versus logic and analysis. The pure architects may laugh at all this (as they may laugh at us), either because it is indeed nothing new, or because it displays none of the deep meaning, overly egotistical expressions of something that is radically new with one foot outside reality, and generally pretentious with silly pointed bits stuck up from the roofs. Are we saying that, generally speaking, there are two solutions to architecture and the environment; i.e., the way the old people did it, and the way the building boom in the 1960's did it? How absurd. What about *Art Deco* buildings?—and that includes the New York skyscrapers. This strikes me as being the last decent movement in architecture that was worth commenting upon, but it used traditional materials and a traditional approach much of the time, but with a definite aesthetic identity all it's own. This movement seems to have been killed off by the Second World War and such attitudes never fully recovered since. Something has happened along the way (probably embryoed by the post-war austerity years).

Time. Time has given us progress. And progress has sent us to the moon, given us instant hot water and central heating, saved lives through improved medicine, and deposited fantastic electronic machines in numerous households that can cook in seconds, toast bread, record moving pictures from glass viewing portals in the corner then play them back, and shave hair from mens faces without soap and hot water. We can now devise the most fantastic everyday utensils which we all take so much for granted (my typewriter just beeped to let me know I had spelled a word wrong); miracles of design and engineering technology, if you sit down on your front door step, stroke its stone or concrete edge, listen to the birds arguing and the trees rustling, and really think about it. We should preserve what is worth preserving of the old, carefully restore it, or at least contribute to it harmoniously in keeping with it's original conception. But we must go on creating something new. In this way, what should materialize are towns and cities that reflect the best from each movement, each generation, each approach to building. It is fashionable to condemn modernism, skyscrapers, but there are some superb tower blocks that have been built—a few—and they should be acknowledged as such. But we tend to associate modernism with bad prefabricated housing and squalid social conditions. It would have been interesting if there had been a new architectural movement allowed to follow on from modernism beyond the current Post Modernism (nevertheless producing excellence), maybe with the simpler shapes, but with some proper relief detail, some form, some interest, some craftsmanship. Probably through a combination of public sentimentality due to 1960s blunders, and an

PRIMROSE HILL, LOOKING TOWARDS THE RASHCLIFFE FLATS AND HUDDERSFIELD TOWN CENTRE BEYOND

idiotic economic structure of things, architects have largely been frustrated from being able to give it to us yet, although an absolutely stunning new building that is under construction near to the town hall in Leeds certainly looks like it is going to show the way. As we progress technologically, are we regressing culturally? Will something radically new transpire, and impress the landscape in the way the Victorians managed? But just a minute. Time. Time. The Victorians looked to a previous time for much of their inspiration. They ripped off Greek Classical, Egyptian, Gothic, the Italian Renaissance. Is anything new? Is it true that the Italians are the ones with a colour sense, with a real flair for design? Time. Time will tell. As it marches on. And the urban wilderness will continue to fascinate in a way the countryside—wonderful as it is—never can or ever will. The urban landscape tells you about people, it holds the attention because of people, you can define history through its fluctuating design, its constant turmoil sustains the imagination, which is why personally, I can write pages and pages about wet streets and wooden doors and the hub of activity, but I struggle to talk about green trees and fields to any great length. The countryside also reflects the faults of so many attitudes, and as such is the exact antithesis of the long suffering urban sprawl in almost every conceivable sense. For if we are not trying to mock at its existence artificially, we are all too ready to escape to it, rather than attempt to grapple with the problems faced by our towns and cities. If we could lavish some of the affection we hold for fields and trees on the backstreets and buildings of the urban jungle, what towns and cities they would be.

But I enjoy fresh air too, and for once I was inhaling it deeply on a Sunday morning in the spring of 1988, as I thought about the passage of time and contemplated how surprisingly warm the day was for the time of the year.

Everywhere, the smell of freshly mown grass circulated, drifting up from the frenzied sound of the Flymo, fresh out of hibernation. It seemed that first day had arrived—there always is one, as there is in reverse at the end of it—when it suddenly feels warm to the bone, and you know that winter has well and truly finished until next time. The sun was low enough in the azure sky, but only just by mid-morning, to cast darker shadows and model the relief detail of everything pleasingly, so the colours were standing out vividly, crystal clear, as they do all day on frosty sunny days in winter when there is not a cloud in the deep ocean blue sky. By mid-day, the sun had climbed higher, bleaching the earth and the colours and the civilization beneath into a dazzling semi-chalked paleness which made you constantly screw your eyes up in retaliation. Clouds had begun to gather, plucking themselves magically from the backdrop of floodlit deep space, whilst hundreds of miles above, invisible spy and communications satellites orbited the world at fantastic speeds, keeping their electronic eyes perusing the potentially giant powder-keg full of teeming gnats below. The clouds were wispy at first, the tentative steps of a fledgling water-colourist; then they were rolling then piling on top of one another, cotton-woolly in their texture from the broader, more confident strokes of the old masters of oil.

I wasn't strolling through the idyllic countryside that surrounds the town of Huddersfield, I was standing next to an old Christadelphian Chapel at a place called Rashcliffe, on the outskirts of the town centre. Here, a muddled confluence of architectural hotch-potch meets to paint the type of picture you see in the inner urban areas of every major old industrialized town or city the length and breadth of this part of the nation: areas jettisoned from the mainstream.

Putting the craftsmanship back into new architecture? Leeds 1989

Years ago, my Mother worked for the *Rashcliffe Mending Company* a few yards across the road from where I was standing. She was a Mender by trade for almost her entire life which in textiles, to put it simply, is the craft of taking a freshly woven roll of cloth and repairing any tiny defects it may have by needle and thread. This part of Huddersfield's inner urban landscape where it tumbles down from Primrose Hill was then, and is now, marvellously botched: a graphic illustration of the uncomfortable lack of cohesiveness of old and new; the downright slovenliness in planning which exists in those parts of our old industrial landscapes where you always feel that nobody takes the trouble to lay it out with any heart. This is one of those areas made in Huddersfield that are never mentioned when the town congratulates itself and reminds you what a splendid town it is in which to live. But the place isn't half as bad as some of the parts of other towns I've seen. Huddersfield has fared comparatively well: there isn't the aura of stagnant, peeling decay; the stench of frustrated and oppressed humanity coming off from some of those vast post-apocalyptic wastelands scattered with corroding concrete silos that look as though they should be storing missiles instead of housing people.

Of course, inner city decay is one of the catch-phrases of the 1980s, as popular as 'shopping complex' and 'rising prosperity'. I mentioned earlier the England of Old, the England of New. Both these Englands, these Britains, could be ten million miles away when you are in one of the really horrifying pockets of inner city suffering especially the post-holocaust places. They might as well be on another planet. That all-pervading and lingering eternal English watercolour crossed by hedgerows, with the weighty monastic ruins at the end of narrow winding lanes, punctuated by wooden gateways silhouetted against the rising sun on frosty winters' mornings, *is* undoubtedly a certain jolly, light-hearted part of the story, but this other part of England, appallingly tolerated, has the effect of paling the watercolour into insignificance. A friend of mine is married to a lady who teaches infant children in one of the inner city areas of Yorkshire. The Yorkshire her pupils see is not a jolly, light-hearted affair, although of course they do shout and cheer. The Yorkshire they see around them rubs shoulders with dereliction, cracked pavements, with the old foundations of nearby demolished industry and boarded-up shops and crumbling concrete tenements: with poverty on the bottom rung. The children know they are in Yorkshire, West Yorkshire, but it is not the comfortable, romanticized Yorkshire full of brass bands and canalside picnic areas and quaint little town squares, the Yorkshire of the fashionable commuter villages, the Yorkshire of the full page BMW and Mercedes advertisements, the Yorkshire with its folklore of sheep shearing and My Life with the Dales folk, the holiday and good food guides, the historic monuments and the restored country walks. When you take the trouble to go to these kids' Yorkshire, or Lancashire, you develop a better, broader, more realistic perspective to the overall substance which makes up the framework of the county, especially if you carry an English tourist's guide under your arm and sit down to read it on a modern concrete bollard blocking the end of a cobbled street, next to a busy main road by some blocks of flats across from an inner city post office on Thursday mornings. In such places, you realize you are on the counties' shop floor, and you have got to go to them on an intimate level to fully appreciate that they actually exist; to construct a serious, credible sense of perspective upon yourself in the vast scheme of things. I taught some infant children for a few days myself

---

OVERLEAF: NEWBY SQUARE FLATS, WEST BOWLING, BRADFORD, DURING DEMOLITION IN 1987.

once, but in a very prosperous town, much to the consternation of at least one of their regular, well spoken teachers who appeared to instantly dismiss my bestubbled, denimed appearance. The kids were six years olds, and a majority of them spoke better, more eloquent English than I did at twenty-five; the verbal rhythms of one or two of them already showing signs of incorporating the sequence of rehearsed stock phrases that bolt together the framework of all consciously *au fait* middle class speech. They were from very well-to-do backgrounds and the towns almost exclusively residential suburbs. They came into the classroom huddled together in a pack, wearing identical uniforms and little straw boaters. From the moment they spoke, it was obvious their futures had been mapped out for them twenty years in advance. Sometime later, I was walking through a very run down big inner city area, walled in from all sides by decaying concrete but with plushly upholstered cars roaring through on adjacent motorways. I passed along a street which was literally crumbling at the seams. There was an enormous black smudge reaching up the side of a block of flats where somebody had tried to set fire to them. The street was smeared with garbage and graffitti, scattered with discarded tires, and with a couple of moth-eaten mongrels nosing amongst the gutters. A few of the nearby house doors were open, and from one of them, a TV set was blaring too loud for its sounds to be legible. The entire street looked to be only just managing to hold itself up, by supplementary benefit. It was nigh impossible to conceive that the city centre skyscrapers I could see behind the haze in the distance contained air-conditioned offices, computer screens, commercial transactions zipping across the world in a matter of seconds from incredible concoctions of technology and plastic. The good looking men and women spilling out of those skyscrapers at lunchtimes from the offices and receptions and think-tanks smelling of leather, expensive leather, power, lifts without the graffitti only computerized push-buttons that whisk the cubicle hundreds of yards effortlessly in a few quiet seconds: they were as alien to this crumbling street of tenements as the street was from a fax machine. A little girl staggered out of the doorway with the TV inside; she was even younger than the kids I'd taught in the prosperous town. She was barely able to walk properly, her plastic nappie was showing from underneath her skirt. She had pony tails, she showed the potential for growing up to be a very attractive young lady, she was like the little kids I'd taught in that she was innocent and wide-eyed. As I drew alongside her, she smiled and showed me all her teeth, which were still all the same size at the front, emphasizing the frailty of her age. When I'd taught the kids in the prosperous town, one of them had come up to me and asked me, very politely, excuse me sir, I understand you worked on so-and-so, and my elder brother would like to enquire as to whether or not you encountered any major production problems during the making of the film. This from a six year old. I nearly fell over, and I promise you I do not exaggerate the words. The little girl in the inner city area grinned and giggled as she came up to me and said, very politely, forming the words as best she could so young, "You fuck off!". I felt the hello-there-little-girly expression on my face crack and splinter and drop off into the gutter amongst the litter with a hollow clatter, like you see in the old Warner Brothers cartoons. I suppose her future was mapped out twenty years in advance as well. I shivered, even though it was the height of summer, and did.

When my Mother worked for the *Rashcliffe Mending Company,* the sand falling through the outrageously oversized cliff-hanger prop from an old episode of *Batman* had reached about 1971. The company was sandwiched into a long terrace of near derelict Victorian shops and houses that opened straight onto the busy main road. Many of the properties were boarded up or crumbling, with roof slates missing, planks of wood nailed over doors and windows, and plastered with bill-posters advertising pop groups, political marches and religion. I'm sure the buildings must have been condemned for many years. The one occupied by the *Rashcliffe Mending Company* stood in the middle of all this boarded-up neglect. You could tell it had once been a shop itself, but now it had the awkward, fraying look of a building not serving its original purpose. The walls inside were covered with mirrors and tiles, suggesting it may once have been a rather shabby cafe. The mirrors reflected everything, turning the interior into a poor man's weak-kneed attempt to create some gloomy hall of mirrors, well away from the fair. The Menders hunched over the tables looked back at themselves as they turned to fumble for their chalks or needles or take a drink of tea. I could watch the faces of the women I fancied without them knowing. This type of shabby Victorian or Edwardian terrace is typical of much of what you still see in these areas today. They proliferate on the wide main roads plunging through the former industrial suburbs into the hearts of cities such as Leeds or Manchester. But big chunks of them have been bitten away. In the places where many mills once stood, pockets of crammed terraced housing, these bits of shops, and a handful of industrial buildings remain, but between them all is what I can only describe as a lack of big lumps of buildings, a lack of verticals, both in the absence of the former textile mills and of their chimneys. Many towns are comprised only of terraced houses, all sorts of houses, so nothing much else pushes up, but because the way these industrial places were laid out was dictated by what has gone, there is that curious open flatness which does not look natural—too much sky visible too near the ground in all the wrong places—which densely packed Northern milltowns somehow shouldn't have. This is the dilemma they must face: how to recover from the wounds and come to terms with the scars where private money does not want to build and doesn't take much care when it does. The practical consideration to remember when making such an essentially sentimentalized observation is that a lot of the old mills are empty, no longer needed, but this tugs constantly against the stark realization that a milltown panorama without its chimneys and the majestic rising buttes of its mills is like a sailing ship without its masts: at the most it looks unbalanced and incomplete, a familiar contour to the eye out of synchronization when devoid of the proper or a planned outline. Even the newcomers who have never seen such towns in the flesh may be unconsciously aware that something is wrong. They are troubled by an uncomfortable interference to the quality of reception in their vision as they home in towards the derelict patches of ground, the exposed interior walls up the sides of mills with the doorways suddenly sealed up with breeze-block, the overall truncated look to that which they see, or thought they would see. And those shabby rows of shops that remain housing second-hand dealers, fast-food take-aways, laundrettes, video shops, car spares outlets, cafes, vying for attention with their garish perspex signs amidst the mills, warehouses, corner pubs chopped off, and the ubiquitous flat patches of open grass where the other buildings once stood, surrounded by modern council flats of the sheltered and silly roofed type, litter, illicit footpaths ignoring the roundabout route of the designer's somnambulance, speckled with broken bottles and dog muck.

Behind the *Rashcliffe Mending Company* rose Rashcliffe Hill. Originally, this had been a road that branched off the main Lockwood Road at the intersection of tarmac at Folly Hall, a few hundred yards from the mending business. It used to be a steep labyrinthine of terraced houses, snickets, narrow flights of steps, and cobbles. It was demolished en-masse during the 1950's, replaced by blocks of flats rendered grey, five stories high. Rather unusually, these grey flats—now badly stained by the elements and basically looking as though they are going mouldy—have ceramic chimney pots on the top of their flat roofs. Thus, you witness the peculiar spectacle of modern blocks of flats with smoke rising from old fashioned chimney stacks. Besides the washing draped on the tiny balconies outside, the smoke is the only thing that makes them look lived in. Further up the hill, two blocks of high-rise flats watch over a small sea of terraced houses directly beneath. The flats were erected in 1965 and stand at the head of an ancient flight of stone steps with the centres worn into hollows by the feet of generations. Round the other side, if you look closely between the weeds, you can make out bits of walls from some of the houses which used to be there, three,

Executive Housing for the 21st Century: Dod Lea, Longwood

four, and five stories high. A little flight of steps that would have been the outside staircase to a paved landing protrudes from a wall; they are filled up with stone now and only carry your eye—up to an austere fence made from slabs of dull grey concrete like a miniature Berlin wall. Undergrowth has taken hold of what may still be a stone floor beneath a thick tangle of roots. Behind glower the sterile blocks of flats, and over the other side of the main road, behind a knot of pelican crossings and the ever present flowing of traffic, a black mill chimney– leaning somewhat noticeably, wrapped in a latticework of steel bracing holding it together—drives up into the sky, next to a Scandinavian-looking car showroom building and an old pub coverted into a nightclub.

My Grandmother worked around here, in several of the mills that trail off down Albert Street, over a period of some forty years, as a weaver, a burler, and a shader. She was involved in the making of khaki during both world wars, beginning her working life on Tuesday 26th February 1918—the day after her thirteenth birthday—as a doffer in the giant Rock Mills at Brockholes, up the Holme Valley; a valley which runs parallel, more or less, with the Colne Valley over the hill in between. Running down Albert Street starting at Rashcliffe was one of the longest successions of straight terraced houses you would have come across hereabouts (there is an almost identical facsimile as you approach Wigan from Bolton). They were tiny, rickety, ancient dwellings, bulldozed as part of a slum clearance program many years ago. They were built to house the employees that fed the mills straight across the street. My Grandmother had several friends who lived here, and she remembers the little houses very vividly, the women standing in the doorways, the short-cuts through miry cobbled back alleys to the bus stop at Lockwood Bar, the lines of limp washing, the dustbins, the snotty nosed kids running in and out of them all. The last mill she worked at down Albert Street was demolished in 1987. She retired from it in 1968 and shows me photographs of the women she worked with, standing on wet pavements with that 1940's squared-shouldered overcoat and black-buildings-in-the-background-vintage-car look. To this day, across the road from this last mill where she worked, you can see a section of the front walls of a couple of the little houses. My Grandmother's friend Nellie lived somewhere here. Only the bottom half of the walls remain. They must have been tiny, tiny dwellings because I measured the width of one of them and found it to be only about twelve feet. The front doors and parlour windows were walled up so long ago the stone which was used has blended tonally to perfection with the rest of the facade. It is as though the houses were built like this, in the last century, anonymous homes for long-gone anonymous gnomes, with no windows and no doors, only openings cut out then sealed back up. Behind them is a fenced compound filled with stacks of portable gas cylinders: the bit of remaining house forms the front perimeter of the fence. The rest of the houses, except for the odd stone gate-post leading into undergrowth, have gone. Where the houses used to be packed, an uneven mass of modern red brick, brown brick, corrugated sheeting, flat felt roofs, pebble-dash, brightly coloured perspex, car parks with fences framed by little chains, and petrol stations lead across to the better built terraced houses, at the other side of the road, which survived demolition. They are occupied now largely by some of Huddersfield's extensive Asian population, who have established themselves in what to all intents and purposes looks like a sector of the living quarters for the old industrial North. This produces one of Britain's contrasts of culture, and it is one you notice in all the major industrialized textile towns in

Yorkshire and Lancashire. Some of the places I have walked through have small pockets, some even bigger pockets as a matter of fact, where the environment has not really changed one iota visually since it was built. I was in Blackburn last year, walking through some of the dense concentrations of terraced housing just off the town centre. I cut through a cobbled back alley rich in Northern flavour, behind the yards to the rear of some houses, and turned into a street. The street was cobbled, retained its original stone-flagged-pavements, and the two long terraces on either side of me rose very gradually towards a large mill and chimney at the top of the street, watching over its old territory and framed starkly against the sky as it did so. A cliched soundtrack from out of the open window in one of those old British black and white kitchen sink dramas enveloped me; the tumultuous shrieking and laughing of numerous children playing echoed down the alley-ways, the sound of feet scuffling with a football and rebounding from a gable end came at me over my shoulder. Somewhere, a train clickety-clacked slowly over a tangle of pointwork, but without the chuffing, without the familiar whistling from the world when it was recorded in monochrome, only the gear change and short burst of flatulence from a modern diesel multiple unit. The scene was so vividly authentic in its sound, I had to stop for a second and close my eyes. A chill wind felt at my cheeks as I opened them and reminded myself of AD 1987 by looking at the chrome digital watch strapped to my wrist. The only difference between the street of old and the street of new was that all the little children I could see running about were Asian. There was not a single caucasian to be seen. The environment was almost exactly as it had been built, refreshingly so, time stood still, due more than anything, and somewhat ironically, to neglect and then desertion by the original inhabitants. But curiously, there definitely seemed to be an underlying feeling of the old sense of community, an overall lack of social competitiveness. The only thing that had changed were the inhabitants and the cars parked outside some of the front doors, all of which opened out onto the pavements. The children were totally oblivious to me, and the youngsters jostling one another for the football were barking commands in a Northern accent that was even stronger than mine. I've seen such scenes duplicated in every major milltown in the North, from Bolton to Bradford, Batley to Burnley. At Rawtenstall, I was photographing an amazing narrow back alley with a mill and chimney towering at the bottom on the opposite page, and some voices came scurrying up behind me, young voices, tugging at my coat, "Oy mister, will yer tekk us photo", "Ere, tekk one o' me will yer". I turned to a circle of tiny Asian girls, replete with bright turquoise and pink and blue and emerald silks.

The *Rashcliffe Mending Company* has gone. Both it and the rest of the dilapidated terrace attached to it were finally demolished about five years ago. They had all been empty for years. I don't know what happened to the mending company, or the bloke called Raymond who ran it, it closed down so long since. Its windows were boarded-up and then also papered with bill-posters asking us to "PLACE THY FAITH IN HE WHO WILL BE THY SAVIOUR". Right up to the end, the black and white hand-painted sign was visible above the door. It was peeling, cracked, becoming difficult to read, but it was there nevertheless, and I looked at it every single time I went past on the bus. Now the location has been grassed over and 'landscaped'. Sometimes, this patch of green is covered with litter, blowing about. It would blend in if somebody had had the heart to spare to perhaps build a solid stone wall around the edge, a low wall, and maybe make it into some kind of park-like area with seating and a

RAWTENSTALL

proper integration of the green. Instead, it looks curiously contrived, an observation at odds with the lack of effort actually put into it. You always feel that such useless patches of green are devised purely for some esoteric psychological reason, drawn from the dated notion that green-is-good and makes people feel better. Usually, all they would need to make them work is a fence framing them, a fence of quality, a fence that relates to the existing architectural fabric, that helps to link everything together. When seating areas are made in such places, they almost always look hideously crude, ambiguous flower beds and rockeries made from old railway sleepers somebody must have managed to scrounge in this world of money, sculpted into pointlessly meandering shapes. But this is the inner city, and I suppose its story never really changes, only its look. The little scene I was standing alongside at Rashcliffe seems to quantify the changes in this look upon such sites, and numerous others scattered right across the North's industrial towns: buildings, history, people, local architectural styles and towns' identities, blown away by the ever turning wheel of progress and the strong winds of change. When they were built, they must have thought they would last forever; they erected them with some commitment, if the standard of a lot of the buildings was anything to go by. The amiable banter of the textile Menders who were some of the last people to circulate around this particular area of sky that is too near to the ground has gone, dead, buried, like the shops and grocers, cobblers and pawnbrokers, their cash registers rattling and their door bells tinkling in years past as the trams rattled and tinkled on the lines set into the cobbles outside; before change blew in through the shop doors with the last customer and ousted the proprietors into the yellowing pages of The History of the Invasion of the Supermarket. Only this flat green expanse of nothingness remains, a blank space where none of the stone from the terrace was kept behind to build even a paltry little wall. I wondered where that stone might have gone, as I remembered standing at a bus stop on a bitter cold November day a few years previously. It didn't stay here I concluded. Once, I nicknamed such places "Those funny gaps in Oldham" because that town has so many: flat patches, incongruous bites wrenched out of the flow of the urban townscape, or replaced by some modern planner's blunder that is as desperate as it is banal.

I walked up the main road and combed the entire area: graphics, plastic, images, people, sounds, they all bombarded the senses: YOUR PRINTS BACK IN 24 HOURS OR YOU PAY NOTHING, leftover cast-iron, pointed roofed houses, box shaped houses, play areas against more green and concrete with climbing frames painted bright red and yellow and blue, DOG FOOD LARGE 20p, youths boasting gutterally about their exploits between women's legs and with beer, litter bins in KEEP BRITAIN TIDY vac-formed plastic yellow, the inevitable

HUDDERSFIELD TOWN
AFC

BLACKBURN, 1988

KEEP LEFT bollards from Forest City with the blue arrow pointing down and housed in white and backlit perspex orange, BACK STANLEY STREET near a few worn cobbles, Victorian stone speckled with mirrored perspex, blue perspex, luminescent perspex, red perspex, KAM TONG CHINESE MEALS TO TAKE AWAY, young girls squeezed into mini-skirts with bare blotchy legs and ill-fitting stiletto heels scraping clumsily along pavements disco DUMM BOO DA DA DUMM DUMM BOO DA DA DAAA music, a dejected looking botched railway station with most of the buildings sheared clean from the platforms and subways decorated with

TOWN SKINS

and graffitti likening policemen to hogs, BETA WASH COIN-OP LAUNDREMATTE, clashing of real and synthetic roof slates, MY DAY OF SHAME or some such headline hanging outside a newsagent's, THIS IS A COMMUNITY PROGRAMME PROJECT SPONSORED BY MSC, more music somewhere, this time with words worth listening to from a charming young man singing of how miserable he is now and asking why does he smile at people who he'd much rather kick in the eye, MAJOR ROADWORKS AT MOLDGREEN SO EXPECT DELAYS UNTIL DECEMBER 1989, bargains, a BEEP BEEP BEEP BEEP BEEP pelican crossing flashing amber now–you–can–go, signs to Sheffield, signs to town centre, signs to Manchester, signs to Oldham, signs for buses, public conveniences, signs of prosperity driving through the urban muddle back to the escape of the residential hinterlands flourishing beyond, signs of day-glo pink and green and red, signs of *Sex Pistols* still signing walls, signs of AIDS, signs of anarchy, signs of the campaign for nuclear disarmament, signs of old red telephone boxes that have a shape and a design and a humanity, signs of new telephone boxes that *are* boxes in clear glass and aluminium and apple green and the familiar yellow logo looking astonishingly like matter transformation cubicles out of the science-fiction films tempting us from the posters in the video shop windows. (The shift in priorities on an elaborate yet simple scale could not be better illustrated than by these two different telephone boxes). Walking about today's urban pastiche, the urban cosmopolitan, the urban urban, one minute you can be slipping and sliding over worn cobbles through an uneven back alley straight out of Dickens, and the next you cut through a concrete ginnel and step into the vac-formed flocculence of consumer society 1988. Sound, aggression, tumult, energy, pace; I stood and looked across to the mill where my Grandmother retired from, almost completely demolished now, its chimney standing proudly, some grey smoke drifting up from the burning debris. As I craned up to observe the tall chimney gently discharging the faintest plume of black smoke hauling itself up onto the breeze, I could hear, from an open window somewhere, the relentless hammering of machine-guns and bursts of American abuse and glass shattering and wheels screetching and basso-profundo explosions from a film or video ejaculating into somebody's living room. I'm sure that if I could have located the source of the racket, I would have seen thunder and lightening bouncing stroboscopically from the glazed expression of the addict, and would have been instantly captivated myself, aroused by the rhythm of light and noise, conditioned as I have been by the blazing hellzapoppin of the night-club and the pop record and the hero's mouthful of gritted teeth and four-letter words and the fast paced beat of the music and exhaust-pipe media generation.

I called at my Grandmother's when the sun was beginning to be obscured by one of the fledgling water-colourists from the start of the walk who had quickly progressed in his confidence to a bigger brush but had spilled a grey wash clumsily over the entire canvas. My Grandmother has an uncanny knack of expecting me and as a consequence had prepared an old fashioned lunchtime spread which I've associated with her since I was a kid. She pickles some onions and cucumber in an old pressed-glass sugar dish, and I apply these liberally to cheese sandwiches made from brown teacakes purchased by her home help from the baker's down by the railway bridge, in front of the recreation ground. I usually consume them with a strong pot of tea—I only ever drink tea at my Grandmother's because she is the only person I know who can brew it so it tastes like tea and not mucky dishwater. It always tastes extremely refreshing at her house after a long walk. The great British cuppa, sipped piping hot with one eye looking through the faintly rising steam at the numerous shiny leaves of the Aspidistra sat on a table in the corner of the room. "Have you any plain crisps?" I asked her. "I know, and I wouldn't be surprised if it rains later on" replied my Grandmother. She is a little hard of hearing, and sometimes I think she tries to guess what I've said by listening to the rhythm of the blurred noises I make. I nearly always have to say everything twice, so I asked for the crisps again, but louder, and she laughed and reminded me that it must be me who speaks muffled, because she can hear the car doors slamming outside in the mornings, and the old lady in the flat underneath her's who sings out loud to *Songs of Praise* on Sunday nights.

My Grandmother is now eighty-three years of age. She lives in one of two upstairs council flats in a block of four. The estate it is situated amidst was built during the early 1960's. Back then, as they were being constructed, my friend The Jembo—the chap who grew into the Guy with a Thick Man-like Neck but has also been known as Job Chopper, Big Jimminy Chip, Space Pilot, and The Longer Lasting Snack—and myself used to play on the 'muck lumps'—great piles of clay and soil and grass in the fields where the flats were to be sited. The fields were at the bottom of our back garden up the street where we both lived at the time, and were the ultimate adventure playgrounds full of innumerable discoveries of the imagination for two little three year old nippers playing at *Thunderbirds*, or 'Thundbuds' as the spelling on one of Choppers old wax-crayon drawings he's kept signifies. When the construction teams moved in to begin excavations for my Grandmother's estate, it was the contents of Pod 3 from Thunderbird 2 being deposited in our own back yards. They began turning the earth and revving up the Mole and giant machines appeared and scaffolding and wooden huts—Eddie Houseman's construction camp was being unloaded. The washing hung out in the neighbour's back gardens was never clean again because it was in our flight path when we scrambled to get to Tracy Island. On the planking on the scaffolding around the foundations of the new buildings—shining out between the mud and puddles like foundations being unearthed at an archaeological dig—the builders' transistor radios, made from cream coloured plastic encased by maroon leatherette cases and with big cumbersome

A Funny Gap in Oldham

tuning dials the size of small saucers, blared out the simple but sparkling staccato guitar rhythms of songs sounding like Johneeeee Remember Meeeeeeeee, as we scrambled up and down the muck lumps wearing balaclavas (remember those?) and getting our wellington boots stuck in the quagmire. The resultant estate is as typical of the '60's as the spindly-legged furniture and turquoise and purple and blue and orange coloured tomorrow the decade looks to have still been forging towards on the covers of home decor magazines from the period, an edition of which I have sitting on the table next to me as I write, and which hasn't half jolted my memory with a grimace. On the front cover is a settee that is brown and orange with soft cushions in the corners that are striped alternately in bands of purple, blue, green, and turquoise. The room containing the settee has pink and blue carpet, orange and white walls, and brown and red furniture. Heck. It looks like a set out of *The Avengers* or a mixing pallet for pop art. You can picture Emma Peel slinking out from behind the dark blue curtains, having just arrived outside the flat in a bright yellow open top Triumph Stag wearing horn-rimmed sunglasses with the pointed frames and having turned off the radio belting forth sounds from within the car's real walnut dashboard. The photograph on the cover of this magazine and those inside it hit you with a punch, but at least the style was new, whether it looks garish or not. I can vaguely recollect such furniture—we used to have a black and red settee with black legs with chrome nipples—and the similar PVC furniture that made rude noises when you adjusted your position at relatives' homes and everyone coughed to cover up their embarrassment, but my Grandmother's one bedroomed flat in 1988 shows no such radical expression in the way it is laid out. It contains a concise mixture of old and new: Victorian, Edwardian, pre-war, post-war; and modern furniture and ornamentation.

Only recently though, I was standing inside an old lady's house that was time standing still. I had stepped back into the textures and colours and smells and styles of mass-market interior decorating tastes in the England of the 1930's and '40's. Everything was absolutely intact: brown tiled fireplaces, original wallpapers that look mellow not crass, painted woodgrain on doors and windows and built-in cupboards, a cast-iron bath, the sides unflushed, carpets which felt noticeably thinner under foot, delicate bone china, enamelled pots and pans and bakelite this and hammered metal finish like Hammerite that. It was the house of an old lady living in a frozen time capsule; insulated from the computerized, synthesized, stroboscopically lit, snap-together outside world of today with its set pieces on the kitchen table and the ironing board straight out of the heads of the stylists from *2001: A Space Odyssey,* plummeting ever more energetically towards the fantastically futuristic sounding The 21st Century, Century 21, Two thousand and whatever: all best said by a deep throated voice-over artist to the accompaniment of a dramatic, rapturous musical fanfare blasting from the headphones of the personal hi-fi clamped to your head at a cinema near you from Sunday. Not a single kitchen utensil or household electrical item in this old lady's house looked to have been bought after about 1950, except, of course, the electronic full-colour viewing portal in the corner of the living room that was the latest state-of-the-art Japanese import. It stood out like a piece of Tupperware on a banquet table full of Georgian silverware. Her house looked somewhat drab by today's tastes, but there was an instant humanity about it. The crudity of the pots and pans implied they had been made by people; the brush-strokes on the hand painted simulation of wood grain suggested a human hand had been at work, not a plastic press or vac-formed uPVC. The overall browns and beiges and golds in the living room flashed with electronically inspired life as the light from the television commercials bounced computer generated pack shots from the gilt-edged picture frames hanging from the picture rails. It was a thick, dampening day outside the house across the moors, and then a vivid green silence filled the room as a snooker match resumed on the TV screen and two young men with pursed lips were concentrating hard to pot their plastic balls in pursuit of tens of thousands of pounds. "Ohhh, he's missed" said the commentator, the world about to end, "Would you believe that". The player didn't as he reseated himself and felt fame and fortune and credibility sliding from his grip. What sticks in my mind about that old lady's house is the vacuum cleaner, all burnt umbers and chocolate coloured and bakelite and patterned canvas on the dust-bag. The design has changed little today, only its colours have become sickly, more clinical, reminiscent of the interiors of social security offices. The old one in her house had a curious kind of drab sanity to its simple, sad looking colouring from forty years ago. I knew this to be its age, because in the box of tubes and accessories—still attached to the card and never removed—was the original guarantee from when she purchased it, in Bradford, in October 1947. Amazing. But there it stood, in the 'glory-hole' under the stairs, as it had stood for so long. She probably carried it home on a trolley bus, or got off at the local railway station when the entire line was still there, with its goods facilities and coal fires burning in the waiting rooms and porters lighting the gas lamps at teatime so they hissed dimly through the night, illuminating the platforms with their tongued-and-grooved buildings and people and staff giving that reassured lived-in quality even I can recall being distinctly warmed by, traditional, enlightening, human, rather like seeing a policeman riding about on a bicycle. But outside the glory hole, outside her house, the world progressed from the steam age to the computer age to the plastic injection moulded age of hi-tech styling, electric fires rather than coal in the station waiting rooms that are left, machines rather than staff, machines doing the jobs of staff, and fuel-injected 0-60mph one and a half seconds faster than your nearest competitors. Seconds, minutes, speed, agression. We become ever more obsessed with slicing time from our daily routines, but this vaccuum cleaner—like an old steel heater in one of the bedrooms that looked like it came from the sets of the original Buster Crabbe *Flash Gordon* serials: all louvres and bullet shaped—was worth seriously studying because it had been manufactured when the world was moving a little bit slower; only then at the beginning of the age of the spring-loaded push-button. Looking at such products, touching them, smelling them, you wonder if they were created at the half way stage between the old world and the new, comprising the genesis of the technological advancements of one with the hangover from the primarily aesthetically inspired styling and textures and shapes of the other. I'm looking at a 1930's bakelite radio I have in front of me, comparing it to the equivalent of today. The old one first and foremost has a shape, a design, a visual sense of expression which comes from the designer's grasping of form, which must have been such an instrument's primary means of attracting attention at that time, and thus garnering a sale. The new one sounds like the most amazing audio experience you ever heard; it has rows of flashing LEDs and graphic equalizers bouncing up and down, but it does not have an aesthetically pleasing shape. Preference is given to the displaying of its gadgetry, and as such it looks sterile and lifeless and, now this is a curious thing, seems possessed of an underlying sense of aggressiveness. It does more than the older one, it is easier to hold because it is significantly lighter, but no way does it *look* as good, in my opinion, as the older one. It is though its technological progression has outweighed consideration for the human input to the design of its casing. The new one looks to have been designed and made by machines, not men.

I know of a house elsewhere, last decorated in 1915, that is still gas-lit in the late 1980's. And next door, computer programmed disco music of the syn-drum and beat-machine type *Badoomphas* out of a hi-fi stack crammed full of micro-chip technology flashing with its chaser sequencers and graphic equalizers in unison with the sledgehammer of noise that erupts from the set of however many megawatt speakers as you take a journey into sound and *pump pump pump up the volume.* When you approach some shops excited by more *dumm boo da da dumm dumm boo da da daaa* spilling into the street, it is increasingly confounding to reach out to open the door and find it suddenly whisked from the air in front of you by a little electronic senso-pad under the mat that has detected the weight of your foot and performed the task in an instant for you. But sometimes, it is wonderful and spiritually enlightening to open a door that creaks slightly, that smells of polish, to hear a bell tinkle; to board an older type diesel multiple unit in the railway stations by opening a door and turning a chromed handle; to sit down on faded upholstery and listen to the clickety-clack of the train's wheels, if the tracks have not been replaced with complete lengths of welded line several hundred feet long that give off nothing but a constant monotonous metallic drone so the vehicle can go faster faster faster. I cherish the simplicity of adding a few precious seconds to my day, the absurdly exultant sensation of turning a big chunky bakelite knob rather than depressing a concaved stud, igniting the gas ring on an old cream-enamelled gas cooker with bright-red dials and chrome beading which I bought from a junk shop because I bought it for its *design,* its almost naïve *humanity,* for the pleasure of participating in its function by igniting its rings with a box of matches, revelling in the operation of a basic machine but running my fingers over its exquisite paintwork, its bulbous edges, then *blowing the match out!* Occasionally, it is gratifying and most stimulating to revel in the ecstasy of using your hands and hearing old sounds, smelling smells, feeling bumps, hearing hollow rattles, rather than looking at objects which somehow belong on the worktops in an operating theatre. It is rewarding to raise two fingers against the onslaught of the push-button and the senso-pad.

But who am I trying to fool? The only reason I am typing so fast as I write this now is because of the touch sensitive keys of this sophisticated electronic machine sat in front of me. It can do virtually anything in generating the production of efficiently typed manuscripts, except extract the words from my head (no doubt we are busy formulating a device to do this). In its built-in, computerized memory, it can store every single word I type as I type it, to perfection, more than my own humble memory could ever hope to do. It beeps at me when I spell a word incorrectly. At the press of another button it shows me how to spell the word on its screen. It erases these errors for me and leaves the page clean. With this machine I can type faster, more efficiently than I can on a manual one. On a manual one, I cannot type very well because every other letter tends to come out lighter than the preceding letter, due to my not being able to depress the keys with equal pressure. On a manual typewriter—now that I am used to modern technology—I curse and swear when I

WINTER SUNLIGHT, BRADFORD, CHRISTMAS 1987. THE CITY'S NEW SHOPPING COMPLEX IS TO BE BUILT IN THE MIDDLEGROUND

make a mistake, the aggression factor creeps in at the inducement, the familiarity, of speed; I have to consult the dictionary if I make a spelling mistake rather than pressing a button and checking a screen. I have to insert paper in the manual machine by hand; on the electronic typewriter, I merely place the sheet of paper onto the top of the rubber roller, press another button, and watch it as it is drawn magically into the machine, aligned, and the printing hammer positions itself ready to begin producing pages for a book. If I type out a page, but decide I wish to remove some words, or insert a completely new paragraph, I can consult the typewriter's memory, tell it what to do, then go and make myself a cup of coffee whilst, at the press of yet another sequence of buttons, the internal electronics miraculously print out the page again as I sit back and watch. The machine is an invaluable tool, it makes the task of writing, of setting writing down, easier, faster, more tolerable, more economical timewise, more technological. But looking at the modular plasticity of its styling, its lack of awareness for the potential of colour, its bland prefabricated texture, I wonder sometimes whether it ought really to be typing its reams of paper from the bridge of a science-fiction film set overlooking the vastness of the Earth slowly revolving below; an observation that stems from the picture created in our minds by such films that suggest whiteness, food pastes, 'living quarters' with built-in toilets under hand basins, and a clinical non-existence without the tab-ends generally.

Self-doubt crept into my mind as the cakes tin entered the room in my Grandmother's hands. (And I have the audacity to pummel a good friend of mine verbally for being unable to resist the temptation to ignite tobacco). Confusion raced as the cakes tin was deposited on the table beside us. I gritted my teeth secretly in defeat. I have a terrible, childish weakness for chocolate cake, and I knew the enticing lump of cocoa sponge would triumph moments from then. Indeed, it is the association with childhood with really makes the special pleasures of sweets so attractive during adulthood. As the lid of the cake tin was opened, the aroma of a fresh batch of thousands of very tasty home-made calories was released into the room with the temerity of a butterfly being released into the air on a spring day. It is sometimes easier to resist temptation in a cafe or a restaurant, but in the house of an elderly person, you are cajoled into submission by the very nature of the cosy environment, the slowly ticking wooden clock on the mantlepiece, the smell of polish and the playing of the daylight across the examples of Victorian furniture sitting next to you under the window. There is a comforting escape, a sort of momentary release from time, when you sit and enjoy a cup of tea in the house of an old person. It's the smells that I always notice the most. Even in this relatively modern council flat that my Grandmother lives in today, she has succeeded in bringing with her the polished living room smell, the shiny wooden furniture smell, from the old pre-industrial revolution cottage she lived in when I was very small, where we used to toast crumpets on the end of a long brass fork, in front of the open coal fire, before it was all razed to the ground. This is a sore subject with her, and I avoided the temptation to encourage her to reminisce nostalgically then, as I looked at the framed photograph of her old village on the living room wall, as it was when it stood, as it was how I can remember it with the uneven pavements, the gas lamps, the curious compacted homeliness that everybody who was uprooted when it was demolished pines after even today. Many of the tenants who were living on the new estate when my Grandmother came to it had been rehoused with her from the slum clearance. You don't dare refer to it as a slum though; this was merely the excuse given by the propogators of what she and her old compatriots regard as an idiotically inspired, hare-brained scheme that never even came to fruition. It is important to remain objective when considering an argument, to resist the temptation to let emotion run riot, but standing on the great patch of useless green that is left today where her houses once stood, I have to be perfectly honest, and conclude that I cannot for the life in me even remotely comprehend the mentality that destroyed the village. Like many such schemes, it seems the instigators were struggling with the visual, with the environmental, the commonsensical, as hopelessly ineptly as if struggling with algebra on a piece of paper. If you make your way through the dense undergrowth which has taken hold where the old footpath and stone steps were that ran down through the centre of the village, you come upon a lone gas lamp standard still standing after all these years, being consumed by crawling ivys, incredibly corroded. The horse has bolted as they say, and I should think it unlikely it will bolt in such a manner again, mainly because the type of old housing developments that made up my Grandmother's village are now extremely desirable on the property market. In some respects, such places that have survived have still bolted, because they are now very fashionable; the prices demanded often very high. The houses are well manicured, in picturesque settings, up steep hillsides with views, clustered appealingly in leafy glades around narrow winding lanes. They are labelled, and venomously defended, as conservation areas, even if conservation is of a rose-tinted, idealized, and wholly bogus variety that allows for the installation of dreadfully ugly thick concrete roof slates upon 18th century cottages, the castration of chimney stacks, the siting of incongruous one-off detached villas which never quite seem to know whether they are trying to be a Scandinavian chalet bungalow, a Victorian folly, or a Spanish apartment, but which generally receive planning permission provided they are made from stone.

Many of the tenants on my Grandmother's new estate yearned for gardens they could call their own. A good number had left behind cherished rose-beds and tiny lawns, cultivated to perfection through years of patience and hard work. In desperation, they have planted rows of flowers in tiny bands of soil only a few inches wide which run underneath the flats' windows around the edges of the vast municipal lawns surrounding the development. At least one elderly gentleman mows this council lawn outside his flat, even though a large motorized machine trundles up and down once a week; he is simply desperate for a garden to tend to. I am told that the same gentleman has in his possession a home movie he shot of the bulldozers flattening his previous environment twenty-odd years ago. Other tenants tend veritable greenhouses sprouting in their living rooms on the inside windowsills. At times, I have visited my Grandmother and been unable to use the bathroom comfortably, due to the profusion of foliage being watered in the bath and in the sink. But my Grandmother's chocolate cake has, thankfully, remained unchanged. Taste her baking with its hard chocolate topping applied spatula-like with a knife, and the buttercream and cocoa filling that is making my mouth water as I type this now, and you'll never touch the plastic tasting artificial stuff with the mysteriously long shelf life ever again. Synthetic pre-packed silage tastes exactly like what it is after the delights of her real cake. The secret lays, apparently, in the quantity of flour to margerine, and consuming the cake whilst it is fluffy and fresh. Even now, in my mid-twenties, I can scrape bowls of her raw cake mix out, before baking, like I did as a kid, and sod etiquette or being 'grown up'. The teachers encouraged us to grow up when we were at school, but fortunately, or unfortunately as the case may be for them, I was one of those who didn't grow up and I must confess that I hope I never do. If adulthood means disconnecting yourself from such enjoyably juvenile characteristics as licking bowls of cake mix out with a teaspoon, give me a pair of short trousers any day. Speaking of teaspoons, I have got into the habit of looking at where things are made whenever I use them (to the extent that terrified waiters in restaurants think you have found dirt on the cutlery), and as I turned the teaspoon over to examine it after I had stirred the milk into my second cup of tea, I noted that it had been MADE IN SHEFFIELD, because it was an old one. I lifted the relatively new fork out of the bowl of pickled onions and cucumber, and squinted to read its embossed stamp in the afternoon sunlight filtering through the living room window: MADE IN KOREA.

Ramsden Mill Lane, Milnsbridge

7

Suitably nourished and refreshed, with a mixture of onion, cake, vinegar, cheese, brown bread, and tannin sloshing around in the slop-pail of the stomach, I left my Grandmother's at about one-thirty. Encouraged by the Indian summer of the morning, the water-colourists upset had been wiped clean and the afternoon was quickly turning itself into a steamy rendition of the great British Sunday. I walked up through a modern residential housing estate, surrounded by the aroma of spring flowers and the aerosol deodorant activated underneath my armpits. The sun was fierce and beamed down at me from high upon its zenith, determined, it would have seemed, to try and ignite the shirt across my back. I noted the plastic urns full of flowers outside the front doors of the houses, the ever-present calling of a cuckoo from high in one of the mature trees around which the development expanded and that dominate nearly every garden. I listened to the constant monotonous drone of electric lawnmowers and hedgetrimmers, the dazzle of the gleaming new cars, some in pairs on the neatly manicured driveways, the red and yellow dots of burglar-alarms speckling the houses, defending it all. Radios and hi-fi stacks played with plenty of bass and hardly any treble in the front rooms, spilling out through the open mock-Georgian windows, circulating around rockeries and bird tables and crazy paving and mock-Spanish fences and gateways. In the back gardens, a number of people were roasting themselves like human beetroots, sipping the proverbial cans of beer, lolling in deck-chairs, frolicking on bath towels laid on the grass. A few of the older bathers were asleep with their heads tilted, at peace, outside toilets and dirty old milltowns and zinc baths in front of the fire things of a bare-stoneworked and subjugated Northern English past. All around the heat positively reeked, an outdoor sauna, pressing down, uncouth in its remorseless baking properties. The overall browns and beiges of the buildings and greeness of the lawns against the backdrop of white and blue was broken up at sporadic intervals by hundreds of little cushions of bright yellow alpines flourishing on the rockeries and on top of the walls framing the gardens.

This, then, was Great Britain in the year nineteen hundred and eighty eight. One nine eight eight. Healthy youngsters were rushing about on their bikes wearing wholesome expressions on their faces and high quality thick soled training shoes on their feet. The surrounding hillsides glowed to the soundtrack, the peace and quiet serenity of English greenery, and birds and the magnificent hazy atmospherics of that hot summer's sound of Sunday silence. The hillside pubs would be filled with lunchtime patrons out for three course Sunday lunch, the clinking of glasses, the puther of smoke, laughter, embellished by the stereophonic middle-of-the-road Val Doonican or Country and Western issuing from the speakers above the horse-brasses and beaten copper jugs hanging from the exposed wooden or fibreglass beams. The verdant landscape was filled with pleasure, eating, sex, music, drink, four-wheel drive, stiletto heels, high-street sun tans, garden centres, religious worship, greenhouses, the love of flowers, happiness and dinnertime political programmes on TV. Through the kitchen windows of the houses surrounding me there would be the fully fitted interiors, the mug trees on the worktops, the toasters, herb-and-spice racks, jug

TEXTURES OF NEW: 'LONG MEADOWS', MILNSBRIDGE

kettles, cordless kettles, coffee makers, extractor fans, the smell of pork and beef and apple sauce and stuffing rising from the non-stick pans sat on the wipe easy hobs embedded into the authentic cottage styled units. Nearly every house living room would have its stone fireplace, its nest of hi-fi stacks, record libraries, colour televisions, video recorders. Without wishing to stare through the windows, but pretending to scratch my neck so I could, I occasionally caught glimpses of leopard-skin and cow hide and tapered copper canopies above log-effect gas fires, and those paintings of wide eyed Mexican girls looking sad with the big tear drops on the cheeks.

I used to live near here many years ago, down on the main road below the railway goods yard. It would be about 1968, and I suppose the Sunday afternoon landscape was still filled with pleasure, sex, drink, the pill, but the dinnertime political programmes on TV were in a fuzzy-edged black and white, instead of crystal-clear full colour video with amazing computer graphics and digitized music during the opening credits. My mates and me used to play where the houses I was passing through were built, when it was all lush meadow full of staring Fresians and peppered with their associated pats, which we stuck lighted Bangers in when they were available from the newsagents before Bonfire Night. We trudged warily between the cows to reach a nearby millowners house and forage for frog-spawn in the ponds in the huge coniferous gardens, until abuse was aimed in our direction comparing our hasty departure to urinating, and ourselves to fatherless little children, as we piled over the nearest blackened dry-stone wall. Now I had the intruder's sensation of analysing everything I saw with a fresh eye. I was retreading footsteps in streets I had not taken for some time. Everything was a lot smaller than when we'd played in and around them all as kids. I walked down an old footpath, barely able to move between the enclosing undergrowth, enveloped by a pleasantly acrid aroma of warm foliage, perfumic, faintly seething with flies. Our old house also looked smaller, strangely forlorn, even slightly embarrassing somehow. Bits of uneven black walls came back in an instant, and suddenly I had a vivid recollection of the marbelite handles on the living room door, on top of their chromed mounts. Distances were ridiculously foreshortened. How the area had been when we used to run about in gangs had been compressed and absurdly abbreviated. A distance of what I used to think was about half a mile I now covered effortlessly in a few strides. Most of all, I was conscious of looking at it all from a much higher plane, which I suppose I must have been, having elongated in height quite considerably since then. I distinctly remember being on the same eye level as the top of some wooden fencing I was passing, when I used to deliver bread on the adjacent council estate on Saturday mornings: now I was a good two feet above it. And if I tried to do a turnover on the handrails at the bottom of the footpath today—which certainly appeals, as does a good old fashioned game of *Japs and Commandoes*—I would probably rupture myself through being too long to completely revolve.

It is strange how visiting childhood pastures like this seems to be to gamble on the fine line between elation and downright depression — well, when visiting scenes of unpleasantness, that is, because the first few chapters of this book certainly don't hold distasteful memories. But here, in such places as the one I was walking through on this hot afternoon, there is an immediate tendency towards self-pity. Here, in this busy suburb, we used to run a corner shop for some years after my Father died. It went bankrupt when the area was redeveloped and the shop's custom was immediately castrated, similar to the way in which Sunnybank Mills affected the shop at the end of our terrace when it closed down. I can remember the dark old houses, the lace curtains behind the misty windows, the scoured doorsteps, the corroding enamel signs bolted to our shop front, and poverty. I say poverty because, for some years after the shop was demolished, we were at times genuinely penniless. My Mother was a widow, and any widow reading this will remember the way in which income tax was always structured (this may have changed now) in such a way that when there was a rise in state benefit (the widow's pension), a corresponding amount was doctored in your wage packet, so you were not really any better off at all. Money was merely shuffled about at the expense of the employer and the employee. Our poverty was, of course, relative, and it fluctuated, but was never very far above the breadline. I say relative because, although there were occasions when we literally had only a few coppers to last a week or a fortnight, and I was wearing hand-me-down clothes with patches sewn on the knees of my trousers to school, and we had to borrow money from my Grandmother to tide us over, there was still the television in the corner of the living room, and our house was clean. There were other impoverished households I can vaguely remember going into very occasionally, down damp backstreets in parts of Huddersfield I can no longer identify, which were genuinely poverty-stricken. This was the late 1960s, when yards full of sagging outside toilets were still commonplace in the shadows of vast mountains of scaffolding from which were emerging futuristic tower blocks. This handful of poor houses seemed to perpetually exist on cold overcast days (nonsense, of course, but that is how they *remain* in one's memory) and, I recall being taken for a ride in a motorbike and side-car—the side-car was completely home-made from hardboard—and inside some of the houses themselves, with their frowzy smell of chicken-stew blended with the aroma of dog sweat and babies.

I must emphasize this point about our own poverty being relative. The mention of poverty, and these loose reminiscences here, will have brought to mind a bread-and-margerine picture of some gloomy industrial suburb during the 1930s. Yet within a stone's throw of our own street, there were newish semi-detached houses, brand new cars, and fields quite close by to that. Our own household may have been broke, but we queued for fish and chips in the same shop with the company foreman and his wife, and there was *UFO* blowing my mind to pieces on TV. Things never got quite so bad that we had to dispose of major household possessions to make ends meet, although on a couple of occasions, the old car we ran had to be sold off, and once, when things got abysmally bad, I sold some of my toys to raise a few pounds. Notice how poverty is generally defined in terms of goods which could otherwise be considered as items of luxury. How does one measure poverty today, in the post-war consumer world of the West? Our poverty *was* genuine at times, but it was relative to what was the average standard of living of the day. The rest of the time we were 'merely' poor, which is to say we didn't go hungry, but never had the money to afford luxuries. And, you will have noted, I had access to further education and was able to decide on a career a long way from what would have been accepted as the norm in an old industrial suburb in a Northern town. Here it is that you come upon an extremely important point when considering the under-privileged in today's world—this being that these days, life is generally regarded in *standards* of life, rather than quality of *life*. The placing of the italics is very important here. Our neighbours, and our relatives were unaware of our situation at the time, because we skillfully avoided arousing any suspicions

Blackburn 1987

of such, and were still able to keep up a type of parody upon comic-gentility in our appearance. We were always respectable, but we were poor. The obvious question is: does poverty, extreme poverty worse than we knew, exist in contemporary Great Britain? The answer is yes, of course it does, and only an idiot with blunt sensibilities stands up and pretends that it is otherwise. But you have got to take the trouble to go and seek it out to be sure of this, because there is a conscienceless political conspiracy which will try to convince you it is otherwise. Poverty in Great Britain during the 1980s really exists as unofficial history, systematically denied during television interviews and glossed over in certain magazines. Like unemployment, it has been re-defined as a social rather than an economic problem, which is the key to the heart of the dilemma. Even when you go to the impoverished places, or what appear to be such, you can be thrown by some of the contradictions you see, and which reflect the confusing mish-mash of social furniture comprising the layout of the age of false values in which we now live. As a small example, look at the photograph opposite. Here is a cliched image from contemporary Northern England. This scene exists in the booming, affluent Britain created by Mrs. Thatcher, where standards of living are supposedly higher than at any time during British history. Several ingredients are present in this picture which will have aroused the wrath of many sensitive social observers. The decaying cobbled street, the wholesale demolition of an enormous sector of Blackburn on a scale I cannot remember having witnessed since the slum clearances of the late 1960s. Even the cold-looking grey sky deliberately adds to the overall flavour. Noddy housing and standardized living must surely belong to another planet which somehow behaves differently to the one depicted.

Now study the knot of young figures huddled at the base of the Victorian lamp-post. These bubbly and energetic youngsters were actually gypsy children, who immediately converged upon me and requested I take their photograph. Slum children, you may ask? Not necessarily, because all is not what it seems. They may have had dirty knees, so to speak, but behind where I was kneeling to take the shot were the caravans where they lived. They were those really impressive-looking, multi-wheeled aluminium mobile homes which appear to have been inspired by 1950s American cars, and which I understand cost a great deal of money. Parked outside several of these caravans were absolutely brand- new, state-of-the-art sports cars, with all the attached frills and trimmings. These people are supposedly working class, but how does one define 'working class' any more? Again, notice how the easiest way to put across your point today is to talk in terms of luxuries. To talk, in other words, not in terms of human beings or their emotional substance, but in terms of what is essentially a form of social plumage which everyone unconsciously fastens on to as the means to judge each other by, thus jettisoning the need to bother with character or sensitivity. Or, to put it another way: *Image and Envy*—over-riding the need for human integrity, thereby encouraging the development of a classless, quasi-brutalized robot gradually being stripped naked of all its spiritual essentials in the way it relates to, and forges, social relationships. And who has not watched the documentaries on TV about the 'poverty stricken', those supported by the Welfare State, and failed to notice the fully fitted kitchens the people are sitting in as they are being interviewed? Or noted the comments about how the mortgage repayments for the modern chalet bungalow are falling dangerously behind? And how the video recorder, then the colour television, then the car, then the package holiday have all had to be reluctantly sacrificed? The truth of the matter is that this is only one ambiguity in the overall confusing picture. Real poverty exists for both young and old alike, not only of the type you see when you emerge from Charing Cross station late at night and pass beneath that huge railway bridge just there. The little girl I mentioned earlier in the inner city suburb exists as a kind of symbol of another part of the story for me. Personally, that incident was one of those sudden instalments of your life which catapult your thinking off onto a totally different tangent, with the combined impact of a well-written political book (an extreme rarity, by the way) and a paper bag being exploded in your face. It affected me at the time because up until about that point, I was still astonishingly naïve. After that, though, it was like suddenly understanding the simple plot to an extremely complex story, clearly, and for the first time.

Walking near our old house, I thought back to school. I saw the place where I had once been spotted playing truant by one of the peevish neighbours, and recalled the whipping I received with the dog-lead as a result. I was also peculiarly irritated by the new streetlamps. From quite a young age, I have had an innate fascination with street furniture. It is one of the quickest ways of categorizing the atmosphere of a given moment. Study the gradual deterioration in the quality of streetlamps and you see a concise mini-history exemplifying the overall shifting in social and economic priorities over the past fifty years. From the ornate gas-lamp to the absolutely perfunctory galvanised metal tube in a few generations. Utterly featureless poles illuminating streets full of miniature Edens lovingly massaged to individual perfection within garden boundaries. It is a little story which says so much; one of the numerous cosmetic elements going on all around you which help to accurately define the age in which you live. Looking back over some of the earlier chapters I have written, I see there have been a number of occasions where I have placed emphasis upon what many observers might classify as insignificant details. It is important to understand that most people who criticize the deterioration of environmental standards are not necessarily talking about the inferior product itself—that is merely a formality of circumstance—but the flaws in the philosophies at the root of it. It is no use dismissing such things as unimportant. For it is precisely the same attitudes which have never been irritated by seemingly useless bits of apparel as inferior street furniture, or tasteless building materials from which fortunes are being made, that will be arranging sight-seeing trips via the space shuttle to view the world from orbit as it is being slowly destroyed by the Greenhouse Effect.

Curious, how topicalities change. At the time we all used to run about these streets I was walking in, the 'world threat' which shaped the background to your world-view was atomic war. Anyone over twenty-five will remember the Sunday papers with their nauseating diagrams of the strike patterns of nuclear warheads depicted on the ends of huge arrows aimed at the British Isles. Or the absurd talk at school where everyone perpetuated the myth — in other words, tried to convince themselves — that hiding behind a sheet of newspaper would shield you from the blast. Or the uneasy way in which your young mind tried not to notice the news reports about Soviet submarines being sighted off the Scottish coasts again, as you played with your toy tanks. Now the world is supposed to be slowly, inexorably burning up, and in the classic tradition of humankind, we are aware of rather as we would if it were only a drawing-pin caught in the planet's enormous collective shoe. A little twitch and it will go away. Angle your foot to one side and you can still move forward agreeably. And why? One does, of course, somewhat cynically wonder. I have heard it claimed emphatically on many occasions that nature probably *will* have the last laugh after all. Sometimes, I wonder though. There will no doubt be a way to twist the Greenhouse Effect to commercial advantage somehow, thus saving the world from doom.

Thinking of this prompted me to do something they say you should never do—I looked up at the sun. Whenever you do this, it always seems to suggest without any shadow of a doubt that the world is really some huge, ridiculous theatre stage. I first remember considering this perspective during my 'teens when I read hundreds of books, nearly all of which were of a science-fiction nature. Obviously, at school this was balked at. Science-fiction was not 'proper' writing, just as pop music was not 'proper' music. But yet, what science-fiction writing (and film) inevitably forces a sustained reader into acquiring is a world view. Because it continually speculates towards the world's future, it speculates politically, which tends to leave the effect upon the reader of subconsciously considering subjects across the entire social spectrum, from technology to people to international affairs. It arouses a 'sense of wonder', and this was largely what happened when I used to look up at the sun (I would not recommend this), sometimes so hard I could have sworn the flames were leaping from its surface.

Once you have imagined the Earth as what it really is—a large blue-green sphere some twenty-four thousand miles in diameter, hanging in space ninety-three million miles from the sun—and experienced this with that peculiar combination of detached humour and bemused contempt, coupled with a momentary qualm of utter helplessness, it somehow becomes increasingly difficult to take all the petty social grievances occurring upon its surface very seriously, although many need taking very seriously indeed. One well-placed meteorite the size of the one they reckon might have caused the extinction of the dinosaurs forging through space towards it, and suddenly, it would probably find it could get on with itself, as nations tend to find they can during times of war when snobbery becomes eclipsed into the emotionally immature absurdity it really is.

This same light was shining now. All around, the birds chatted and the day smiled, heated up by the light being relayed across that inconceivable vacuum of silence at a hundred and eighty six thousand miles per second. That distant source of life thrashed and writhed, a colossal ball of molten energy comprised of a power that would make the atom bomb look like somebody striking a match. Place the Earth next to Jupiter, the biggest planet in our solar system, and to imagine the correct scale, it would be something like placing a golf-ball next to a beach-ball. The Earth is the golf-ball. Place the Earth next to the sun, and you would need to reduce it to something the size of a pea, if still using the beach-ball to scale it by. But here it is, this 'big blue marble', silently revolving, ninth planet in the constellation of whichever galaxy, seasons coming, seasons going, all at the convenience of that distant sun; this tiny planet playing out its turbulent history against an intergalactic compound of a million million other suns which we call stars.

There was a cat neatly folded on somebody's windowsill, dozing and meditating. Probably it would be keeping one eye on the chatting birds. The birds in turn would be keeping one eye on the insects moving in the grass. And all around, beneath my immense size-eleven shoes crashing down upon the tarmac with each stride, more microscopic predators, the other tiny parts in the same chain reaction of endless preying and survival:

each one deadly serious about its own self-contained little universe, oblivious to the shadows of a pair of feet forging towards it.

Probably, a scientist could prove I had flattened several self-contained universes in the few minutes it had taken me to walk up this street.

I turned about face and made my way up through the old streets and footpaths, aware that it is often crazily worthwhile to experience that curious intangible sense of melancholy generated by the recollection of past times, and which so poignantly reminds you of your positioning in the present. I remembered the absurd hopes pinned upon those sheets of newspaper; the creased old photographs in the tatty shopping-bag at home, the trees noticeably smaller behind the foolish young faces grinning at the camera in that far-off time when the world was only a huge silly adventure story out of *Boys Own Adventure.* I shook my head resignedly. The place was beginning to turn my stomach. For a hideous second, I felt I could have blasted it all with a flamethrower. I visualized the rainy day we came away after the removal van and waved two fingers and said good riddance. Mentally, I was doing the same thing now and made straight for my old school, out of sight at the other side of the hill above me.

I sat on a seat at the edge of some playing fields near the school and surveyed the lush green valley spread out in front of me. The seat was surrounded by worn, hardened earth, and a sea of battered sweet-wrappers and bent cigarette ends. It was covered in felt-tip generated graffitti and splodges of bird muck. I studied the scrawled signatures and rough language and references to young rock musicians, searching for witticisms, until I found the only one:

Roses are red,
Violets are blue,
I'm skittserfrenic,
And so are you.

Spelling complete and unabridged. Somewhat inspired momentarily, I looked at my notepad in front of me and chewed the end of my pen. I contemplated writing some poetry, and made a few vague scribbles, but gave up half-heartedly before I had even really begun, embarrassed at such weak attempts sitting on a Huddersfield hill-top. I thought back to the time I spent in the school behind me. The type of poetry we wrote—or I should say I wrote—seemed to be the most banal rubbish you could imagine, with lines such as 'The hippo grunts and opens its huge mouth and yawns' (taken from a poem I have just dug out, written inside those buildings) and other such nonsense. Genuine creativity was just not encouraged, much less nurtured. It was almost something to be semi-ashamed about, a kind of school mascot brought out onto classroom walls during parent's evenings. My school days seemed to be suspended beneath a vaguely totalitarian atmosphere, forever discouraging you from thinking or expressing yourself individually. The best thing about them was a cast of the most incredible characters, young and old, that I shall make use of in one form or another at some point. Talking of individuality, at art college, things often went too far the other way. There was a lecturer, a typical bearded hyper-intellectual, his conversations

Textures of old: Mankinholes near Todmorden

laced with "didactic" and "existentialism" and "eclecticism". He once argued with me, as we did from time to time, that when an art student does a piece of work that he or she hates and wishes to throw away, unconsciously, they really love it without realizing it, because the spontaneity of the ambiguously autonomated neo-eclectic transcriptions that structure the very creative impulses that the human mind must expound if it is to survive the illusionment of disillusionment—or something like that–shaped the very thought structure of the act of generating new ideas that are not restricted to the reality of reality. This may have been a valid point, but I reminded him that when I wished to throw a piece of work away, it was because I considered it to be a load of rubbish. Actually, I never used to throw paintings or drawings or sketches away. I would throw paint at them, or beat them with a rolled up tabloid newspaper, or set fire to them in my sketchbook.

I wrote a poem some time since, when the TV screens were still showing the demolition and decay, and which expressed my anger at the time. It is based upon a paragraph from chapter one and more or less sums up what the people in the street were saying and thinking as they lamented the decline of the old industrial North.

All around a kingdom's man-made cliffs of stone,
    Confessing to the melting light,
With angry refrain, and anguished fractures
    of a lost faith,
As the boot of a greedy Demon
Stamps flat the tortured carcass of
    a stone eternity, Or so they thought.

It was, when once it formed a gigantic belching
    Chunk
Of a landscape's grisly energy,
    Throbbing cloth and sweat and muck
into purposeful streets, convulsing with
    mesmerised light, playing with a gulping
Urgency upon
    Heavenly rhythms, infatuating a claustrophobic
little backstreet corner, Despite the
    Dirt, in the sun-bleached past of rainy days;
In the past of shrivelled days standing at
    Bus stops bolted against pitch black walls,
Alive.

But knowing now this New single imbecile's
    Laughter,
Screaming with a greedy necrophiliac's sordid pleasure,
    upon a stupefied North, so flat,
So senseless, or so the ignorance said,
    As it used to laugh, and now it did,
As a blue or grey day stretched in to envelope
    All
Whilst spewing forth harkening sounds of a new
    Emphatic sky, Rheumatic with the pain of a
Great block of Industrial Time,

Devoured ruthlessly, without the jury of
Purposeful faces to say
Spare The Agony Of An Old Face's Murder—
Bugger elsewhere! Heathen fatherless swine,
Raping confidence roosting within a framework
Of green and roughened landscapes and sculpted
blocks of hand-shaped domicility,
And now a mill's old debauchery, fallowed
by a callous
Hunger. It was gone.

For where once watched the implacable solidity
of austere frowning from all sides,
Now swallowing up the wound of this new space,
Flagrant with a bloody animosity
from which emerged a new void
Huge, pregnant
With a racing confusion, never compensating
For the lost motions
of emotion and sustenance consumed by
Death in another ugly form,
Claiming from the land now the ubiquitous
Oldness of an old land lost,
To the depthless god of an ugly ignominy;
to need this piece of broken compensation
Lost within a new view of a house.

This house, these rows, these havens
skewered strong to attention
As long as these chunks of Northern now
reported lost had done so too,
Before being taken back to the greedy iniquity
Of time from whence they sprung,
transcended by a new Time, hungry for new
Spoils,
To scavenge and ravage in a gluttonous orgy
of self-inflicted orgasmic prophecy.
It disgorged forth from the seething pleasures
Of angels lost and crosses smashed
Upon unnoble heads banging with hunger,
Upon the face of this ravaged land
Lost and torn asunder amongst the calloused
episodes no longer attuned to the new Demons,
Whose blankets of stormy sorrow closed up within
sheets of callous morals, suspiciously stripped
Bare, of emotional essentials sucked dry
Upon the arid mud-bank of deepening unchange,
and joking whilst feeding, upon peevish
Thoughts? No.
No emotions piled high upon the gibbering
Empty jars upon a shelf stocked full of gold

With scorched souls strong only from the
Pride of an intangibility.

Now this past dirtied over with the sacrosanct
Scum of lost corpses festering inside
This vibrant pulse of angry rumours lost,
The emptiness,
of a village,
Filled with a new standing to attention soon
To Be
Put to the test as a mouth huge
strips away the screaming and grinding
on the end of calculating strings;
Of belching concrete and a roaring bloody
Yorkshire, its spine snapped,
Or so they said,
Before the bits of tin spawned forth from the
empty jars of an ephemeral pledge; propped up
the swaying serenity of new flimsy breezes
catching the sunlight,
like these rotten pieces of history lost,
angry, ruptured and torn, jettisoned with
The aftermath of a hundred bloody years lost
Faith. These damned bloody jaws snapped off
great
Slabs of the North's drugged afterbirth of an
eternal slimy toil. Or so they said,
Its figures prudent and now askance but not
deterred. As the irony of a new stone and tin
filled land exploded into the hungry light of
a new blazing plastic sun, Or so they said;
pretending those who saw the glozing sun's
hollow worth; studying the irony of a million
Angry ghosts ripped out and bleeding, in a
Memory of no magna-charta signed here.

This soul,
rampant with a cliched submission, fodder for
TV visions, who at least saw the battle
At no time of mercy, at a time of greedy
Purpose's slaughtering indecision.

Before the arraigned scavengers rammed home
Their feeding squabbling greedy fighting
Tearing, amidst an orgasm of thrashing sound
and tumultuous demolition exploding across a
Huge place in the old playgrounds lost to an
arrogance breathing down upon all those
Ruptured fellows,
Now brutalized by the inevitable
Dawning of the years of a lost conscience,

Few could see it, never some winds of strongest
Blow, or so they said as no clouds parted
To shine a new light, As this light of old,
who swore blind this present would live, who
Couldn't face the change of needs to false
New fires for old stenches, cajoled behind
The new affronts upon hollow insides,
No numbness needed to feed them before
A sledgehammer to a head came filled with
exploding, blasting, wrenching, screaming
Nerves snapped across a vision of this falling
sky collapsing in,
With cracking eggshells of a million skulls,
Split by thunder and a great enclosing smoke,
Then a knife slicing and tearing too,
gouging up to the hilt, comprised of no flimsy
Tin or make-believe life but the pretence to
Defy.
With both hands firm upon a bloody hilt.

They would succumb but they would not.
Or so they said. Before the ironic rewinding
Of history cleared spaces for a disparaging iron,
No more emancipation of a vicious unrelenting
Here. Ripping across the lower part of a village
Heart and a big land, with as ferocious an
Impact on the skyline

As when the mills and that land were first built.

Or so they said! Bugger elsewhere! Or so
They said! But who listened?
Only an empty staring sky. Or so it said.
With that land still watching false clean fires,
Striking matches for old stenches anew.

As when the mills and that land were first
Built.

2

My shirt sleeves flapped in the strong breeze that was whistling ever so slightly on the edges of my ear lobes. In between the trees at the opposite side of the valley, the roof tops of houses from all the different generations that had made Huddersfield glistened in the sunlight. The crumbling concrete tenements of the street where the little girl had come up to me smiling and announcing some of the first words she had learned to speak so proudly, so much so as if she expected me to put a tick at the end of her page and give her a gold star, were a long way from where I was sitting that warm afternoon. The trees had only recently come into bloom, and from this distance, they looked like a great mass of lichen hiding the join with the backscene at the edge of a model railway layout. Similarly, I could see a smooth field full of model cattle, grazing way off over to my left, where my Grandmother had lived so long ago before her village was demolished; and where my Mother had been born into one of two cottages since converted and sandblasted and yuppified into one. Pushing up from the trees were a couple of old mill chimneys, some church steeples, and a few blocks of high-rise flats, incongruous, alien looking, but even their pomposity was emphasized and looked good because of the glorious sunny weather.

Two young lads came up over the crest of the hill, accompanied by a gasping, lolloping labrador. They were kicking what I took to be a rugby ball around for it, and it galloped after it, excited, nattering disjointedly to itself under its breath, tongue slavering and covered in pieces of grass, impersonating an overweight yellow greyhound, a bad simile if ever there was one. I'd registered that I'd thought the rugby ball an odd stripey colour, but it wasn't until it bounced in an unbalanced, one sided manner a couple of feet from where I was sitting that the "YANKEE CATZ", or some other such blurb on it, told me that it was actually, surprise surprise, an American football. The dog pounced on the ball then suddenly bolted upright with a serious expression: a mongrel was staring at it threateningly from about twenty yards away, and they approached each other, the football abandoned, muscles tensed. They took turns to sniff each other's backsides then were instantly engulfed in a slavering, ferocious tangle of growling and high-pitched yelping that lasted only for a split second. Foul mouthed abuse was turfed very matter-of-factly by the two young lads, comparing the labrador crudely with sexual intercourse and being fatherless again; then the football was kicked high in the air and bounced to become the focus of attention once more.

I was only about two miles from Milnsbridge, but the scene spread out in front of me could have been almost anywhere. In some instances, walking through such places it is impossible to stifle the feeling that you are definitely not in England, let alone the North of it. You are in a little pop-up imitation of a continental Beaujolais town from a kiddies' fairy story book—cardboard looking, without the proper details, only mocked, painted-on, suggested—or a middle-American suburb from a Steven Speilberg fantasy movie, with the tapered gable-end chimney stacks made from crazy paving slabs. But you are not in England, at least not in the country you have looked up to and learned to recognize from books and from passing through since you were young. If you are still in the same country when you pass through these new environments of today, somehow you cannot help but feel you are witnessing an England that is gradually losing the ability to create its own inspirations, except possibly in teeming and lading. As I had come up through the residential estate earlier in the afternoon, I had been walking through a scene from the Steven Spielberg movie. At any moment, the sky would darken, and the children racing about on bicycles would skid to a halt and shield their eyes as they gazed up in wonderment at the monstrous alien spacecraft disengaging itself from a pure white cumulus. Their bicycles were of the BMX type, all bright yellow and blue frames. Even the knobbly thick tires were cast in matching rubber colours. Others skooted about on skate-boards—back in fashion—dressed in multi-coloured tracksuits playing at the *A-Team* and *Knightrider:* just as we had played at *Batman* with our duffel-coats fastened only around our necks for the cape; and thrown each other across the desks in mock simulation of slow-motion cybernetic strength, because we'd been playing at *The Six Million Dollar Man.*

Back at home, the uncleared mess that used to be the mills behind the house was becoming rather too much to bear. I had decided that change was necessary. The place was beginning to depress me, looking out across the same tangled clumps of weed infestated carnage. The place I had lived in for fourteen years was to be left behind at last. I'd got the orange "BROOK BOND TEA" sign from the wall of the closed corner shop, as I'd determined I would, but the bedroom that once looked across the mills, the bedroom with the single bed and its early explorations of the female body–they had become largely meaningless. Now I was moving into another house, still the same sort of terraced house, but in another environment altogether. I had recently taken some final photographs of the old mill site because now there were fresh rumours brewing of new developers moving in to build. But I was getting out. The place was dead, or at least devoid of the life it had. Again, my sentiments were based purely upon knowing how it used to be — alive — and it was this that dictated such a reluctant evaluation; but there was an atmosphere of stagnation which needed attending to, and there had been little evidence given over the past five years to instigate its immediate cessation. It was absurd, absolutely inexcusably absurd, that a piece of derelict, half cleared ground on such a scale should have been left to rot unattended for so long. Whatever the reasons, whatever the excuses, I do not see how this state of affairs could have been given credence for so long, and let it be said. Some years back, one of the neighbours heard that with such a mess behind their properties, the occupants could claim a reduction in rates from the local authority. Forms were distributed, gossip circulated—primarily in the hope it would encourage a speedy clearance of the land—visits were made by local government officials. A young lady came to my house and told me I would be receiving a reduction of £2.00 in my annual demand — I think it was this figure approximately: it's so long since, and was such a waste of time, I cannot remember the precise amount. Five years ago, when the town received the main gutting of its industrial intestines, you could make an easy comparison between it and the more guarded fashionable areas. These were being preserved against wholesale bastardization and prefabricated intruders, like the best tea service which you had bought as a wedding present and which was immaculately kept, viewed once or twice a year when you felt as though you wanted to enjoy its special elegance. But Milnsbridge was moving with the hardened edge of the times. It wasn't being treated as the best tea service or with delicate hands. It was becoming chipped and cracked, the patterning scratched and faded, because it was the cheap crockery used every day throughout the year and, as with any everyday set of mugs and eating utensils, it was not being given special treatment but was thrown about, dropped, used as a makeshift ash-tray, used for mixing paint in, used even as a coconut-shy at times, until some of its pots became so soiled the handles dropped off and they were thrown away and a new one was added in that obvious, tasteless manner; and then there was the awkward look of a town that was damaged, patched up, stained, and comprised of so many different elements, with so many chips missing from the edges, it no longer had a continuity. I watched it happen. Should the mess up at Longwood have been cleared, it would have represented a more positive sign; if something worthwhile had been erected in the old mills'

Rochdale

place, or if it had merely been tastefully landscaped and bedded back in and turned into some kind of park area. To anyone with any imagination, if imagination could only find the space to manoeuvre with any semblance of genuine enthusiasm, there are untold variations on numerous themes that would work. But maybe this was the root cause of such problems and why it is that they consistently refuse to go away: in the modern world you feel there is increasingly less room allowed for the manoeuvre of the imagination in this sort of instance. To care costs money, and the equation is always such that you are never able to care fully, only half-heartedly. Emotion rears, as always, providing the psychological crash-barrier from which to bounce one's thoughts, lunging with savage reposte at your objectivity and subjectivity—the mental yardstick from which to rebound your measurements.

Yardstick.

Yard.

The back yard at home was terribly overgrown now. I hadn't tended it, so maybe I was no better than the tangled mess of mill wreckage over the wall. Much had transpired since I'd put the dead cat in the dustbin several years previously. Big gaps had opened up in both the spirit and the structure of the suburb, turning it—I cursed for admitting it—into a crumbling mockery of its former existence. That was it. Something had gone, probably the same thing that goes, the non-descriptive nothingness, that hangs over the town after it has been bombed and is pulling itself together in the old post-war films with the contrasty lighting shot on location in central London, with the shattered remnants of bombed out buildings behind the kids playing on the waste ground reflecting in the craters full of sludge. This need not have happened in places such as Milnsbridge if a more positive, more planned strategy had existed for the years ahead. We are encouraged by the commercials on TV to save our money, to store it, build it up, take out pension schemes, life assurance, to think to the years far ahead, so why not the same with towns? I think I know why, but there was, and is, no need for areas of decay, and there was, and is, no need for incongruous new buildings to be erected that always stink like somebody begrudged them reluctantly, because of the lack of enthusiasm that is part and parcel of their appeal in the economic system, where inferior products are a 'necessary' counterbalance to superior products. But things can be done right, because they are done right in fashionable areas. But it is nearly always only the fashionable areas where things are done for any real reason other than glum function anyway. Milnsbridge is not fashionable. It never has been.

If you are a newcomer to the town, or are hurtling past it in a railway carriage across the impressive viaduct on your way to or from the busy polished and well fed commercial centres of Leeds or Manchester—about twenty miles away in either direction—you cannot fail but notice the great gaps that have opened up in the flow of the town's layout from this angle. But oddly enough, the reflection from all this is that the place has a distinct lack of pretentiousness, in some respects, it could even be seen as a sublime vitality, its atmosphere at once easy going and completely genuine. This is probably the only originality it has left, which I think is its most priceless asset of all. The town is still unmistakably working class, as I have always known it, although this is of course almost wholly the reason why it has been undermined. Some of the social mannerisms discernible elsewhere have not settled here, at least not in the straight narrow streets branching off Market Street and up by the overgrown canal. Milnsbridge has not been gentrified, possibly because people on lower incomes have traditionally to concern themselves with basic living and do not possess either the resources, or the time to spare and organize pressure groups to lobby elected representatives about something as relatively trivial as tidying up the run down industrial areas of the town where they live. Having said that, the people living in the area immediately surrounding the Sunnybank Mills bombsite have certainly spoken out and lobbied corporate bodies, but still there has been no impact. Only photographs of faces in the newspapers showing concern and giving more promises about compulsory purchase orders which never seem to materialize. The way I was brought up, I was taught that to give a promise was to mean to keep it. Your conscience was troubled if you didn't, and this last you weren't taught. Despite this, it is worth remembering that the reason such places as this town, and numerous others scattered right across the North's old industrial areas, maintain a genuine spirit at all is through a combination of being under-privileged, neglected, but essentially undesirable on the property circuit, and not a great deal more.

Milnsbridge does, however, continue to be a relatively busy little industrial suburb. Although environmentally somewhat neglected, its shopping facilities are reasonably comprehensive (it stocks everything from vegetables and basic food provisions to furniture, carpet, pets and one of the finest Indian Take-Aways I know of, considering the perpetual weakness I have for Asian food), but, like many such places the length and breadth of Great Britain, its real manufacturing potential for the future remains untapped. Doubtless, there are in this area, as in hundreds of others, craftsmen working quietly down backstreets, satisfying their creative urges to design, to make, to produce, their own original British products such as, say, furniture (I know of several myself). But they are largely frustrated from offering it to the mass market in their own country because of cheap imports fellow 'countrymen' are bringing in, in gigantic bulk loads from elsewhere. Labour costs in their own nation, and the price structure of the economy, looks to be piled against them. The best story I heard connected with this concerns inlaying wood into furniture. Because of labour costs in Great Britain, one of the large well-known furniture manufacturers in this country imports vast amounts of components from a South American country, where labour costs are significantly cheaper. To combat this, a British citizen has now devised a machine which can print the *effect* of inlaid wood onto furniture, without having to physically do it. It is so convincing, I am told it is nearly impossible to discern it from the real thing. Now this erstwhile British citizen has patented his invention and will make a fortune, because he can even undercut the labour costs of the South American country: because he can do it all with a few buttons and a few machines, but—most significant of all—only a few people. This has to be good for Britain. It reflects human ingenuity, it must generate more wealth, however proportionately small, for the nation. But is the sad epitaph to this little story not the simple absurdity of it? That people in this country cannot do the job with their own hands, even if they were there and wanted to do it, and to bring the job back into Great Britain, only a machine can be devised to *simulate* the effect? It is so hilarious as to be almost incomprehensible, but it is a disturbing indication of the direction in which we are inexorably heading linked, as always, to uncontrolled market forces and technological progress, which nearly always work unconsciously hand-in-hand to cut each other's throats constantly. Think of this progress and visualize an immense neck being strangled ever tighter. It has—it has *got* to be—wild exaggeration—surely it will never get to this stage:

THE ORIGINAL UNION MILL, TANYARD ROAD, MILNSBRIDGE, GRADUALLY DECOMPOSING DURING BRITAIN'S BOOMING ECONOMIC YEARS OF THE LATE 1980s.

things will always readjust themselves—but when does the pressure upon the neck reach the point where it cannot be squeezed any tighter? What happens then? It is obvious what happens if you squeeze a neck as hard as you can, and this is why I sometimes shudder to think of the consequences. Let us hope the neck being strangled puts up a damned good fight.

In a document I found in Huddersfield reference library that was published in 1984, it is stated that Milnsbridge lost a higher proportion of textile jobs during the Recession than any other town in the whole of West Yorkshire. Maybe now it has another claim to fame. Textiles does, however, continue to be a major source of employment in the town (about 500 jobs are left from the original several thousand of a few years ago). But the amount of textile industry left within it has, when compared man for man and mill for mill to how much of it there used to be, sunk to the bottom of manufacturing industry's ocean bed of oblivion. Statistics and the profits made by the biggest remaining textile company have gone out the window here. Growing up in a place and noticing the holes, as yet unfilled, is the yardstick I use to take my measurements this time. The remaining mills shine out, largely unused, glaring, the few lost ships connected with another age, the few lost ships left in a once busy ocean of industry that made, conceived, designed; the shipping lanes of which were congested with mighty vessels full of Huddersfield woollens, masts held high. Many of them sailed into the present decade, but by then they had finally run aground on the sandbank of textile recession and were empty and rusting, waiting to be scrapped. Books and the local press say that textiles are doing well again; there are as many people working in the industry now as there were in 1968, that the production of Yorkshire cloth has contracted about as much as it can do. I passed a textile business last week that only recently set up. It actually had VACANCIES advertised in its window for passers by in the street. It is a long time since I saw this. Most of the old vacancy boards tacked to the outside of such buildings have grown dusty and cracked. The industry has been making record profits; it has had to prune itself and increase productivity to compete in a modernized, highly technologisized world. Computers now control the modern looms, replacing the old familiar rattling of cast-iron with sophisticated hums, whines, chatters. A friend of mine, who has worked in a local mill since he left school in 1977, is at the moment undergoing training to operate new machines being installed that are made in Switzerland. Technology. Programming. But within Victorian outbuildings. There is an upsurge of optimism (at the time I write), and now there is interest in preserving old buildings connected with the industry for sentimental reasons, now the clatter and rattle is also becoming a thing of the past. Up the rest of the Colne Valley, textiles appear to be doing well. There are two dozen or so mills left standing, and a majority of them continue to be engaged in the production of, the *making* of cloth.

But what about this place? It took a real hammering, more than any other part of the valley. Instead of cleaning up the detritus, adapting it to new uses, tearing the mills down even and using the stones to build something in their place, rumours abound and threats proliferate that even more of it must go. Is this place the butt of some obscene joke? If it is, it isn't funny any more, and I speak with the best qualification of all: as a resident. What is left of Milnsbridge should be preserved, if only because it is unlikely that what it is made from will ever be built again: and certainly nothing better. If the alternative is today's average depressing industrial landscape, with its acres of defeated looking corrugated sheds, it is amazing that such nonsense can even be considered seriously. Merely retaliating that utilizing the mills which are left is financially unrealistic refuses to grapple with the real problem, which goes far, far deeper than financial statistics and refurbishing mere structures of stone and steel. Moreover, the stumbling block arises out of the lack of genuine emotional objectivity which is integral to this perpetual economic friction existing in the first place. With potential resources we could not hope to duplicate today (which is a nonsense of course, because we could), it is absurd to throw these assets away in an age of energy conservation, if nothing else. If I was to throw a drawing away, or screw a photograph up, or rip some sheets of writing to bits, or whatever, it would only be after I've tried my absolute damndest to make what is already there work. If I detect any sign of potential, assuming I can identify it; if I see the basis of a good solid framework that needs only attention and perseverance, I work at it all the more. This is an important element of self development, and it is my instinct to pursue it. If I fight it, the terror that all creative people live in fear of begins feeling it's way into the corners of the brain: self doubt. It is this constant dreading of self doubt, the sense of failure at giving in, that fuels any genuinely artistic person forward: the ultimate sense of vanity, especially during the formative, competitive, self-centred years of the young. Once you stop having to ward off the self doubt, once you begin to cruise, you have ceased to be original because you no longer have to grasp in agony at any potential.

From where I was sitting I could see the old textile mill in the distance where my Grandmother worked during the textile boom just after the First World War. She hated it there. It was the only mill she ever worked at where she loathed the management with contempt, because the employees had to clock-off and clock-back on each time they wanted to spend a few minutes going to the toilet. A few minutes. Whenever I see an old mill being demolished I don't think of the mill owners, they never really enter into it. I think of the people that worked in them. The steps worn into hollows up to each floor—visible against the sky as the walls come crashing down—make me think of those who fought for better conditions, better pay, better life. They fought against greed, tiny cogs in a vast greedy machine. And this is what saddens me when I see old mills being pulled down. This is what angers me when I see their old workplaces being pulled down and flogged to the highest bidder for easy money. This is why I want to see more genuine commitment given to the part of Huddersfield where I've grown up, for to pull such places down is to kick their memory in the face, to say these people didn't really matter at all, that the part they played in building us into what we are now meant absolutely nothing.

3

"Give over, Russell!" shouted a bloke to his son who was scampering about over my shoulder, trying to see what I was scribbling. The playing fields of my old secondary school shimmered across the surface with the breeze. I caught a whiff of cigarette smoke and women's perfume, brought over to me with the movement of the grass. I turned to see the man and his family, two up two down, clustered around him in a tight posy of pink and turquoise slacks, white t-shirts and thick-soled training shoes; him with the other infant perched atop his shoulders. The daisies blowing in the breeze shimmered with the cropped grass, a natural improvised pile against green at the blurred edge of my vision in a sparkle of tiny white and yellow dots. I turned to face the rest of the valley again. The model railway layout cattle a few miles distant were not motionless after all. Since last I looked at them, they had moved over to the left, under the shadows of some glowing, backlit trees that were glittering at the edges of their foliage as they flowed down into a hollow. I concentrated hard, trying to see if the cattle were moving, but it was as frustrating as studying the hands of a clock: any movement is imperceptible to the naked eye until after it has happened and you can relate the positioning of the hands to the space of your previous marker.

Then I thought about unemployment—as suddenly as that. Like poverty, I had thought about it many times during the course of my assessment of this part of the country in which I live—at times, it was thrust into your face so forcefully only a fool could remain oblivious to it. But I had, up until then, felt a certain guarded reserve at including it in this itinerary. Doubtless, my reasons were those born of the reluctance of being drawn into the dreary arena of politics. But everything, I concluded very quickly, is political. The mere expression of opinion could be seen as political, and I had definitely expressed many heartfelt opinions thus far.

But politics was not the reason why I wished to observe unemployment as I sat on the seat that hot Sunday afternoon. I thought about unemployment because, once again, it was an impulse that arose caused by environmental contrast: in this case, the contrast between such a peaceful landscape and some of the places existing in the inner city areas of Northern towns. More than this, I felt I had to include it, to comment upon it's existence, to paint the complete picture I had been trying to describe through words and pictures so far. There is so much looking back at the present moment in time, nostalgic romanticization, to the extent that we are almost becoming oblivious to the here and now, or at least are only feigning a coming to terms with certain aspects of it. I had set out to try and capture the essence of the Lancashire and Yorkshire millscapes as they are in the 1980's at a crucial point in both their's and the nation's history. I would, I knew, be condemned by certain blinkered quarters; for talking about that boring old subject, now so well worn: the decline of the industrial North. But this dereliction and decay exists, just as the beautiful areas exist, the unspoilt areas, the new prosperous bits, and I wanted to put them all together at the same time, because it is important to view things as a whole before evaluating them visually and mentally. And I knew, as I had known for a long time, that I would never be able to write one of those delightfully charming little books where everything is positively wonderful and beautiful and the sun always shines, and the sheep bleat, and the larks call, and the water trickles, and nobody swears or has a heart attack if somebody turns their car around in somebody else's drive down a cul-de-sac.

Huddersfield in 1988, then. West Yorkshire. The North of England. Homing in from outer space towards the Earth at full speed we recognize the map of Great Britain, we see it as a geologist's drawing with the different land levels picked out in varying shades of colour. There is a section that runs the length of the map that is lightest of all because it is up to several thousand feet above sea level. A great mass and jumble of squares, lines, horizontals, and roads shows itself and we recognize the mark of civilization sprawling about halfway up, underneath us. We roar in to the outer atmosphere past the spy satellites, the wind whistling in our ears now, through the parting clouds and between the aircraft and the birds

THE POST-INDUSTRIAL LANDSCAPE: SALTAIRE, NEAR BRADFORD, FROM ROBERTS PARK ON A SUMMER SUNDAY AFTERNOON. In the background is the New Mill, part of the impressive factory village erected by Sir Titus Salt between 1850 and 1870. Today, it is one of West Yorkshire's lesser-known tourist draws. The mills stand largely empty, redudant of textile production since 1985.

and then we abruptly decelerate with a strain and a judder and now recognize a traditionally industrial manufacturing town situated almost midway between the Yorkshire city of Leeds at the top of the M1, and the Lancashire city of Manchester which, at one point during the course of British history, was more important as an industrial and commercial centre than the City of London. As I visualized this approach, I realized more than ever before that in the fast-paced high-tech world all around me, unemployment is something you really are not consciously aware of in the Huddersfield of the late 1980's unless you are either without a job, or unless you deliberately seek it out[1]. You walk about the town centre and it looks, to all intents and purposes, reasonably well fed. Generally speaking, there is an air of comfortable prosperity, by no means the prosperity of the well-spoken women in the Harrogate antique shops, but the prosperity of that great big wedge of the lower middle market variety—the 'new middle classes' which have evolved from the marinating of the old middle class and the post-war prosperous working class into today's gigantic groundswell of public opinion—ticking respectfully over, probably almost entirely on the never-never, but in the modest capacity of being in a position to secure such terms in the first place. The shops are bustling. The cash-points outside the banks have their immense queues of plastic making withdrawals on Saturday afternoons. The building societies flourish, the national and local news bulletins reporting that savers are depositing more money in bigger volumes than ever before in queues that snake several times around their interiors in the mornings. The property shops and the estate agents display their slowly revolving tabernacles, enticing with offers of investment in Spanish apartments and Ye Olde bijou cottages fully restored with uPVC doors and windows to their original Georgian or Victorian splendour near the motorway exits. The short-haired youths emerge from the teenage clothing shops, bordering on the serious mating and night-club phase now, and showing more interest in their attire than I ever do in mine, wielding polythene bags with the pink and yellow graphics full of imported cheesecloth and shuffling in spotty groups along the pavements with that big-footed, I've-not-quite-widened-out-into-a-man-yet look. Huddersfield town centre has its fair share of good buildings, mediocre buildings, redevelopment, but it looks clean. The women, even the older women, are looking curiously sexier every year, with their bare tanned legs and stiletto heels and tinted hair-dos and comfortable affluent, semi-affluent, and aspiring affluent expressions. The multi-storey car parks and the shoddy makeshift car parks on the sites of long demolished terraced houses with cobbled streets visible through the dust like lost relics from some ancient civilization, bulge with an ever increasing number of newer and newer and more and more futuristic cars and the ubiquitous four-wheel drive. But what you are seeing is the reasonably, if moderately, prosperous part of the town's inhabitants; the huge consumer part, the part that is doing quite well, the part which has money in its pocket both to spend and save; the part that I am no doubt hoping some of whom will have the money to spare to buy this book.

But one day last week I passed through the entrance along the bottom side of the redeveloped market hall, a typical 1960's structure with it's sculptured and scalloped walls and garish murals. I had not walked down that part of the town centre for some considerable length of time. There are some steps just there, at the head of slabs of dirty concrete, and skinned with black rubber matting. It nearly always smells of urine at that point, and has done for years, it was a running gag even when I was at school in the mid-

[1]Huddersfield has a population of approximately 125,000, just under 7,000 of whom are unemployed.

seventies and it had only been up for a few years. As I descended the steps, noting the concrete has eroded on each after only twenty years, so that rain collects in puddles in the hollows, forcing some Huddersfield citizens to use them in a peculiarly tentative manner, I glanced over to the Unemployment Benefit Office at the other side of the ring road, right on the very edge of the town centre, as social benefit establishments nearly always are. Possibly, by chance, it was the busiest day of the week, but it was teeming with people. People sitting on the wall outside. People streaming in and out. Women pushing plastic prams and their denimed young men resting one hand on the handle. It took me back with such a start I actually paused momentarily and swore to myself instinctively. I was swearing at my own ignorance. What made such an observation all the more preposterous was that some of the students circulating around the nearby polytechnic were visible amongst the groups of obviously unemployed. Two different futures clearly visible, etched into facial characteristics. In fact some of the students, particularly the young women, looked decidedly affluent in comparison to the destitute expressions on some of the paler faces of the unemployed. At the bottom of the steps there was a bestubbled old down and out, with a glazed countenance and a dark-green bottle and a six-pack. He asked me for a light mate, but I apologized because I didn't smoke. I was making my way towards the Huddersfield County Court building on Queen Street, to summons a company who owed me money (and were obviously and deliberately delaying payment) for work done enthusiastically and wholeheartedly many months previously. The contrast between the bustling town centre behind me, the indoor market hall with the majority of its patrons probably just keeping afloat; the Unemployment Benefit Office, the students, the traffic teeming along the ring road in front of me, and the multi-million pound company who owed me a measly few hundred quid from their air-conditioned, plushly upholstered offices with the glamour-girl receptionists was jolted starkly into perspective as I stood there and contemplated it all on the steps at the bottom of town.

There is a lot of talk these days about the North-South divide. This is probably spoken of in economic terms and used as a political strong-arm tactic, but I would definitely like to hear a little more talk about the North-North divide: just as I'm sure a great deal of people below Watford would like to hear a bit more talk about the South-South divide: as would a great deal in between, too.

I remember when there was constant talk in the village around our house of some other long established textile firm going under. For a brief few years, it was a theme forever permeating the air, forever exchanged over the counters in the shops and in bus queues and over tables in pubs. Relatively speaking, the town momentarily held it's breath, with the same kind of uneasy trepidation it would if it awaited the news of the outbreak of war, or of the results of the FA Cup final, if it's non-league team happened to have gone to play in the final at Wembley. There was, at least amongst the textile workers that came to and from our house, an apprehensiveness about who would be the next to be felled, eagerly discussed over cups of tea, through clouds of smoke, and to the rustling accompaniment of packets of *Bourbon Creams*. It also extended into other professions. Engineering, for example. It was a theme unconsciously lodged in most people's minds: Recession. Where would it bite next? Then it was unemployment, the figures steadily rising on the news bulletins and in the newspapers with a viciousness that seems to have abated somewhat. The theme you are

Primrose Hill, Huddersfield

definitely aware of today, in the town centre and in a lot of pubs, is one of inspired affluence. I am not making political statements here, but merely observing a social essence that is there for all to see. This has been heightened even more by the recent explosion in property prices. People who are in work are doing well, seems to be the underlying message. But what of unemployment? We seem to have grown so used to it, you could argue that we now accept it as some kind of tolerable necessity. We become aware of it mildly, during our evening meal, when the ITN news says another seven jobs have been created in Gateshead, three in Bognor, and fourteen in Rotherham. Then it says thirteen have been lost in Sheffield, six in Cardiff, and one at a food processing factory in Blackpool, so a net gain of four new jobs. This may or may not be wild exaggeration, but it serves to underline my point.

Unemployment therefore had to be included to paint the realistic picture, but it has to be placed in the correct perspective, the way it registers upon the conscience of the nation, its relevance to the current social atmosphere as a whole. And it is obvious it has receded into the background, lingering in political programmes on TV and at election times and around dole offices only. In fifty years time, how would an historian analyse unemployment in Great Britain in the latter part of the twentieth century? How would he balance it? Firstly, he would probably already be armed with the knowledge that a sustained body of unemployed is a natural by-product of any *laissez-faire* capitalist economy. Fifty years *ago* three million people were unemployed in Great Britain. But the relevance of that amount of unemployed had a different significance to the rest of the nation at that time. There were fewer people, tens of millions fewer. The world was entirely different. There were two distinct and far greater social divisions within the nation. But one fact remains the same now —whatever the change in technology, lifestyle, videos, moonshots—as it did then: this being that several million British people remain jobless, idle, and unable to participate in the *standards of living* a majority of the rest of the people are enjoying. This is precisely as appalling now as it must have been then. No matter how overall standards of living have improved, this one fact remains the same. So why does it continue? I had tried to identify some of the reasons so far in my book, I saw the pointers, and I concluded swiftly that it remains so simply because we are prepared to tolerate it. There is no doubt whatsoever that there has been an increase in prosperity in this nation—generally speaking—over recent years. This is good. But it seems to me—perhaps I'm totally ignorant, oblivious to some startling facts—that it is only the part of the nation in work that has been getting more prosperous, the part which, in theory, was enjoying a certain degree of prosperity anyway. As all this has been going on, new jobs have been created for the unemployed: the members of the sociological pack viciously driven out from the clearing of busy activity and concealed in the crumbling concrete foliage around the edges. But several million remain jobless now, as then, before the rise in prosperity. Why? All this money has been conjured from somewhere. And if a lot of it has been borrowed, it has still come from somewhere. It doesn't just materialize out of thin air. It must have been there, vast amounts of it, waiting in the shadows, doing absolutely nothing, whilst millions of people did absolutely nothing.

The peace and quiet was overwhelming. Inhaling it all, its warm air, its hedges, its shining fields, it was impossible not to take it seriously without mentally inhaling a whiff of its secret class structure, its demolition, its decay, its unchanging hardcore, its new found prosperity, its unemployment, its ingrained anachronisms. It struck me that it is also impossible to seriously contemplate only one aspect or the other of all this and ignore the rest unless you have one foot rooted firmly outside reality. I had seen certain social conditions that were enough to convince me beyond dispute that it is an affrontary to a civilized society to steadily maintain a sort of social and economic sub-caste whilst talking about booming prosperity. I'm convinced that the people who utter it really know they are somehow pulling the great national leg. Moreover, it is an insult to the intelligence of any decent, law-abiding, tax-paying individual. Incredibly, though, I have even heard it argued that anyone who complains about social injustice or unemployment is doing so out of a kind of moral duty. To appreciate the significance of such emotional immaturity, you have got to understand that it is an attitude born of the most contemptible arrogance. I would guess that most thinkers of the Centre and the Left—and a fair number secretly on the Right for that matter—*do* consider such things first and foremost from the ethical point of view, which still has to be the best and most justifiable one. But most genuine thinkers are also contemplating the deeper sociological repercussions in the mid to long term, something that is hardly ever discussed convincingly, but which holds extremely serious implications.

A few people I have come across have said it is a waste of time to discuss such things as these—the negative aspects of society. This strikes me as being something of an admittance of intellectual pacifism, a half-baked desire to grumble but not to really see anything changed. Let somebody else sort it all out. I emphatically disagree with this mentality. To me it is useless to deny the existence of such things as under-privileged conditions when the evidence is there before you; to blithely assume that everyone is like that because they are degenerate and don't know anything better. It is impossible to remain integral to oneself if you do. It is impossible to seriously sit in a tea-room without feeling a slight tinge of embarrassment when you contemplate the pretty-patterned crockery. *That* is when you know you are on the real planet Earth. And the moment you feel this, you have begun to develop a conscience. And then you have made the first positive step towards change. There is more, a hell of a lot more, forever scratching away at one's conceptions of morality. There *are* the steep Shaftesbury lanes; there *is* the pleasant summer haze behind the grazing Fresians, but there are also a lot of dirty smells. It is futile to separate one from the other. Each time you do, you stamp on the face of frustration and increase the crime figures by ten.

Here had been a glimpse of a major part of this land. Here had been a glimpse of this part of the peaceful land, the green and pleasant land. I felt as though I had picked up a fairly large sociological stone and skimmed it across the surface of the country, but caused a big ricochet somewhere between Lancashire and Yorkshire, although I knew some other parts reasonably well too. And now I had decided that it was essential I must look at the rest, but closer in. And I know with some certainty that there are groups of people living in the South of England who genuinely believe that the North is stuck in some kind of everlasting sepia-toned photographic quagmire, still living in the age of the cloth cap. A friend of mine once told me that when he started at art school in the South East some years ago (admittedly before the Recession, which brought the North to national prominence once again) there were members of his group—and this seems impossible to take without a pinch of salt, but I

Halifax on a December afternoon from the graveyard of St. Thomas's Church, Claremount

relate it as it was told to me—who still thought people travelled about on horses and carts up here, a permanent embellishment to cobbled streets, factory chimneys at the end, and sleepy derelict barns. If such people happen to be reading this book, I hope I've managed, through the writing and the photographs and the limitations of space, to give a fairly rounded picture of what it is like, at least in this part of the North, in the 1980s. The cobbled streets have been almost completely tarmacced over; the factory chimneys have nearly all gone and, with the exception of a few scrap dealers plying their trade on the backstreets and ring roads and a museum in Halifax, the horses and carts have all gone too, replaced by cars cars cars. And most of the old barns have been ambiguously converted into chic executive dwellings, whilst the contents and incumbent birds have been shovelled across the fields into asbestos or corrugated tin replacements sometimes condemned as not keeping with the environmental feel of the newly conserved area. I am only sorry I have not included more photographs of modern housing estates, but the public does not warm to the prospect of buying books full of pictures of new houses and motorways (there has to be a moral in there somewhere), and this book is still a commercial venture I am afraid. Mind you, if you were to put all the various visual characteristics of this area into one of those circular pie-charts you see bearded lecturers gesturing to on *The Open University,* the 'original look' of the North would still take up the biggest chunk, with the landscape itself equally as prominent, so maybe the visual balance of the book isn't too far out. And take my word for it that there are very few people wearing cloth caps up here these days. And, as I have indicated over the previous pages, take my word for it that there is wealth. And squalor. And the big lump in between. Just like anywhere else. Take a look at the multi-storey car-parks off Deansgate in Manchester, only a stones throw from the teeming multitudes of shoppers on the one hand, and the forests of mouldy concrete across the river on the other. Couple this with the fact we are living at a crucial period, and you realize that the subject of class looks likely to become something of a recurring one. It is too big a subject to discuss in any depth in these particular pages, but suffice it to say that quite possibly, *if* things carry on in the direction they are going, there is a chance we will begin to see the sort of overt class hatred which existed in this country before the First World War re-emerge in various sections of today's population, but inculcated with certain bizarre twists. In fact, there are implications of this already. And looking back over the bulk of this book so far, it is impossible to seriously contemplate all that I have written without realizing that the social hierarchical structure of contemporary Great Britain loiters in the background to almost everything I have described. In the same way that the textile industry is the enigma around which West Yorkshire still exists, etched indelibly upon the landscape and embedded into the place's soul despite the concrete and the new pace jostling for attention, so it is that the inherent social hierarchical structure of this country is the underlying theme which binds this book together, despite the number of washing-machines and crowded wardrobes in infinitely more households, whatever the changes in the past forty years.

Indeed finally, considering the vast social and political changes of the past decade, your mind buzzing with the whole crazy gamut of contemporary Great Britain, you examine the pros and cons and conclude that certain things never really change at all. As you contemplate the country basking in the glow of its tracery of yellow flowers, the high-rise flats and the new bypass tucked safely out of sight behind the cathedral in the background, if you are of reasonable intelligence and possessed of a fairly sound imagination, if you are aware, you cannot help but conclude that this is a nation which definitely sustains severe internal problems. Still the same old cliched comments. Still the same old fashioned cliches which refuse to go away. Still the same old fashioned, absurdly simple—though natural—human impulse mixed up with a means of exchange at the root of the whole gigantic social hierarchical muddle.

And contemplating the changing but unchanging attitude which used to make those millworkers who toiled with my Grandmother clock-off and clock-back on when they went to relieve themselves, you cannot help but conclude that it is still political indifferentism and closet-greed in too many high places, which ought to possess the emotional maturity to know better, that are the underlying reasons why several million British people have remained under-privileged for so long, many suffocated by disgraceful poverty and a feeling of worthlessness in a world geared towards work and success.

There were no yellow flowers as I sat on the seat near my old secondary school in 1988. There were no cathedrals either, but I could see several blocks of flats and just make out the omniscient hum of nearby traffic. The sun was blazing, the children were playing, and a few dogs were yapping at the other side of some Scandinavian-type bungalows which had recently been refitted with brand-new uPVC doors and windows moulded in the Victorian style. All the pros and cons of booming contemporary Great Britain, contemporary England—they seemed further away, yet closer than ever before, complex and difficult issues requiring far more space than these pages will allow.

But for a moment, whilst contemplating the sterile uPVC and equating it to that all pervading English watercolour, but most significantly, contemplating the previous few pages of this book, it was difficult not to feel the very deepest sense of dismay.

Thank God I still maintained the faculty.

WRIGLEY HEAD MILL, FAILSWORTH, OLDHAM, DURING DEMOLITION IN THE AUTUMN OF 1988. After being vacated by a builders and plumbers merchants, the mill was so badly vandalized that when would-be purchasers approached, its cost-effectiveness had so diminished the only serious alternative was to pull it down. Only the staircase tower remains, awaiting detonation.

MARSDEN

endpiece

1

Dumfounded, but not really dumbfounded in the slightest, I stood up and made my way down through a council estate, to reconnoitre locations for photographing ready for publication. Then there was another residential housing estate spreading out, concocted from the usual hastily prepared recipe, pebble-dash dappled with a few plastic stones, fibre-glass Corinthian columns, Mediterranean railings, plastic coach lamps, frilly garden umbrellas, barbecue patios, fish ponds with plaster-cast gnomes fishing between the lillies and plastic toads, more sound effects of electric lawnmowers and hedgetrimmers and vacuum cleaners and spin dryers and babies crying and Mothers swearing inside open doorways, and two people lolling full length on an upstairs mock-Spanish veranda. The rest of Huddersfield spread out before me, steaming in the distance through the pleasant aroma of spring flowers: the classic Northern panorama with its trailing rooftops stepping steeply down the hillsides, chimney-pots old and new and gone, some mill chimneys, some viaducts, some big concrete boxes, some figures kicking balls about on some distant grass: all perfectly aligned for a telephoto lens shot of some kids arriving at my old school with the urban vista foreshortened in the background, and the concrete street lamps standing out starkly against the sky as they do down Primrose Hill, and the larking about and the abuse and the goggle-eyes joking over how they'd like to get their laughing gear around the ends of so-and-so's juicy great knockers.

I had a sudden crazy urge to listen to an old record I'd played for the first time in ages the previous evening. It played now in my mind, the sounds of birds-twittering-and-children-larking summer gradually losing themselves and fading out. I cursed for not bringing my personal hi-fi tape player like a smoker who forgets his cigarettes. I imagined the record instead and clenched my teeth, a morbid soundtrack of saxophones—real saxophones played by human hands with a few duff notes–but then even they were fading out, into the background, and a deep reverberating machine was booming frustratedly to the fore. Suddenly, I saw the whole wide world as a gigantic model railway layout, and wondered if, underneath the surface, it was all held together with pink string and sealing wax on a timber framework of 2x2; and somewhere else, a sardonic supervillain out of one of my old superhero comics—with an army of faceless, unquestioning, mechanical employees—was laughing at me in the most bellicose, lingering, salivating manner imaginable. Laughing all the way to the bank. Then a propeller driven aeroplane hummed intermittently overhead, lazy and lingering, into that British summer's day distance which always evokes memories of goose-spit and long grass and hot dusty pavements and the smell of creosoted garages during childhood. Much nearer the ground, birds of the feathered variety stood out starkly as black silhouettes, gliding in front of the greyish background haze hanging like scrim between me and the rest of the diffused valley beyond. Over in the distance, at the edge of my picture, at the back of the landscape, a bus moving slowly up the rolling green hillside suddenly caught the sun and reflected it for an instant like a mirror. I thought spontaneously of an old episode of *The Avengers* where a scientist had deciphered some crazy new weapon which paralyzed its victims with just such a bright glinting of white hot energy. The instant passed and a tiny green-and-cream speck was moving in the dazzle's place instead. Specks. There were specks everywhere. Specks of houses. Specks of birds. Specks of moving cars. Specks of noise. Specks of dust. There would no doubt be tiny specks moving silently through space high above, circling the earth. It's funny. The mill chimney I could see down in the bottom of the valley was one we used to play around when we were kids, before the specks began circulating the planet. I remember the first moon shot, the Apollo lift off, the trip, the landing on the dusty satellite; I remember my heart being in my throat, the visits to the toilet every five minutes from the adrenalin of listening to James Burke commentating and my sense of wonder aroused at men being thrust into space. Science-fiction into science-fact. Drawings of Lunar modules and planetary diagrams on the blackboards at school. In summer. Summer was here now as I walked. Summer was beaming. And beyond, as always, the Pennine moors lifted up, beyond even the tiny speck of the bus crawling up the papier-mache hillside flocked green. The moors rose in a misty cut-out, a steeply rising bulk behind the scrim; windswept desolation, a perpetual bloated grimace of prehistoric land formation. Way over there, beyond the smudges of mixed buildings and towns and villages in the foreground, out above Marsden, the last outpost at the end of the Colne Valley seven miles from Huddersfield, there comes a point where your entire field of view resembles a gigantic smoothened lava flow: the petrified aftermath of some colossal primeval volcanic eruption that gushed molten Pennine down from a long vanished mountain above. Smooth, undulating moorland etched only by the browns and purples of heather in autumn and the greens of ferns in summer, untouched by man except for a sprinkling of the white crumbs of his sheep, sweeps rhythmically away from you at the opposite side of a peat gully, rising slowly towards Buckstones with the M62 slicing through it, somewhere over the horizon to the right. Looking across this seemingly endless vista of utter desolation, you feel to be glimpsing a piece of West Yorkshire landscape which does indeed belong before history. The covering of wiry grass or heather or ferns—there is not a single tree and hardly a single bush, only heather, grass, heather, grass—could be the beginnings of forests that will sprout tens of thousands of years hence. This piece of West Yorkshire could be at the dawn of time, the gashes in the low ceiling of grey cloud with a gilt edge of glowing sunset blasting through late on a winter's afternoon are the storm clouds gathering at the command of some inestimable extra-terrestrial force of creation: the steam that rises off it after the summer rains the smoke fresh from the explosions of recent creation. In the civilization sprawling on either side of the backbone of England, centuries of industrial turmoil, pulling down, reshaping, rebuilding, have long since deflowered virgin landscape. But there, on the misty silhouette of the Pennine Chain, up their above, the landscape is intact. Up there Earth herself is well and truly in charge. Some days you can be in sunshine in the lowlands of the valleys on either side, then, as you climb upon her, you can suddenly be engulfed by dense fogs as baleful as those she breathes down around the rooftops of the houses on a cold winter's day. And if it is winter, and it is raining in Huddersfield or Oldham, you can be sure that at the high points above, nature's exhaust pipe will be gusting a veritable monsoon, and more than likely great torrents of sleet. It is the tremendous amplification of the more

Storm Clouds over Pole Moor

inclement weathers up there during winter that remind man he is the insignificant passer through, and he knows it and she knows it. Nature keeps man out as best she can and as only she knows how—she frightens him with her climate. The cash registers of the brain of commerce have not sloshed their way through the mud with any degree of significance, except when they built the motorway twenty five years ago, and then she gave them a good fight, swallowing the contractors' bulldozers into her mud overnight if they were parked in the wrong places. Man's constantly revolving wheel of progress and evolution has hardly left its collective imprint in the mud up there. She won't let him, except maybe for the odd row of electric pylons marching off mysteriously in either direction as they do between Ripponden and Rochdale. The Pennines have not yet been undercut. The backbone of England, cutting defiantly through the massive industrial connurbations of Lancashire to the west and Yorkshire to the east with a ruggedness and sheer presence that is impossible to ignore. From the tops, the towns trail off down the long gullies carved in the earth by

More Storm Clouds over Pole Moor

ancient glacial activity like satellite photographs taken from low orbit. From up there you stare, transfixed, narrow footpaths trodden by the feet of enthusiastic hikers in search of good health and clean air and breathtaking panoramas thread their way across the heather which rustles unceasingly under cajolery from the breezes before disappearing invitingly out of sight over the crests of little peninsulas. Up there you can escape, the thick penetrating quietness and absolute stillness broken only by the occasional shrieks of a curlew high on the wind, as they say; the grass rustling under the constant breath in the air; the sudden swish of a passing car. In another second the wind presses against your face making your eyes water, and then your previous reverie is shattered to be replaced by another as the landscape takes on a fantastic swirling shape in the blur of tears flooding your vision; and that gently curving horizon line, which you were so sure was just an endless morass of peat and bog and heather, elongates then stirs ominously; then it is rising up to reveal itself to be the belly of an immense creature of the moors formed of the very land before you, hypnotizing you whilst you gazed upon its uncompromising bleakness before wrenching up to swallow you in a huge, bog-like maw.

The backbone of England. Millstone grit country. Millscape country. Oldham, Blackburn, Bolton, Accrington, Nelson, Colne to the west, Huddersfield, Bradford, Halifax to the east: names which sound like they were hacked out of the stone or moulded in the bricks that all of these towns were built from. Now they are spliced with concrete and glass, connected to each other by more tendons of ferro bodged with tarmaccadem. But the moors. They do not change. Road, river, canal, and railway jostle for space where the going gets narrow and she squeezes them together to suit the whims of her evolution. Outcrops of blackened rock eroded into fantastic other-worldly shapes, project from the smooth hillsides, or are scattered in heaps down craggy slopes, aimed at the townships clustering in the hollows. Years ago, a man interviewed in Batley, West Yorkshire described the North of England as a great fat old sow laying on its side, and the South was the litter of greedy piglets feeding from its udders. Probably he was not intending to insult a great mass of erstwhile Southern citizens in a similar predicament to himself, but was referring to a tiny parasitic minority. But he spoke in a different time. Such comments can still arouse fierce snarls of hostility amongst the older inhabitants from here all the way up to the North East and beyond. The nipples of the big old sow have been drying up for some time, she herself, the venerable guardian, grew damn near impotent, unable to feed the piglets any longer. Moreover, maybe the piglets escaped from the pen, became fed up with the same old milk and decided to try a dehydrated version elsewhere, abandoning the fat sow in favour of richer bearers and push-button transactions instead: but built up ready to grow into maturity, nourished with strength garnered from the old satisfying elixir all the same.

Perhaps the history of that fat old sow—at least down here where she lolls on either side of the backbone—could never have existed in the form we know it without the silent, watchful moorlands rising high above, dourly keeping their eye on those funny black smudges oozing smoke and people down below. Perhaps even the Pennines themselves could not be possessed of the enigma they have created for themselves if not for their contrast against what transpired—what *transpires*—in their immediate shadow. Maybe it was the knowledge of this vast kingdom, its ironies, its constant controversy for people who do not know it, that prevents them from being only rugged outcrops of land somewhere but nowhere, other than at geographical reference points on some anonymous map. The most noticeable thing when you are up on the moors, on your feet, standing up, breathing, is the peace, the easing of pace, the serenity of calm, the sense of escape from squabbling and dispute, sneering and underhandedness, conniving and manipulation. Breathing in the air up there is to experience a decrease in the pulse-rate of your own metabolism. Relaxation. Awareness of senses. Quiet. Slow.

On the other hand . . .

2

I changed from third gear back up into fourth and eased the accelerator pedal down to the floor. The lumbering yellow juggernaut snarling up the flow of traffic streaming through the coniferous suburb passed me in a roaring blur on my left-hand side as I indicated and moved out from behind it to overtake, now that the road was widening and the wind-tunnel was clear. I checked my rear view mirror and saw the queue of pursuing vehicles filing out neatly into the jetstream. I moved back into the left-hand lane again, in front of the juggernaut, which was now a rapidly diminishing dot falling away from me in my mirror as the sections of the Apollo rockets spiralled away from the command module in the classic footage.

Released now, the Granadas and Cavaliers and XR whatevers leaped past me at mach-ten, then swept out of sight around the bend in the wide, villa lined road, probably heading ultimately for a place called Cardiac Arrest. Surprisingly quickly, residential bijou blended with long lengths of Victorian and Edwardian. Then they petered out, becoming tatty and boarded-up amidst the usual smattering of video and washeterias, greengrocers and graffitti in both English and Urdu, overtones of unemployment and deprivation; the last outpost of civilization for a few minutes before I hit the stifling blandness of the Leeds ring road conglomeration in the no-man's-land of asphalt that used to be a packed industrial suburb on the outskirts of the city centre. Only a 1930's library remains with any degree of real credibility. Scores of traffic lights and overhead destination gantries, interspersed with a tangle of dual carriageway homing in from all directions, encircle the landscaped patches with their rows of ugly council flats both along and up—a long way up—painting the archetypal picture of inner city depression we tolerate so unflinchingly as we commute to and from our own little green and pleasant hinterlands coming into bloom beyond.

I pulled up gently behind the same Granadas and Cavaliers and XR whatevers at the glut of traffic lights in the middle of it all, easing my foot gradually down onto the brake pedal. Sheepscar was another insane parody in this whole wide world which is really a giant model railway layout. This time it was mimicing a complex junction at the throat of one of the big main-line stations. The vehicles I could see were all the different trains, the lorries all the different goods wagons, uncoupled but shunting themselves independently in a different sort of marshalling yard altogether. The trains didn't have flanged wheels any more, but rubber ones instead. The roads were the tracks, but without the rails, only endless corroding tarmaccadem which is a lot more cumbersome to lay and expensive to replace and maintain, and much shorter lasting. Somebody once wrote a letter to the local newspaper along the line of this theme, suggesting an inspiring but simple solution to combatting the problem of increasing urban congestion in our major towns and cities. It was brilliantly simple and would have lent itself quite significantly to adaptation for the movement of traffic over long distance on the motorways. The correspondent proposed that if we fitted road vehicles with flanged wheels, especially the obtrusive lorries and juggernauts, and laid rails in the surface of the roads, it might regulate the flow of traffic, ease the confusion, enforce an orderliness and saneness to that of hurry hurry hurry. On these long distance journeys, timetables could be introduced, but most of all, the goods could be transported at much greater speed, more efficiently and with less damage to the environment. It might also relieve the immense cost to the taxpayer of maintaining roads in their present form, because pieces of hardened metal last much longer, bearing in mind the future, which is always worth thinking about. It seemed to me a very good idea, and I'm surprised nobody has snapped up the rights to the correspondent's suggestion before he patents the entire

COTTON MILLS IN OLDHAM

concept. It makes you wonder, though, why it has never been thought of before, especially when we tend to evolve by creating machinery that makes the task of progressing quicker, less stressful, more economic, faster, tighter. It seems odd, this.

I looked in my rear view mirror again and saw the yellow juggernaut thundering down behind me through a succession of pelican crossings, enlarging in the frame as it tore in from Chapel Allerton. For a terrifying second I thought its brakes had failed. The rest of the vehicles all around me hummed, the day humid and glaring. The music blaring from the cassette-tape player in my car reached a crescendo before the singers' next chorus and his relating about how he'd come to wish somebody an unhappy birthday because they were evil and they lied. The traffic waited, wound up like a dynamo, me with it, then the traffic lights changed to amber and the starting pistol of the motoring world was fired and we all thrust forward, separated, and peeled off down the slip roads. I saw the lorry in my mirror, lumbering and blocking the flow again, then suddenly, from nowhere, an old dark-green Austin A30 zipped past me and nipped in front of my car, it really did. I couldn't believe it. The final chapter began to collect together in my mind. The bulbous shape was there again after so long. A picture of doing one up all those years ago with the coal wagon driver when I was a kid flashed through me; both of us replete with our war-paints of grease and engine oil. The dark-green memory parked in one of the dim recesses had burst out from the doors of the old garage in my head—asbestos lined, with a yale padlock and a corrugated apexed roof, surrounded by a bed of nettles and the yellow sprinkling of dandelions in summer—out into broad daylight in Leeds 1988. I turned the volume up on my cassette-player and pursued the A30 up the hill towards the concrete and glass from Mies Van Der Dallas scowling at the top. The vehicles bunched up at the next set of traffic lights, the dynamos rewound, the starting pistols being reloaded. I switched lanes and drew up alongside the A30, eyes devouring it. It was perfect, gleaming, antique, the chrome and the beading so good it must have been replated. Everything was exactly as I remembered it: the whining engine from the old episodes of *Mysteries of Edgar Wallace* was music to my ears: the simple radiator grill shaped like a louvred toilet seat: the design exquisitely crude but charming and refreshingly clear. Incredibly, the car was being driven by a girl who looked much younger than me — too young to have remembered A30's nostalgically when they proliferated on the British roads of the 1950's and '60's. She was attractive, faintly blond with the face of the young tennis player earning millions at Wimbledon; the girl with the tanned smooth face when I was a kid who lived in a crescent or a grove or a cul-de-sac, and who I always wanted to go out with but never had the courage to ask because her parents drove a car that was too big and too new for me to be taken seriously. She glanced at me with an intelligent expression, the look now of the Sociology or English student; the face called Lindsey or Victoria or Sandy for short; the face on its way to a degree, although I would't have been at all surprised if she'd been scribbling away in a back room of the advertising agency in which I'd just consumed my umpteenth cup of caffeine stimulation during my third meeting so far that day. She caught my eye but quickly turned away. She needn't have bothered. My eyes were lusting after the magnificent little glass bubble she was piloting. It stuck out like a sore thumb. It was too rounded at the edges in comparison to the buildings, too dumpy in comparison to the rest of the vehicles and the lifestyle spreading out all around her. But she seemed not to be intimidated by the likes of Mr. Sierra or Mr. Nissan or Mr.

BMW or Mr. Cavalier grumbling in a cloud of carbon-monoxide to front, side and rear. The lights changed and the vehicles surged and more concrete loomed, this time the set piece for the yarn unfolding in the alternate prefabricated nightmare, with soulless creatures skulking about with shaven heads and somnambulistic expressions, being whipped by leather-clad security officials into pools of urine stagnating in the icy cold stairwells that always stink halfway between public toilets and hamburger caravans outside night-clubs or football grounds.

The traffic gushed down the incline towards another part of the ring road, full of vehicles blazing in from the outer planets of the M1 and the York Road. The gaping maw of the underpass which plunges beneath the ferro-grey of the multi-storey car park, the playhouse, and the university yawned and swallowed us all up as we slipped into the main jetstream and blended with the flow. Horns blared somewhere behind me and I saw some headlights flash on full-beam for an instant in the distance in my rear view mirror. Another horn retaliated with two fingers, but then my attention was switched back to the A30 in front of me. She indicated cheekily, swapped lanes, then was away, disappearing into the anonymous multi-wheeled crowd. Up until then, I'd hardly ever set eyes on a car such as her's in years. They had only been available to me from that fraying picture library of the mind of when-I-was-a-kid. The past that the old dark-green A30 of our's had lived in with its snippets of the edited highlights of Uncles and Aunts and Mums and Dads standing on front doorsteps holding babies with a gas lamp on the street behind: with its distant holidays at Mablethorpe and Sutton-on-Sea captured on those Box-Brownie snaps with corner shops and mills and beating of looms outside sashed-and-leaded bedroom windows—all caught fire and began curling up into little black, shrivelled rose-heads of paper and nothingness. The past moth-balled, when even in my wretchedly short time and empty experience, I was convinced it had moved that little bit slower, had been that little bit less prefabricated, a little more lean, a lot less fat. Now it was very prefabricated. It was in full colour; colours I knew well, with a great many benefits and hardly any outside toilets. Black and white had gone, was dead, finnito: like most of the Uncles and Aunts, Mums and Dads on the charred remains of those tatty wretched photographs burning in the stupid furnace of the head. It was moth-balled alright, but there in front of me in 1988, was a bulbous four-wheeled stupid idealism, a memory telescoped together with more Box-Brownie snaps; there in front of me in 1988, there to be seen as the stupid nostalgic hogwash it really was, had been an old Austin A30, not in black and white but in full colour green driven by vivacious full colour blond. Now it too had gone. The cars of the rip-roaring 1980's raced through the underpass, catching my imagination in their fervour. The pacing quickened, the editing of the sequence stacatto and punchy. More engine fumes entered my car through the air-intakes on the dashboard, squeezed in at me by the confined space of the concrete corridor with its orange lights chasing past me in a pulse of flashing florescence. I wound the window down. The volume of roaring engines—stifled underground—was turned up all of a sudden and blasted in at me, rushing and screaming and adrenalin inducing as I'm sure would happen if I happened to climb out onto the roof of a train bulleting at full pelt. No way was I driving through England, this green and pleasant land. I was driving through Los Angeles. The cars throbbed in a great teeming pack, blurring at the fringes of my vision down the underpass, overlapping outside the open window into a single tumultuous drone. At any moment, an

Arnold Schwarzenegger-like man-machine would lunge at me from the window of the car alongside, smashing straight through in a crash and spray of sugar-glass fragments, wielding an oversized futuristic sub-machine-gun in a suitably musclebound posture, his face torn wide open exposing chrome and steel and green and red diodes and spitting circuitry for tendons and gears and cogs and sinew and microchips and reams of splashing cybernetic blood trailing down the side of his car. I gripped the steering wheel harder as the images around me were recorded and stapled together in my head. The music on the tape blared in my ears: synthesizers: bass guitars and electric guitars gouging and grazing away at the soundtrack: syn-drums: real drums *Badoompha-ing:* adrenalin pumping: senses turning razor sharp: hairs bristling at the nape of my neck. The ammunition was being loaded, the magazine being snapped into place in the machine-gun of the mind. The finger was on the trigger of the brain. The barrel swung and sprayed. It started. There was no blimp to soundproof me. Marker pens scribbled fantastic shapes over the previously blank sheets of

THE CHANGING URBAN LANDSCAPE: BRADFORD

INNER CITY DECAY NOW DEMOLISHED, BRADFORD

paper before my mind's eye. Strange forms took shape. The mass of vehicles surged out of the underpass. The daylight dazzled and stunned. The destination gantries flickered overhead wielding directions to the other Northern millscape towns of yesteryear, saying it in back-lit green perspex with the writing picked out white and yellow and blue for the motorways and framed by grey sheet steel. The giant digital clock fastened to the prefabricated nipple at the top of the *Yorkshire Post* building announced the temperature and said 16.27 *flip* 16.28. More traffic fed in from the other slip roads. A high speed 125 train meandered across the Holbeck viaduct on its way up from Kings Cross only two and a half short hours away now and soon to be squeezed a few minutes shorter with electrification and billions of pounds. Lorries tore towards the motorway intersections and dwarfed the tiny cars and youths spat compulsively on the sidewalks and young women with harsh features pushed double-barrelled prams across the concrete footbridges strobing overhead. As I neared the viaduct I caught a glimpse of the first class carriages of the 125 with their firm-faced occupants and tanned middle-aged women in the leather dresses with the smooth shiny legs heading back to Harrogate, knodding and drinking animatedly, and the orange curtains, and the big number ones on the doors, and the men with their ritualistic perusals of the peach-coloured newspapers and the RRR-OOOOOAAAARINGG of the power car as the end of the train passed over my roof in blue and yellow and a cloud of pulsing vapour that made the graphics on the side shimmer as through a heat-haze. Leeds city centre winked at me in my rear view and side mirrors, banks, finance, prosperity, designer-accountant gaudy spectacles in bright yellow and red and white and blue, tower blocks, Arndale Centre, 19th century, 20th, sham Gothic, the ugly modern swimming pool straight out of the title sequence to *Stingray* with its angled inverted flat roof and harshness and dirty concrete and bad after-taste. Then the freeway ended and became the M621 on its way up to join on to the M62 at Gomersal. Leeds city disappeared behind me, a mass of grey and tower blocks now winking on the misty horizon three miles away, embellished by its futurama of steel and tarmac and glass. The main bridge of the M62 flashed overhead with the roofs of its scalextric track of vehicles shooting left and right. I dived under it and joined the main carriageway for a few miles, then this too disappeared at another great tangle of spaghetti-like intersections and old Northern skylines, truncated, spilling down the adjacent hillside towards a huge roundabout running under the motorway. The M606 opened up before me, a short piece of motorway functioning exactly like a branch line on a railway joining onto the main line of the huge model train layout. An old stone farmhouse glowed beautifully in the afternoon sunlight at the opposite side of a sea of buttercups, butted up to the Euroway Trading Estate, another corrugated glimpse of tommorow today; spreading out on either side of the six lanes divided by the crash-barrier and the central reservation with the regiment of tall lamp standards filing past in a rapid blur with both arms outstretched. I saw the next stage of the reshaping of our civilization, of our society, our England, our Britain. The seeds have been sown, the new industrial estates are gathering at the motorway junctions, pressed up to their edges, feeding them, the transport life-lines, heading straight for politically manipulated seizure, the buildings going up wherever you look, like *Meccano* sets, just as quick, just as pretend. I visualized the massive new leisure and shopping complexes costing tens of billions of instant pounds that will come; the retail shopping parks that must inevitably follow, away from the old towns and cities which were becoming so congested, so difficult in which to do our shopping, so impractical to accommodate the automobile. My automobile. And then we would have spread out even more and the giant complexes would form the cores of the new towns and cities, and more little fields full of dolls' houses would pop up near to the motorway junctions, as they almost always are, rush, speed, hurry, pace, fast, fast, rush, hurtle, fast, fast, fast, and they would all grow alongside the life-lines, hand in hand with the ginormous retail, industrial and leisure parks, speed, square, glass, corrugation. Then the other parts of this futuristic era were before me, the guarded bits, the Ripons, the Yorks, the Canterburys, the Cotswolds, the grand country houses with the Corinthian columns, undefiled, cocooned, isolated at the ends of their commuting tentacles to and from The Cities whilst the rest of the dirty old new plastic England was stamped out ten to the neat and tidy vac-formed dozen, without the details, only those fast screeches around nearly every modern manufacturing corner, back-lit, bubble-packed, with a ten year money back guarantee, and NO STAFF IN ATTENDANCE so suit yourself. I saw the even sleeker cars, even more remote-controlled windows, above all I saw a greater although acutely calculated overall competitive affluence, the happy faces, the contented units; but I also saw little glass bubbles climbing up the mirrored walls to enjoy its gigantic corrugated boxes containing indoor plastic leisure parks, its plastic tropical jungles recreated here from there, its mock-Tudor made from moulded plastic, its dead tree trunks with thousands of holes drilled along the dry branches and replaced with imitation plastic leaves giving them an eternal blooming, without the need for real life-giving water, life-giving sunshine, life-giving chlorophyll. I saw its fun parks, its holiday parks, its joy, its laughter, its cocktails around swimming pools with the topless bathing, its monorails shooting around its stalks of elevated concrete with its tinted windscreens and tinny background department store music from the train with another view—and just beyond the edge of the landscaping and the neat little rows of brightly coloured plastic shrubs planted next to the immense car parks with spaces for hundreds and thousands of vehicles, I could see an old mill chimney poking up behind a day-glow perspex sign at the entrance to the fun and joy, welcoming you to the mystery and adventure, and two steeplejacks were hammering scaffolding onto the summit of the chimney, ready to pull it down, ready to nail it firmly into the coffin of a dirty stinking forgotten past, ready to be buried in a graveyard full of tiny coffins, coffins full of wretched little pairs of rotting, decomposing hands, men's hands, women's hands, skilled hands, hands no longer needed, hands no longer relaying skills and sensitivity to brains. And there was a futuristic robot at the back of the graveyard with a demoniac slit for a mouth, an evil hole-in-the-head jammed full of needle-like teeth and with a searchlight attached to its plated skull, and the searchlight was sweeping from side to side because the sun had suddenly gone out and it was dark and grey and miserable as mist, and there was a dreadful mournful synthesized trilling and droning of electronic noise, and the robot was ripping up the earth with its slender metallic fingers and was tearing the dead hands to pieces and devouring them as ravenously and as frantically and as messily and as sloppily as a school of frenzied starving piranhas, turning them into ground-up stumps of so much human sludge. And beyond even this dark dismal hell-hole of dying rancid flesh filled with distant wailing and screaming voices like the worst jolts from the most horrifying nightmare bursting at the seams with monsters and goblins and demons and ghouls, the light glowed from the Happy City, the city of light, rolling ever onward with its plastic foliage, its constant pretend indoor this and indoor that, its high-speed food jack-knifing in the intestines, its superquick building now reduced, at long last, to a few buttons and a few vac-forming presses, its massive robo-controlled multi-national corporations with feelers shooting out in bursts of effervescence like cursors over a computer graphics simulation of a globe of the world. Even babies would, I concluded, all eventually be born into life in that futuristic world I was imagining, with a good start, into the universal affluence, quickly growing into tanned bikini-clad youngsters mating up beneath the plastic fruit trees around the edges of the swimming pools under a dome of eternal tropical sunshine. But they would be unquestioning, because there would be nothing left to question, because those babies would be born with exactly the same teeth and fingernails now moulded from uPVC.

And beyond the dome, beyond even the dome's vision, the other children with real teeth and fingernails but broken and smashed, broken and smashed from clawing and pressing against the dome's impenetrable glass, broken and smashed from covering their heads, broken and smashed from preventing the omniscient foot of a forgotten humanity forever stamping on the face of their eternal frustration.

I turned the cassette-tape over, a rapid-fire fix of new images and clinical environs invading the familiar environs of my mind, my nostalgia, my confused present, my hometown suburb that sometimes strikes me as being regarded as a sort of stain in the underpants of Huddersfield. I contemplated the size of the spare tyre around my stomach which had miraculously inflated since I'd stopped walking as much as I did when I was traipsing around the towns and cities and villages and hillsides with my camera. Spare tyre. Fat. Food. *Food!* Then food made me think of the early hours of the morning the previous evening, whether or not the spare tyre had been noticed. As at all such moments, when the potentiality of serious thinking is suddenly embarrassed at the behest of the naked provocation of the sex drive, ever the victor and ever the controlling *thrust a la tour de force,* I smiled contentedly and flushed it all down the toilet of the mind, anticipating instead the slow arousel that would be coming during the evening meal a few hours later that day, in the moortop restaurant above the old Yorkshire milltown sparkling in the dark belly of the valley below, the one so neglectfully wrecked–but then the motorway and the three minute syndrome ended abruptly at a roundabout and I wanted to urinate instead. I was intensely aware of every tiny detail all around me: the concrete, the asphalt, the waiting fields, the cats-eyes bump-bumping under the wheels of my car, the white road markings flickering, the electric pylons marching, the brutalized drivers compulsively overtaking, the angular bridges from the United States, the green laid out on either side of West Yorkshire, Heckmondwike, Cleckheaton, down at the bottom of the undulating green with a couple of lost mill chimneys sailing from their lost industry — fast cuts in a documentary of observations laced with the ever-thumping soundtrack of music from the speakers in my car.

The ring road and DIY superstores of another old textile city began, one which the postmarks on the letters I receive from it declare is 'bouncing back'. Huddersfield, Milnsbridge, Sunnybank Mills–they were made twelve miles away, carved out of another Northern hillside, not dissimilar to the one unfolding itself before me now amidst the usual confusing mixture of high-rise, classical and corinthian, a splendidly refurbished theatre, Gothic, steel, community programmes, an old chapel converted into a Muslim girls' school, tinted glass, a few wretched mill chimneys, and some blocks of flats being demolished which the city will be paying off the loan from their original construction only twenty years ago until goodness knows which year whenever. A sea of terraced house rooftops, punched up from in between by more multi-storey verticals, trailed away down into the heart of the city, changed into a voluminous outline of more high squares and boxes and horizontals, then cascaded up the rolling hillside at the other side in reverse. More traffic surged, the congestion multiplying again. The beautiful profile of the old Wool Exchange building peeped at me between the big cubes and boxes thrusting up at the bottom of the newest section of recently opened ring road, and intersections, and more overhead destination gantries telling me how far it was now, and which lane I should be in, for the other Yorkshire millscape towns, muddlescape towns. And have a nice day, I thought, and enjoy your fast food, and keep on the sidewalks, and don't forget to wear your sneakers to kick your funny shaped rugby ball about, and be careful of the kids playing on the BMX bikes and the skateboards or they'll be bouncing all over your hood like squashed tummaytoes, old bean. The last track faded out on the cassette, then good old Radio One erupted into my ears as the tape ran on to the end of the spool and ejected itself from the machine. No matter where I was, there was always rock music, and I couldn't live without it, conditioned by it as I have been, amongst other things. I readjusted the volume and then I was putting another tape into the mouth of the machine, a softer music, more mellow, relaxing, my audio-cigarette, Ella Fitzgerald's soothing vocals singing volume one of Cole Porter *Alllll through the Niiiight.* Over in the Great Horton direction I could have sworn I caught a glimpse of a mill under demolition, before it disappeared behind some blocks of flats looming in the foreground. I saw the familiar white patch of exposed interior wall against the black cut-out of the chimney. Wings had flexed and the demolition men had descended again. The roof slates had gone and a few greasy timbers would have been stacked ready for sorting before being bundled onto the backs of the waiting lorries. But now they were finding fewer and fewer

NORTHALLERTON ROAD, WAPPING, BRADFORD

carcasses on which to feed. The frenzied squabbling of five or six years previously had abated, textiles having contracted about as much as it can do, I am told, but continuing to provide a major bedrock of industry that has receded into background of this new West Yorkshire.

The second song from Ms Fitzgerald began, the very first words she sang to me so perfectly applicable to what I was contemplating at that precise moment through my car windows I would not be seriously believed if I set them down here. So I shook my head disbelievingly and changed from fourth gear down into third as I neared the congestion at the heart of the city, and my meeting to discuss doing some preliminary work pertaining to the giant new shopping complex they are going to build on the site of the Midland Railway's old Forster Square Station down Cheapside. If I got the job it would be a big one, and I would have to draft in several very expensive colleagues from London to help me do it in so short a space of time, to achieve the standards I always set myself, to do it right.

I was in Bradford 1988, my head ached, and didn't I know it.